Nicaragua
a country study

Federal Research Division
Library of Congress
Edited by
Tim L. Merrill
Research Completed
December 1993

On the cover: The almost perfectly shaped cone of
Momotombo, one of the many active volcanoes in
western Nicaragua

Third Edition, First Printing, 1994.

Library of Congress Cataloging-in-Publication Data

Nicaragua: a country study / Federal Research Division,
Library of Congress ; edited by Tim Merrill.—3rd ed.
   p. cm. — (Area handbook series, ISSN 1057–5294)
(DA Pam ; 550–88)
   "Supersedes the 1982 edition of Nicaragua: A Country
Study, edited by James D. Rudolph."—T.p. verso.
   "Research completed December 1993."
   Includes bibliographical references (pp. 251–269) and
index.
   ISBN 0–8444-0831–X
   1. Nicaragua. I. Merrill, Tim 1949– . II. Library of
Congress. Federal Research Division. III. Series. IV.
Series: DA Pam ; 550–88
F1523.N569 1994   94–21664
972.85–dc20   CIP

Headquarters, Department of the Army
DA Pam 550–88

Reprinted without alteration
on acid-free paper

(∞) ™

Bernan
Lanham, Maryland
December 1994

Foreword

This volume is one in a continuing series of books prepared by the Federal Research Division of the Library of Congress under the Country Studies/Area Handbook Program sponsored by the Department of the Army. The last two pages of this book list the other published studies.

Most books in the series deal with a particular foreign country, describing and analyzing its political, economic, social, and national security systems and institutions, and examining the interrelationships of those systems and the ways they are shaped by cultural factors. Each study is written by a multidisciplinary team of social scientists. The authors seek to provide a basic understanding of the observed society, striving for a dynamic rather than a static portrayal. Particular attention is devoted to the people who make up the society, their origins, dominant beliefs and values, their common interests and the issues on which they are divided, the nature and extent of their involvement with national institutions, and their attitudes toward each other and toward their social system and political order.

The books represent the analysis of the authors and should not be construed as an expression of an official United States government position, policy, or decision. The authors have sought to adhere to accepted standards of scholarly objectivity. Corrections, additions, and suggestions for changes from readers will be welcomed for use in future editions.

Louis R. Mortimer
Chief
Federal Research Division
Library of Congress
Washington, DC 20540–5220

Acknowledgments

The authors would like to acknowledge the contributions of Jan Knippers Black, Jack Child, Mary W. Helms, Julian C. Heriot, Jr., and Richard L. Millet, who wrote the 1982 edition of *Nicaragua: A Country Study.* The present volume incorporates portions of their work.

The authors are grateful to individuals in various government agencies and private institutions who gave of their time, research materials, and expertise in the production of this book. These individuals include Ralph K. Benesch, who oversees the Country Studies—Area Handbook Program for the Department of the Army. None of these individuals, however, is in any way responsible for the work of the authors.

The authors also would like to thank those people on the staff of the Federal Research Division who contributed directly to the preparation of the manuscript. They include Sandra W. Meditz, who reviewed drafts, provided valuable advice on all aspects of production, and conducted liaison with the sponsoring agency; Marilyn L. Majeska, who managed editing and production; Andrea T. Merrill, who edited figures and tables; Barbara Edgerton and Izella Watson, who did word processing; and Stephen C. Cranton and David P. Cabitto, who prepared the camera-ready copy. In addition, thanks go to Sharon Schultz, who edited chapters; Beverly Wolpert, who performed the final prepublication editorial review; and Joan C. Cook, who compiled the index. Thanks also go to David P. Cabitto of the Federal Research Division, who provided valuable graphics support and who, along with the firm of Greenhorne and O'Mara, prepared the maps; and to Wayne Horne, who did the cover art and chapter illustrations. Finally, the authors acknowledge the generosity of the individuals and the public and private agencies who allowed their photographs to be used in this study.

Contents

List of Figures

Preface

Like its predecessor, this study is an attempt to examine objectively and concisely the dominant historical, social, economic, political, and military aspects of contemporary Nicaragua. Sources of information included scholarly books, journals, monographs, official reports of governments and international organizations, and numerous periodicals. Chapter bibliographies appear at the end of the book; brief comments on sources recommended for further reading appear at the end of each chapter. To the extent possible, place-names follow the system adopted by the United States Board on Geographic Names. Measurements are given in the metric system; a conversion table is provided to assist readers unfamiliar with metric measurements (see table 1, Appendix A). A glossary is also included.

Although there are numerous variations, Spanish surnames for men and unmarried women usually consist of two parts: the patrilineal name followed by the matrilineal. In the instance of Daniel José Ortega Saavedra, for example, Ortega is his father's name; Saavedra, his mother's maiden name. In nonformal use, the matrilineal name is often dropped. When a woman marries, she generally drops her matrilineal name and replaces it with her husband's patrilineal name preceded by a "de". Thus, when Cristina Chamorro Barrios married Antonio Lacayo Oyanguren, she became Cristina Chamorro de Lacayo. In informal use, a married woman's patrilineal name is dropped (Cristina Lacayo is the informal usage.) In the case of the patrilineal Somoza, we have retained the matrilineal on occasions when there may be confusion about which individual is being discussed. A minority of individuals, William Ramírez for example, use only the patrilineal name in formal as well as informal use. The patrilineal for men and unmarried women and the husband's patrilineal for married women are used for indexing and bibliographic purposes.

The body of the text reflects information available as of December 1993. Certain other portions of the text, however, have been updated. The Introduction discusses significant events that have occurred since the completion of research; the Country Profile includes updated information as available; several figures and tables are based on information in more recently published sources; and the Bibliography lists recent sources thought to be particularly helpful to the reader.

Country Profile

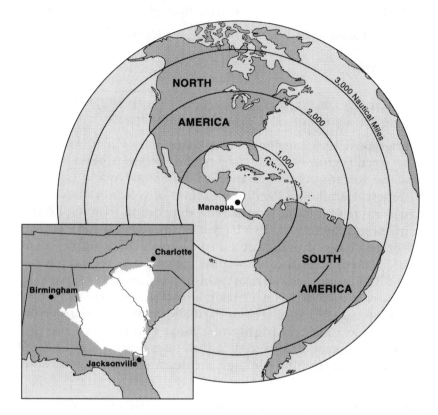

Country

Formal Name: Republic of Nicaragua.

Short Form: Nicaragua.

Term for Nationals: Nicaraguan(s).

Capital: Managua.

NOTE—The Country Profile contains updated information as available.

Date of Independence: Only September 15, 1821, from Spain, observed. July 1, 1823, from Mexico and April 30, 1838, from the United Provinces of Central America noted but not celebrated.

National Holiday: Independence day, September 15.

Geography

Size: Largest country in Central America with 129,494 square kilometers. Land area 120,254 square kilometers.

Topography: Three major geographic regions. Pacific lowlands or western region characterized by flat terrain broken by line of active volcanoes between the Golfo de Fonseca and Lago de Nicaragua paralleling Pacific coast. East of volcanoes lies large structural rift forming long narrow depression from Golfo de Fonseca southeastward. Two largest freshwater lakes in Central America (Lago de Managua and Lago de Nicaragua) also located in rift. Caribbean lowlands (or eastern) region covers about half of national territory; this region consists of tropical rain forest and pine savannas crossed by numerous rivers flowing to Caribbean. Between Pacific lowlands and Caribbean lowlands are central highlands, most extensive in north. Western Nicaragua situated at juncture between colliding tectonic plates, resulting in high incidence of earthquakes and volcanic activity.

Climate: Warm and relatively humid with some regional variation; temperature variation mainly function of elevation. Pacific lowlands generally more salubrious than Caribbean lowlands. East receives high average annual rainfall; west drier. Rainfall seasonal; May through October wettest months. Caribbean coast subject to destructive tropical storms and hurricanes from July to October.

Society

Population: In 1993 population estimated at 4.08 million. Rate of annual growth calculated at about 3.4 percent—one of highest in Latin America. Population density 32 persons per square kilometer in 1990—lowest in Central America. Most of population concentrated in Pacific lowlands; Caribbean lowlands sparsely settled. Population 55 percent urban, with urban growth nearly twice that of rural areas.

Ethnic Groups: Although definitions imprecise, approximately 76 percent of population mestizo, 10 percent European, about 3 percent indigenous, estimated 11 percent Creole or African. Indigenous, Creole, and African populations dominate in east; ladinos (culturally Hispanic mestizos and Europeans) mainly in Pacific lowlands and central highlands.

Languages: Spanish official language, spoken by almost everyone in Pacific lowlands and central highlands. English predominant language in Caribbean lowlands. Miskito predominant indigenous language, also spoken in east. Spanish widely used as second language in east.

Education and Literacy: Education system underfunded and generally inadequate. Access to education improved during 1980s, with introduction of free education, but large majority of population was not completing primary schooling in 1993. Literacy reported at about 50 percent at end of Somoza regime. Literacy campaign in 1980 reportedly raised functional literacy rate to about 77 percent.

Health and Welfare: Health indicators generally poor; life expectancy at birth 62 years in 1991; infant mortality rate 72 per 1,000 live births in 1989; high incidence of malnutrition; high incidence of infectious diseases, mainly enteritis, malaria, and tuberculosis; relatively low incidence of human immuno-deficiency virus (HIV). Health care system inadequate despite modest improvement during 1980s. Welfare indicators generally poor; approximately 70 percent of population below poverty line; nearly 50 percent unemployed or underemployed; access to safe drinking water and basic public services generally poor, especially in rural areas and Caribbean coast; quality of housing poor in urban shantytowns, with acute housing shortage in capital.

Economy

Salient Features: Formerly mixed economy undergoing extensive market-oriented structural adjustment, mainly by means of privatization of state enterprises and downsizing of public sector. Restoration of economic stability and reconstruction after eight years of civil war major concerns. Production dominated by primary commodities, mainly agricultural, for export and domestic consumption. Small manufacturing sector produces mainly for domestic and regional markets. Debt and political instability hampering growth and preventing return of foreign capital in early 1990s, despite dramatic progress in reducing inflation since 1990. Economy heavily dependent on foreign aid.

Gross Domestic Product (GDP): US$1.6 billion in 1992 (US$425 per capita), one of lowest per capita figures in Western Hemisphere. Economy contracted sharply during late 1980s and stagnant since 1990, with real GDP growth at minus 0.5 percent in 1992. Slow recovery expected by mid-1990s.

Agriculture: Mainstay of economy, accounted for approximately 29 percent of GDP in 1989 and an estimated 24 percent in 1991; employs about 45 percent of work force. Production heavily oriented toward export of coffee and cotton, which generate about half of total export revenues; bananas, sugar, tobacco, sesame, rice, and beef also important export commodities. Domestic-use agriculture robust, but increasingly supplemented by food and basic grains imports. Approximately 80 percent of agricultural production controlled by private sector, following expropriation and redistribution of large landholdings during 1980s.

Industry: Small industrial sector producing for domestic and regional markets; experienced substantial growth during 1960s in response to tariff protection and intraregional trade expansion under Central American Common Market (CACM) but declined precipitously thereafter. Industrial production as share of GDP peaked at 23 percent in 1978, dropping to 19 percent by 1989. Agro-industries dominate, accounting for 75 percent of total industrial output; other domestic use industries include cement production, chemicals processing, metals processing, and petroleum refining. Industrial recovery impeded during early 1990s by outdated and inefficient equipment and production methods, fuel shortages, lack of spare parts, labor unrest, and lack of supporting infrastructure.

Minerals: Mining not significant economic activity; accounted for 0.6 percent of GDP in 1990. Gold, silver, and salt mining main sources of mineral income; known deposits of copper, lead, iron, antimony, tungsten, molybdenum, and phosphate remain unexploited. Mining sector, nationalized in 1979, remained under state control in 1993. Offshore oil and natural gas exploration being undertaken off Pacific and Caribbean coastlines.

Energy: Domestic energy needs met by petroleum imports, as well as by hydroelectric and geothermal electricity generation. Imported oil, mainly from Mexico and Venezuela, satisfies approximately half of domestic demand. One geothermal and one hydroelectric plant in operation; a second, 400-megawatt hydroelectric plant under construction. Electrification uneven, heavily concentrated in urban areas. National power grid damaged by civil war.

Foreign Trade: Exports valued at US$343 million in 1991, dominated by coffee, cotton, bananas, sugar, and beef. Imports valued at US$650 million in 1991, mainly petroleum and its byproducts, other raw materials, nondurable consumer goods, and machinery. Soviet Union, Eastern Europe, Cuba, the European Community (EC), now the European Union (EU), and Latin America major trading partners during 1980s. Trade conducted mainly with EC, United States, Latin America, and Japan since 1990. Balance of trade characterized by sizable deficits since 1980.

Balance of Payments: Total debt estimated at US$10.6 billion in 1990. Experienced highest per capita debt in Latin America because of chronic fiscal and current account deficits during 1980s, resulting in approximately US$4 billion owed to former Soviet Union and approximately US$6 billion owed to Western nations and multilateral lending institutions. Granted substantial debt relief beginning in 1990.

Foreign Aid: Most economic assistance provided by United States, EC, and multilateral agencies since 1990. Major recipient of aid from socialist countries during 1980s.

Currency and Exchange Rate: Gold córdoba (córdoba oro— C$o); US$1 = C$o6.55 in April 1994.

Fiscal Year: Calendar year.

Transportation And Telecommunications

Roads: 26,000 kilometers in 1993; 4,000 kilometers paved, 2,200 kilometers gravel. Pan American Highway runs north to south for 369 kilometers. Roads highly concentrated in western and central zones, with no paved roads linking Caribbean and Pacific coasts.

Railroads: 373 kilometers, 1.067-meter narrow gauge, linking Managua to León and Granada. Section from León to Corinto unusable.

Ports: One principal, suitable for deep-water berthing at Corinto; secondary port at Puerto Sandino for offloading of petroleum; two smaller ports at Puerto Cabezas and Bluefields.

Airports: One international, Augusto C. Sandino International Airport in Managua; ten secondary airfields.

Telecommunications: Eight television, eleven FM, and forty-five AM radio stations. Total number of telephones in 1993 estimated at 60,000, or 1.5 per 100 inhabitants. International communications to other Central American countries via Central American Microwave System (CAMS), to rest of world via International Telecommunications Satellite Corporation (Intelsat) satellite ground station near Managua and via former Soviet Union Intersputnik system.

Government And Politics

Government: Under constitution promulgated January 1, 1987, republic with three independent branches. Executive elected for six-year term (Violeta Barrios de Chamorro became president on April 25, 1990). Unicameral National Assembly elected to six-year term concurrent with that of president.

Politics: Numerous political parties, most based on personalities rather than political philosophies. Largest and most cohesive single party, leftist Sandinista National Liberation Front (FSLN) headed by Daniel José Ortega Saavedra, entered into opposition in 1990 after almost eleven years in government. Since 1990, government ostensibly held by National Opposition Union (UNO), loose coalition of fourteen parties united to oppose FSLN. Relations between government of President Chamorro and UNO leadership strained over government support for laws guaranteeing transfer of expropriated properties to Sandinistas and continued FSLN influence within police and armed forces. Political process marked by violent labor militancy and sporadic political violence by rearmed

Contra and Sandinista guerrillas. Presidential and National Assembly elections scheduled for 1996.

Judicial System: Judicial system consists of Supreme Court, which handles both civil and criminal cases, courts of appeal, and courts of first instance at departmental and municipal levels.

Administrative Divisions: Nine regions, subdivided into seventeen departments (fifteen full departments and two autonomous regions in Caribbean lowlands). In accordance with 1988 Law on Municipalities, 143 municipal units functioning in 1992.

Foreign Relations: Since 1990 Chamorro government has greatly improved relations with United States and supported Central American integration. During 1980s FSLN government aligned itself with former Soviet bloc and supported leftist causes, straining relations with United States and neighboring Central American countries.

International Agreements and Memberships: Membership in Organization of American States (OAS), Central American Common Market, System of Central American Integration (Sistema de Integración Centroamericana—SICA), and United Nations (UN) and its specialized agencies. Important treaties include: 1947 Rio de Janeiro Treaty of Mutual Assistance (Rio Treaty), Treaty for the Proscription of Nuclear Weapons in Latin America (Tlatelolco Treaty), and Central American Peace Agreement (Esquipulas II).

National Security

Armed Forces: In 1993 consisted of Sandinista People's Army (EPS), with ground, air, and small naval elements. Reduced to 15,200 personnel from peak strength of 97,000 during 1980s. Mandatory military service and reserve and militia forces eliminated in 1990. EPS nominally subordinate to civilian authority but in practice enjoys substantial autonomy within political system; maintains strong links to FSLN.

Major military Units: 13,500-member army with ground forces organized into six regional commands; 500-member naval element with sixteen patrol boats; and 1,200-member air element organized into one squadron.

Military Equipment: Most weaponry supplied by former Soviet

Union, with some older items purchased from United States prior to 1979. Some naval craft acquired from People's Democratic Republic of Korea (North Korea).

Defense Budget: Estimated at US$210 million in 1993, about 14 percent of GDP.

Internal Security Forces: 11,000-member National Police, formerly Sandinista Police, under Ministry of Government.

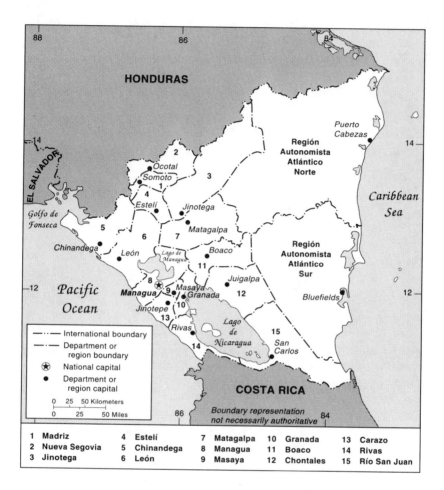

HONDURAS

2

Ocotal
Somoto
1
4
Estelí   Jinotega

Matagalpa

5
6   7
Chinandega
León   Lago de
Managua
11
8

Managua   Masaya
9   Granada
10
Jinotepe
13
Rivas

14

3

Región
Autonomista
Atlántico
Norte

Puerto
Cabezas

Caribbean
Sea

Región
Autonomista
Atlántico
Sur

Juigalpa

12   Bluefields

Lago
de
Nicaragua

15
San
Carlos

COSTA RICA

EL SALVADOR

Golfo de
Fonseca

Boaco

Pacific

Ocean

—--—··— International boundary

—··—··— Department or
region boundary

⊛ National capital

● Department or
region capital

0   25   50 Kilometers

0   25   50 Miles

Boundary representation
not necessarily authoritative

1	Madriz	4	Estelí	7	Matagalpa	10	Granada	13	Carazo
2	Nueva Segovia	5	Chinandega	8	Managua	11	Boaco	14	Rivas
3	Jinotega	6	León	9	Masaya	12	Chontales	15	Río San Juan

Figure 1. Administrative Divisions of Nicaragua, 1993

Introduction

NICARAGUA IS A COUNTRY OVERWHELMED by its history. Since colonial times, Nicaragua has suffered from political instability, civil war, poverty, foreign intervention, and natural disasters. Successive governments have been unable to bring political stability or significant economic growth to the country. Personal and foreign special interests have generally prevailed over national interests, and repeated foreign intervention in Nicaraguan political and economic affairs has resulted in nationalistic reactions and a legacy of suspicion of foreign governments and their motives.

From precolonial times through the present, the broad central mountain range that splits the country in two has also divided it into two culturally distinct areas. Before the arrival of the Spanish, western Nicaragua was populated by indigenous peoples related to the Maya and Aztec in the north; eastern Nicaragua's earliest inhabitants were believed to have migrated to the region from South America. The fertile volcanic soils and more salubrious climate in the west attracted Spanish settlers throughout the colonial period. As a result, most of Nicaragua's present-day population lives in the western part of the country. The eastern Caribbean coastal area with its sultry climate and nonfertile soils attracted only a handful of English settlers and pirates and some blacks (many of whom were runaway slaves) from the West Indies.

Europeans first saw what is now Nicaragua when Christopher Columbus sailed south along the Caribbean coast on his fourth voyage to the Americas in late 1502 and claimed the entire area for Spain. Several land expeditions were launched in the 1520s to subdue the indigenous population, but in general the Spanish were more interested in exploiting the vast riches of Mexico and Peru than in settling Central America (see Glossary). The population of the area dropped precipitously in the sixteenth century. Incoming Spanish settlers were few, and the indigenous population was all but wiped out by exposure to new diseases, with the remainder forcibly sent to Peru to work the silver mines. Administratively during this period, the region became a backwater province of the Audiencia of Guatemala.

The seventeenth century proved no more auspicious than the previous century. Although the population of Nicaragua grew somewhat because of the introduction of livestock, the province's economy was devastated by trade restrictions imposed by Spain, by natural disasters, and by foreign attacks. The local government neglected agricultural production, preferring to import food. The economy of Nicaragua also suffered because of the massive destruction caused by three powerful earthquakes during the period. During the second half of the century, Nicaragua was subjected to bloody incursions from English, French, and Dutch pirates. In 1668 and 1670, these buccaneers captured and destroyed the city of Granada, center of the province's agricultural wealth. Control of the eastern half of the country eluded the Spanish, and the English declared eastern Nicaragua to be a protectorate of the English crown.

The eighteenth century saw the beginnings of economic growth based on agriculture but also the birth of a pernicious political rivalry that was to plague the country for two centuries. By the 1750s, a powerful elite was well established in the cities of León and Granada. The landowners in León concentrated on cattle raising and the export of animal products, and Granada became the center of regional agricultural trade. Although these local elites agreed on promoting Nicaragua as the site for a transisthmian canal linking the Caribbean Sea and Pacific Ocean, they differed violently on the trade policies of the province (free-trade or protectionist). During the colonial period, these two cities fought for political control over the province. After independence, the rivalry only intensified, often breaking into open warfare. The hatred between the two factions, the liberals, or free-traders, in León and the conservatives, or protectionists, in Granada, became so institutionalized that the factions often forgot the original philosophical difference that had spawned their rivalry. The violent conflict between liberals and conservatives was one of the most important and destructive aspects of Nicaraguan history, an aspect that would last until well into the twentieth century. Politicians frequently chose party loyalty over national interest, and the nation was often the loser in interparty strife.

Establishment of an independent Nicaragua came in several stages. The first step occurred when the Audiencia of Guatemala declared its independence from Spain in 1821 and became part of the Mexican Empire. Separatist feelings throughout the isthmus grew, and the United Provinces of Central America declared their independence from Mexico in 1823. Under a weak federal government, each province of the new nation created its own independent internal administration. Efforts to centralize power led to civil war between 1826 and 1829. The federation finally dissolved in 1837, and Nicaragua's independence was formally declared on April 30, 1838.

The mid-1800s were marked by unstable national governments and a rivalry between the United States and Britain to bring Nicaragua under their spheres of influence. The goal of both foreign powers was control of a transisthmian transit route, either overland or via a new Caribbean-to-Pacific canal. Continued domestic turmoil in the 1850s provided the opportunity for William Walker, a soldier of fortune from the United States, to take over Nicaragua. The struggle to expel Walker was long and costly, ultimately involving intervention from all of Nicaragua's neighbors, the British Navy, and an invasion by the United States marines. The Walker affair left a bitter legacy in Nicaragua and was the first example of what was to become a common occurrence in the country: a penchant for Nicaraguan politicians to call on the United States to settle domestic disputes and an eagerness by the United States to respond by military intervention.

Nicaragua's thirty-five-year period of relative calm under conservative administrations was broken in 1893 by liberal José Santos Zelaya. Zelaya's rule proved to be one of the most controversial periods in Nicaraguan history. Zelaya, a ruthless dictator who managed to stay in power for sixteen years despite strong foreign and domestic opposition, was responsible for the creation of a professional army and the growth of strong nationalist feelings. Zelaya opened the country to foreign investment, expanded coffee production, and boosted banana exports.His government promoted internal development and modernized Nicaragua's infrastructure. During his tenure, new roads and seaport facilities were constructed, railroad lines were extended, and many government buildings and schools were built. Opposition from conservatives eventually erupted into a revolt that, with the support of United States marines, drove Zelaya from power in 1909.

Zelaya's fall ushered in another era of political instability and foreign intervention. The United States, flush with its new colonies in the Caribbean won after the Spanish-American War (1898), entered a new era of interventionism in the Caribbean and Central America. The United States marines who helped topple Zelaya remained in Nicaragua to support subsequent conservative governments. United States banks lent money to Nicaragua on the condition that these banks would retain complete control of Nicaraguan customs and all revenue from the railroads and steamships. By the end of World War I, United States military presence and supervision of the economy had turned Nicaragua into a near United States protectorate.

As isolationist sentiment grew in the United States in the 1920s, there were increased calls in the United States for removal of the marines from Nicaragua. United States officials decided that an honorable way to withdraw forces was to create a national Nicaraguan constabulary, the National Guard, to maintain order after the marines withdrew. The National Guard was formed in June 1925, and the last United States marines withdrew in August.

The worst predictions regarding Nicaragua's future after the departure of United States marines soon came to pass. The Nicaraguan government dissolved into chaos, and liberal-conservative fighting erupted anew. The United States, fearing a full-scale civil war would result in a leftist victory, as had been the case after the Mexican Revolution (1911–17), sent the marines back to Managua in January 1927. This time, however, the rapid buildup of United States forces led only to increased mayhem. The fighting did not stop until massive United States power and the growing strength of the National Guard forced most combatants to sign a truce. Out of this latest struggle would emerge two of the most influential Nicaraguans of the twentieth century, Augusto César Sandino and Anastasio Somoza García.

Sandino was the only major player who refused to abide by the truce. Initially a combatant for the liberals in the fighting, he turned his forces against the United States marines and the National Guard, which he considered merely a tool of the United States, after the implementation of the peace accord. Sandino led a force of several hundred who engaged in classic guerrilla warfare in remote rural areas. Never a serious threat to the national government, Sandino's forces nevertheless proved a drain on the economy and a constant gadfly and embarrassment to the National Guard. Sandino's hit-and-run tactics were also the excuse that allowed 2,000 United States marines to remain in Nicaragua.

Once again, domestic events in the United States had powerful repercussions in Nicaragua. The deepening Great Depression, outrage in the United States over the growing number of names on marine casualty lists, and a desire to improve relations with Latin America in the face of a growing threat from Japan and Germany resulted in president Herbert Hoover's withdrawing all marines from Nicaragua in the waning days of his administration in January 1933.

The National Guard and its new director, Somoza García, immediately moved to fill the power vacuum left by the departure of the United States. Recognizing the potential power of a strong army in a weak nation, Somoza García rapidly began consolidating power within the National Guard and soon was acting independently of his uncle, President Juan Bautista Sacasa, who was nominal head of the guard. In January 1934, upon leaving the president's house where he had been conducting peace negotiations, Sandino was assassinated by National Guard associates, who had acted without approval of the president. As Somoza García's power over the National Guard strengthened, his control of national affairs became more evident. Finally, in June 1936, Somoza García forced his uncle to resign as president and instructed the Nicaraguan Congress name him as his uncle's replacement. A Somoza dynasty that would last for more than four decades was hence founded.

For the next twenty years, Somoza García was dictator of Nicaragua, always in control of the National Guard and ruling either directly as president or indirectly through a hand-picked and compliant family associate who held the post of president. A weak opposition was tolerated but only to give a democratic facade to the regime. Real opposition was met with incarceration, torture, exile, or assassination. A clever politician, Somoza García maintained power by changing roles to gain the support of one or another influential group in Nicaragua, while keeping the support of the United States. He, for example, expressed sympathy with fascism in the late 1930s in order to win support from the business sector and the upper classes. However, he was an ardent supporter of the Allies in World War II and was rewarded with large amounts of United States military aid. In the late 1940s and early 1950s, domestically he supported labor (generally on the left politically), while keeping a fervent anticommunist stance in international forums.

Control over the country also meant almost complete control over its economy. The 1940s and 1950s were boom times for the Nicaraguan economy as coffee prices soared, but most of the country's profit went into the pockets of Somoza García and his cronies. (Somoza García is reported to have quipped, "Bucks for my friends, bullets for my enemies.") They bought or expropriated farms, mining interests, and companies until by the late 1940s, Somoza García was the nation's largest landowner. He owned most of the country's cattle ranches and coffee plantations and, as well, owned or controlled all banks, the national railroad, the national airlines, a cement factory, textile plants, several large electric power companies, and extensive rental property in the cities. Somoza García's policies made him many enemies, including a disgruntled citizen who assassinated him in September 1956.

Somoza García had changed the presidential succession so that it devolved on the director of the National Guard, a post held by his older son, Luis Somoza Debayle. Luis Somoza Debayle immediately assumed the post of president, and his younger brother, Anastasio Somoza Debayle, took over as director of the National Guard. The brothers' different personalities soon became apparent. Although both had been trained to take over as president in turn, the older Somoza brother appeared to favor a slight liberalization of his father's repressive style of governing. The younger brother, in contrast, lacked his father's political skills and increasingly commanded the National Guard through brute force. Because of the older brother's poor health, Anastasio Somoza Debayle assumed more and more power.

The formal transfer of power came in 1967, shortly before Luis Somoza Debayle suffered a fatal heart attack. Decades of pent-up grievances against corruption and repression had created opposition to the Somozas. Having none of his father's ability to finesse the opposition, however, the new president, Anastasio Somoza Debayle, reacted to any criticism by increasing political repression. Instead of being trumped as in the past, opposition forces now seemed only to be strengthened by Anastasio Somoza Debayle's repressive tactics. For the next dozen years, a cycle of active opposition to Anastasio Somoza Debayle's regime and the regime's ever more ruthless response threatened to destroy Nicaragua's economy and society.

As the 1970s progressed, all sectors of Nicaraguan society joined the opposition to Anastasio Somoza Debayle's regime.

The turning point for many was the December 1972 earthquake that destroyed Managua. National Guard members joined in looting the city after the tremor, and it was later revealed that most of the international aid after the earthquake enriched the Somoza family instead of reaching the victims. As a result, almost all political figures drifted over to the opposition. The president was nominally identified with the liberals and therefore was opposed by the conservatives from the beginning of his rise to power. Anastasio Somoza Debayle's loyalty to family, cronies, and the National Guard over party, however, gradually alienated former fellow liberals. The country's rapid economic decline after the earthquake lost him the support of labor, the middle class, and Nicaragua's elite. The left and student groups had long been vocal opponents of the regime. The Roman Catholic Church and elements of the press, especially the influential *La Prensa,* also became outspoken in their condemnation of the government's repressive actions.

The group that was eventually to take the lead in opposing Anastasio Somoza Debayle, the Sandinista National Liberation Front (Frente Sandinista de Liberación Nacional—FSLN), was formed in 1962. Taking its name and much of its ideology from Sandino, the FSLN grew from a group of university students to a small Marxist revolutionary organization operating in rural areas. Fueled by growing disenchantment with the dictator and foreign help, the FSLN was militarily challenging the National Guard throughout the country by the late 1970s. Despite the collapse of the economy and the loss of all domestic and international support, the tenacity of Anastasio Somoza Debayle and the National Guard made it increasingly apparent that a change in Nicaragua would come through revolution instead of peaceful reform.

After two years of violent struggle, Anastasio Somoza Debayle finally fled Nicaragua, and on July 20, 1979, the FSLN and other members of the revolutionary force entered Managua. A five-member junta assumed power, pledging political pluralism, a mixed economic system, and a nonaligned foreign policy. The new government inherited a country in ruins; an estimated 50,000 Nicaraguans were dead, 120,000 exiled, and 600,000 homeless. Despite the destruction, most Nicaraguans supported the new regime because they saw the Sandinista (see Glossary) victory as an opportunity to end the repression and economic inequalities of the almost universally hated Somoza regime.

As leaders in the military struggle and the best-organized and most powerful group in postrevolutionary Nicaragua, the Sandinistas rapidly began consolidating their political power. The constitution was abrogated, and the Congress was replaced by an appointed Council of State, dominated by Sandinista members. The two influential non-Sandinista members of the ruling junta resigned, and by 1983 it was clear that Daniel José Ortega Saavedra, a long-time member of the FSLN, controlled the junta. The National Guard was abolished and replaced by the new Sandinista People's Army (Ejército Popular Sandinista—EPS), headed by Humberto Ortega Saavedra. Mass popular groups were formed to represent labor, peasants, and women.

Domestic and international support for the new Sandinista government was not universal, however. The ethnic minorities from the Caribbean coast, neglected by national governments since colonial times, rejected Sandinista efforts to incorporate them into the national mainstream and demanded autonomy. Worried that Nicaragua would become "another Cuba," the United States government launched a campaign to isolate the Sandinista government in 1981. Later that year, the Reagan administration (1981–89) authorized support for groups trying to overthrow the Sandinistas. Using camps in southern Honduras as a staging area, the United States supported groups of disgruntled former members of the National Guard. This effort became known as the Nicaraguan Resistance; members of the group were later called the Contras (short for *contrarevolucionarios*—see Glossary).

As the Contra war intensified, the Sandinistas' tolerance of political pluralism waned, and the government imposed emergency laws to ban criticism and organization of political opposition. Social programs also suffered as a result of the war because the Sandinista regime was forced to increase military spending until half of its budget went for defense. Agricultural production also sharply declined as refugees fled areas of conflict.

Throughout the 1980s, as the war expanded, the economy continued to deteriorate, in part because of a devastating embargo on Nicaraguan goods imposed by the United States in early 1985. In 1987, in the aftermath of the Iran-Contra affair, the United States Congress, however, stopped all military support to the Contras. The result of the cutoff was a military stalemate; the Contras were unable to keep on fighting without United States support, and the Sandinista government could not afford to continue waging an unpopular war that had already devastated the economy. The Contras and the Sandinistas had few options other than to negotiate.

International negotiations among the Central American countries in the late 1980s laid the groundwork for a peace settlement. Elections, originally scheduled for the fall of 1990, were moved to February 1991. President Ortega also agreed to guarantee fair participation for opposition parties and to allow international observers to monitor the entire electoral process.

The Sandinistas felt confident of their success at the polls despite deteriorating socioeconomic conditions. On June 6, 1989, fourteen parties, united only in their opposition to the Sandinistas, formed a coalition called the National Opposition Union (Unión Nacional Opositora—UNO), whose support was drawn from a broad base, including conservative and liberal parties. Despite its determination to vote the Sandinistas out of power, however, the UNO coalition remained a weak opposition lacking a cohesive program.

Despite some violent incidents, the electoral campaign took place in relative peace. In an effort to divert attention from the critical economic situation, the Sandinista campaign appealed to nationalism, depicting UNO followers as pro-Somoza, instruments of United States foreign policy, and enemies of the Nicaraguan revolution. The UNO coalition under Violeta Barrios de Chamorro directed a campaign centered around the failing economy and promises of peace. Many Nicaraguans expected the country's economic crisis to deepen and the Contra conflict to continue if the Sandinistas remained in power. Chamorro promised to end the unpopular military draft, bring about democratic reconciliation, and promote economic growth. The UNO coalition won a surprising victory on February 25, 1990. Exhausted by war and poverty, the Nicaraguan people opted for change.

The new administration inherited a country in ruins. Agriculture remained the country's primary economic resource, but production of the two main crops, coffee and cotton, had dropped during the 1980s. Manufacturing, always a small part of the economy, had practically ceased by 1990. The transportation and telecommunications networks, found almost exclusively in the western half of the country and inadequate even during the Somoza era, were damaged by nearly two decades of fighting. Blackouts were frequent because the electric power system was often the target of sabotage during the Contra war and because the country frequently was unable to pay for petroleum, all of which was imported, to generate electricity. The entire banking system was bankrupt, and more than half the labor force was unemployed or underemployed. A per capita gross domestic product (GDP—see Glossary) of less than US$500 gave Nicaragua the dubious distinction of being one of the poorest nations in the Western Hemisphere. Perhaps the only bright spot in the economic morass was that the collapse of the economy stopped the ecological destruction of the rich forest lands in eastern Nicaragua.

Social conditions largely paralleled the poor state of the economy. Although in their early years in power, the Sandinistas put effort into improving the health and education systems and the literacy rate, diversion of half of the national budget to the military during the second half of their administration largely wiped out the significant gains made in their first few years. Even using spartan standards for what is adequate for survival, official government statistics in 1992 classified two-thirds of Nicaraguans as poor. Only slightly more than half of primary-school age children attended school. Most rural inhabitants (45 percent of the population) and many urban dwellers (55 percent out of a total of nearly 4 million people) lacked access to health care.

The ethnic divide adds to the country's social problems. Nicaragua continues to be ethnically divided in two: the west is relatively homogeneous, Spanish-speaking, culturally Hispanic, and racially mestizo; the east is a multiracial, multicultural, and mostly English-speaking region. Although the people are nominally Roman Catholic, various Protestant denominations have made significant inroads in recent years, particularly in the east.

In addition to its overwhelming economic and social challenges, the new Chamorro administration faced immediate political problems. Almost from the day it took power, the Chamorro government was a stepchild. Even though Chamorro personified the Nicaraguan people's aspiration for peace, neither the UNO nor the FSLN recognized the government as the legitimate representative of its political, social, and economic aspirations for Nicaragua. The strong constitutional powers of the executive branch theoretically should have given the president adequate control over the political and economic systems, but the transition agreements left the Sandinistas in control of the military and police.

President Chamorro's first four years in power were marked by social, political, and economic instability. The economy continued deteriorating. Although the demobilization of the Contras concluded in June 1990, violence continued in rural areas, especially in the country's northern departments. Rearmed members of the Nicaraguan Resistance, now known as Recontras, argued that the Chamorro government did not comply with commitments made during the demobilization process. In the spring of 1991, an estimated 2,000 Recontras rearmed and resumed guerrilla operations in the northern part of the country. They charged the Chamorro government with not fulfilling its promises of land and economic assistance to the Contras as they disarmed and demobilized. The reorganization of the police and the army, as well as the removal of Humberto Ortega as army chief, was necessary, according to the Recontras, for their disbandment.

After the Recontras staged uprisings in support of their demands, demobilized Sandinista soldiers, calling themselves Recompas, took up arms during late August 1991 to fight against anti-Sandinista forces and protect the accomplishments of the Sandinista revolution, which they perceived as being threatened by the UNO government. Recompas clashed with Recontras and government forces and demanded compliance with the commitments made to them during the peace process. Government and army intervention persuaded the two groups to halt the fighting. Ironically, the Recontras and Recompas discovered that they had common grievances and joined forces in a new group called the Revueltos. To achieve political conciliation, the government launched a plan for reconciliation. The government initiative failed, however, to disarm the civilian population. In the spring of 1992, the Revueltos had an estimated 2,000-member force operating in northern Nicaragua.

At the end of 1992, continued confrontation between the Chamorro government and the UNO coalition also threatened the country's democratic institutions. A conflict over politics developed among UNO representatives in the National Assembly. The UNO group in the assembly split into two groups: a larger conservative wing, headed by Alfredo César Aguirre, that demanded a complete rupture with the Sandinistas and began to oppose the president; and a smaller, more moderate group, headed by Antonio Lacayo Oyanguren, that insisted on cooperation with the FSLN as a prerequisite for national reconciliation and continued to support the president's policies. The group headed by César was backed by conservatives in the United States Senate, who threatened to freeze United States aid to Nicaragua in an effort to persuade the Chamorro administration to oppose the Sandinistas more strongly.

The political crisis grew during the summer of 1992, when César launched a political offensive against Lacayo in an effort to implicate Lacayo in fraud and embezzlement of government funds. César also directed attacks on Humberto Ortega and high-ranking police officials. Conflict in the National Assembly heightened when eight UNO deputies broke ranks and began voting with the Sandinistas. This new UNO/Sandinista bloc represented a majority within the legislature, and César, backed by most of the remaining UNO coalition, took over the National Assembly in what many considered a political coup. The Sandinista faction boycotted César's actions by walking out of the National Assembly.

The UNO bloc in the National Assembly headed by César demanded Humberto Ortega's removal from the army and Chamorro's ouster from the presidency. It also demanded property legislation to abolish the Piñata—the FSLN legislation giving the Sandinistas titles to considerable state property put into effect immediately following the 1990 elections. At the same time, the United States Congress froze US$116 million in economic aid to Nicaragua pending restructuring of the police. In an effort to unfreeze the United States economic package, the Chamorro administration negotiated the removal of top Sandinista police leaders, including its chief, René Vivas Lugo. The Nicaraguan president appealed to the courts, which in turn ruled that all legislation passed by the César faction of the UNO was unconstitutional. On December 29, 1992, President Chamorro used her executive powers to authorize a military takeover of the congressional building and the removal of César as president of the National Assembly. The following day, police occupied the National Assembly building and seized all of its assets and documents. The government appointed a provisional administration to run legislative affairs until new authorities were elected on January 9, 1993.

The takeover of the assembly, which César called a coup, marked the end of UNO support for President Chamorro. Ten of the fourteen political parties that in 1990 formed the UNO coalition now openly opposed the Chamorro administration, accusing it of "co-governing" with the Sandinistas. The supporters of Chamorro from the old UNO coalition formed a progovernment center bloc called the Center Group (Grupo de Centro—GC). The FSLN delegation, along with deputies from the GC, elected Gustavo Tablada Zelaya, from the former Communist Party, as president of the National Assembly. The vice presidency of the legislature went to a Sandinista, Reinaldo Antonio Tefel.

After four years of government under Violeta Barrios de Chamorro, Nicaragua faces difficult times on its road to economic recovery and national reconstruction. Its government must cope with insufficient economic aid to carry out economic reforms, lagging growth in investments, intense partisan struggle, and an increasingly frustrated populace. The internal political situation is exacerbated by the need for compromise with the Sandinistas, who themselves suffered a crisis of identity and credibility after their loss in the 1990 elections.

The role of the armed forces remains the center of debate among political forces. Criticized by its neighbors and by the United States because it was deemed too large to be a purely defensive force, the army has gone through a major reduction in force, going from 97,000 troops in 1989 to 15,200 in 1993. However, despite repeated promises by the president that the army chief would be replaced and control be transferred from the Sandinistas to the national government, Humberto Ortega still commanded the Nicaraguan army in mid-1994.

In mid-1994, Nicaragua is still far from enjoying the social and political peace necessary to attract foreign investment and achieve economic growth. The Chamorro administration, as well as the Sandinista leadership and the UNO coalition, are caught between their respective ideals and the need for a pragmatic political reconciliation. Dissatisfaction with the democratic process prevails. Despite its internal conflicts, however, the FSLN remains the strongest and best organized political force in Nicaragua and is the only party with the organizational and political experience to carry out a government program. As the country prepares for the 1996 elections, conditions similar to those faced in 1990—social instability, political polarization, and economic uncertainty— leave Nicaragua with few means for overcoming its political and socioeconomic crisis.

June 28, 1994   Tim L. Merrill

Chapter 1. Historical Setting

Augusto César Sandino, guerrilla leader in the struggle against the United States occupation of Nicaragua in the 1920s–1930s

THROUGHOUT ITS HISTORY, Nicaragua has suffered from political instability, civil war, poverty, foreign intervention, and natural disasters. Governments since colonial times have been unable to bring stability and sustainable economic growth. Personal and foreign special interests have generally prevailed over the national interest, and foreign intervention in Nicaraguan political and economic affairs, especially by the United States, has resulted in various forms of populist and nationalist reactions. The legacy of the past can be seen today in the attitudes toward foreign influence. Although the upper and middle classes tend to emulate North American life-styles and be supportive of United States policies, the Nicaraguan poor are highly suspicious of the culture and political intentions of the United States.

Since precolonial times, Nicaragua's fertile Pacific coast has attracted settlers, thus concentrating most of the population in the western part of the country. Because of its proximity to the West Indies, the Caribbean coast historically has been the site of foreign intervention and non-Hispanic immigration by black and indigenous groups from the Caribbean and by British settlers and pirates. The resulting diverse ethnic groups that today inhabit the Caribbean coast have for centuries resisted Hispanic Nicaraguan governments and demanded political autonomy.

During most of the twentieth century, Nicaragua has suffered under dictatorial regimes. From the mid-1930s until 1979, the Somoza family controlled the government, the military, and an ever expanding sector of the Nicaraguan economy. On July 19, 1979, Somoza rule came to an end after the triumph of an insurrection movement led by the Sandinista National Liberation Front (Frente Sandinista de Liberación Nacional—FSLN). However, the predominance of the FSLN led to the development of a different kind of authoritarian regime that lasted for more than a decade.

During the 1980s, Nicaragua was the center of Cold War confrontation in the Western Hemisphere, with the former Soviet Union and Cuba providing assistance to the Sandinista (see Glossary) government, and the United States supporting antigovernment forces. A regional peace initiative brought an end to civil war in the late 1980s. The Sandinistas lost in the

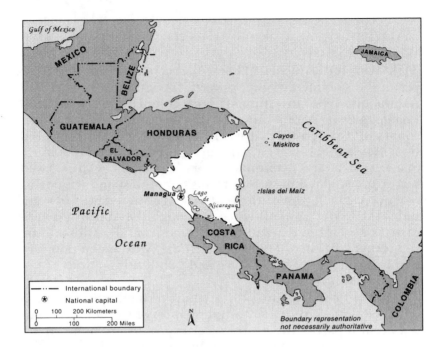

Figure 2. Nicaragua in Its Central American Setting, 1993

1990 elections, and a new government headed by President
Violeta Barrios de Chamorro was installed in April 1990.

Precolonial Period

Present-day Nicaragua is located south of the pre-Columbian culture areas of the Maya and the Aztec in Mexico and
northern Central America (see fig. 2; Glossary). Although conventional wisdom states that the culture of lower Central America did not reach the levels of political or cultural development
achieved in Mexico and northern Central America, recent
excavations in Cuscutlatán, El Salvador, may prove that assump-
tion erroneous.

Two basic culture groups existed in precolonial Nicaragua.
In the central highlands and Pacific coast regions, the native
peoples were linguistically and culturally similar to the Aztec
and the Maya. The oral history of the people of western Nicaragua indicates that they had migrated south from Mexico several centuries before the arrival of the Spanish, a theory

supported by linguistic research. Most people of central and western Nicaragua spoke dialects of Pipil, a language closely related to Nahuatl, the language of the Aztec. The culture and food of the peoples of western Nicaragua also confirmed a link with the early inhabitants of Mexico; the staple foods of both populations were corn, beans, chili peppers, and avocados, still the most common foods in Nicaragua today. Chocolate was drunk at ceremonial occasions, and turkeys and dogs were raised for their meat.

Most of Nicaragua's Caribbean lowlands area was inhabited by tribes that migrated north from what is now Colombia. The various dialects and languages in this area are related to Chibcha, spoken by groups in northern Colombia. Eastern Nicaragua's population consisted of extended families or tribes. Food was obtained by hunting, fishing, and slash-and-burn agriculture. Root crops (especially cassava), plantains, and pineapples were the staple foods. The people of eastern Nicaragua appear to have traded with and been influenced by the native peoples of the Caribbean, as round, thatched huts and canoes, both typical of the Caribbean, were common in eastern Nicaragua.

When the Spanish arrived in western Nicaragua in the early 1500s, they found three principal tribes, each with a different culture and language: the Niquirano, the Chorotegano, and the Chontal. Each of these diverse groups occupied much of Nicaragua's territory, led by independent chieftains (*cacicazgos*) who ruled according to each group's laws and customs. Their weapons consisted of swords, lances, and arrows made out of wood. Monarchy was the form of government of most tribes; the supreme ruler was the chief, or *cacique*, who, surrounded by his princes, formed the nobility. Laws and regulations were disseminated by royal messengers who visited each township and gave their chief's orders to the assembled inhabitants.

The Chontal (the term means foreigner) occupied the central mountain region. The Chontal were less numerous and culturally less advanced than the Niquirano and Chorotegano, who lived in well-established nation-states. Occupying the territory between Lago de Nicaragua and the Pacific coast, the Niquirano were governed by several chiefs, one of whom, chief Nicarao, or Nicaragua, was a rich ruler who lived in Nicaraocali, now the city of Rivas. The Chorotegano lived in the central region of Nicaragua. The Niquirano and Chorotegano had intimate contact with the Spanish conquerors, paving the way for the racial mix of native and European stock now known as mestizos. The differences in the origin and level of civilization of the three groups led to frequent violent encounters, in which one group would displace whole tribes from their territory, contributing to multiple divisions within each group.

In the west and highland areas where the Spanish settled, the indigenous population was almost completely wiped out by the rapid spread of new diseases, for which the native population had no immunity, and the virtual enslavement of the remainder of the indigenous people. In the east, where the Europeans did not settle, most indigenous groups survived. The English, however, did introduce guns and ammunition to one of the local peoples, the Bawihka, who lived in northeast Nicaragua. The Bawihka later intermarried with runaway slaves from Britain's Caribbean possessions, and the resulting population, with its access to superior weapons, began to expand its territory and push other indigenous groups into the interior. This Afro-indigenous group became known to the Europeans as Miskito, and the displaced survivors of their expansionist activities were called the Sumu.

Colonial Period, 1522–1820

The Spanish Conquest

Nicaragua's Caribbean coast was first seen by Spanish explorers in 1502. It was not until 1522, however, that a formal military expedition, under Gil González Dávila, led to the Spanish conquest of Nicaraguan territory. González launched an expedition from Panama, arriving in Nicaragua through Costa Rica. After suffering both illness and torrential rains, he reached the land governed by the powerful chief Nicoya, who gave González and his men a warm welcome. Soon thereafter, Nicoya and 6,000 of his people embraced the Roman Catholic faith. González continued his exploration and arrived in the next settlement, which was governed by a chief named Nicaragua, or Nicarao, after whom the country was named. Chief Nicaragua received González as a friend and gave him large quantities of gold. Perhaps to placate the Spanish, Nicaragua also converted to Roman Catholicism, as did more than 9,000 members of his tribe. All were baptized within eight days. Confident of further success, González moved on to the interior, where he encountered resistance from an army of 3,000 Niquirano, led by another of their chiefs, Diriagén. González

Central Square in León
Courtesy Nicaraguan Tourism Institute

retreated and traveled south to the coast, returning to Panama with large quantities of gold and pearls.

In 1523 the governor of Panama, Pedro Arias Dávila (Pedrarias), appointed Francisco Hernández de Córdoba to lead the Nicaraguan conquest effort. Hernández de Córdoba led an expedition in 1524 that succeeded in establishing the first permanent Spanish settlement in Nicaragua. He quickly overcame the resistance of the native peoples and named the land Nicaragua. To deny González's claims of settlement rights and prevent his eventual control of the region, Hernández de Córdoba founded the cities of León and Granada, which later became the centers of colonial Nicaragua. From León, he launched expeditions to explore other parts of the territory. While the rivalry between Hernández de Córdoba and González raged, Pedrarias charged Hernández de Córdoba with mismanagement and sentenced him to death. González died soon thereafter, and the Spanish crown awarded Pedrarias the governorship of Nicaragua in 1528. Pedrarias stayed in Nicaragua until his death in July 1531.

Spain showed little interest in Nicaragua throughout this period, mostly because it was more interested in exploiting the vast riches found in Mexico and Peru. By 1531 many Spanish settlers in Nicaragua had left for South America to join Francisco Pizarro's efforts to conquer the wealthy regions of the Inca Empire. Native Nicaraguan settlements also decreased in size because the indigenous inhabitants were exported to work in Peruvian mines; an estimated 200,000 native Nicaraguans were exported as slaves to South America from 1528 to 1540. Many Spanish towns founded in Nicaragua during the first years of the conquest disappeared. By the end of the 1500s, Nicaragua was reduced to the cities of León, located west of Lago de León (today Lago de Managua), and Granada, located on Lago de Nicaragua.

Colonial Rule

Although Nicaragua had been part of the *audiencia* (audience or court) of Panama, established in 1538, it was transferred to the Viceroyalty of New Spain when Spain divided its empire into two viceroyalties in 1543. The following year, the new *audiencia* of Guatemala, a subdivision of the Viceroyalty of New Spain, was created. This *audiencia* extended from southern Mexico through Panama and had its capital first at Gracias, Honduras, and then at Antigua, Guatemala, after 1549. In 1570 the *audiencia* was reorganized and reduced in size, losing the territory of present-day Panama, the Yucatán, and the Mexican state of Tabasco.

The five-man *audiencia*, or court, was the highest governmental authority in the territory. During most of the colonial period, the president of the *audiencia* held the additional titles of governor and captain general (hence, the alternative name of Captaincy General of Guatemala) and was charged with administrative, judicial, and military authority. The governor, or captain general, was appointed by the Spanish king and was responsible to him; in fact, the colony was sometimes referred to as the Kingdom of Guatemala.

The *audiencia* was divided into provinces for administrative purposes, and the leading official in each province was generally called an *alcalde mayor*, or governor. León was the capital of the Province of Nicaragua, housing the local governor, the Roman Catholic bishop, and other important appointees. An elite of creole (individuals of Spanish descent born in the New World) merchants controlled the economic and political life of each province. Because of the great distance between the centers of Spanish rule, political power was centered with the local government, the town council or *ayuntamiento*, which ignored most official orders from the Spanish crown.

Throughout the seventeenth century, trade restrictions imposed by Spain, natural disasters, and foreign attacks devastated the economy of the Captaincy General of Guatemala. The local government neglected agricultural production; powerful earthquakes in 1648, 1651, and 1663 caused massive destruction in the Province of Nicaragua; and from 1651 to 1689, Nicaragua was subjected to bloody incursions from English, French, and Dutch pirates. In 1668 and 1670, these buccaneers captured and destroyed the city of Granada, center of the province's agricultural wealth. The Captaincy General of Guatemala was generally neglected by Spain. Within the captaincy general, the Province of Nicaragua remained weak and unstable, ruled by persons with little interest in the welfare of its people.

In the late 1600s, the Miskito, who lived in Nicaragua's Caribbean lowlands, began to be exploited by English "filibusters" (irregular military adventurers) intent on encroaching on Spanish landowners. In 1687 the English governor of Jamaica named a Miskito who was one of his prisoners, "King of the Mosquitia Nation," and declared the region to be under the protection of the English crown. This event marked the beginning of a long rivalry between Spanish (and later Nicaraguan) and British authorities over the sovereignty of the Caribbean coast, which effectively remained under British control until the end of the nineteenth century.

After more than a century of exploiting the mineral wealth of the New World, the Spanish realized that activities other than mining could be profitable. The Province of Nicaragua then began to experience economic growth based on export agriculture. By the early 1700s, a powerful elite was well established in the cities of León, Granada, and, to a lesser extent, Rivas.

Events in Spain in the early 1700s were to have long-lasting repercussions in Nicaragua. The War of the Spanish Succession (1701–14) resulted in the Bourbons replacing the Habsburgs on the Spanish throne. The Habsburgs had supported strict trade monopolies, especially in the Spanish colonies. The Bourbons were proponents of more liberal free-trade policies. Throughout the captaincy general, groups were hurt or helped by these changes; the factions supporting changes in trading policy came to be known as liberals while those who had profited under the old rules were known as conservatives. Liberals generally consisted of growers with new crops to sell, merchants, or export interests. Conservatives were generally composed of landowners who had profited under the old protectionism and who resisted new competition. In time, conservatism also became associated with support for the Roman Catholic Church; the liberals took a more anticlerical stand.

Throughout the captaincy general, cities came to be associated with one or the other of these political factions, depending on the basis of the economy of each. Typically, each of the five provinces of the captaincy general had one city that championed the liberal cause and another that spoke for the conservatives. In Nicaragua, León was primarily involved in exporting animal products such as leather and tallow and soon became the center for free-trading liberalism. The conservative elite in Granada, however, had made their fortunes under the old protectionist system and resisted change. Competition between the two cities over influence on colonial policy became violent at times, and each city supported armed groups in order to defend itself and its ideas. In time, the hatred and violence between the two cities and the two factions became institutionalized, and often the original ideological difference was forgotten. Independence in the next century only exacerbated the struggle as it eliminated Spain as a referee. The violent rivalry between liberals and conservatives was one of the most important and destructive aspects of Nicaraguan history, a characteristic that would last until well into the twentieth century. Politicians frequently chose party loyalty over national interest, and, particularly in the 1800s, the nation was often the loser in interparty strife.

Liberal-conservative rivalry was not only a domestic issue but also an international one. The other provinces in the captaincy general, and later the successor nations, had similar liberal and conservative factions. Each faction did not hesitate to support its compatriots, often with armed force, in another province. After independence, the intercountry interference continued unabated; conservatives or liberals in each of the five successor states frequently sent troops to support like factions in neighboring countries. This constant intervention and involvement in its neighbors' affairs was a second and equally pernicious characteristic of Nicaraguan politics throughout its independent existence.

Nineteenth Century

National Independence, 1821–57

Spain's control over its colonies in the New World was threatened in the early 1800s by the struggle for national independence throughout the entire region. Weakened by the French invasion in 1794 and internal upheaval, Spain tried to hold onto its richest colonies, which led to even further neglect of its poorer Central American territories. Resentment toward the Spanish-born elite (*peninsulares*—those born in Spain and the only persons allowed to administer Spanish colonies) grew among Nicaraguan creoles. The first local movements against Spanish rule in Central America occurred in 1811, when the Province of El Salvador staged a revolt. *Peninsular* authorities were deposed and replaced by creoles, who demanded less repressive laws. Although the Province of Nicaragua officially refused to join the rebellion, a popular uprising soon broke out. Violence and political rivalry prevailed in all of the Central American colonies during the ensuing decade.

Establishment of an independent Nicaragua came in stages. The first stage occurred in 1821 when the Captaincy General of Guatemala formally declared its independence from Spain on

September 15, which is still celebrated as independence day. At first the captaincy general was part of the Mexican Empire under General Agustín de Iturbide, but efforts by Mexico to control the region were resisted all over Central America. Separatist feelings throughout the isthmus grew, and five of the United Provinces of Central America—Costa Rica, El Salvador, Guatemala, Honduras, and Nicaragua—declared their independence from Mexico in July 1823. The sixth province, Chiapas, opted to remain with Mexico. Under a weak federal government, each province created its own independent internal administration. Inadequate communication and internal conflicts, however, overshadowed efforts to institutionalize the federation for the next decade and a half. Efforts to centralize power led to civil war between 1826 and 1829. The federation finally dissolved in 1837, and a Constituent Assembly (see Glossary) formally declared Nicaragua's independence from the United Provinces of Central America on April 30, 1838.

Foreign Intervention, 1850–68

British and United States interests in Nicaragua grew during the mid-1800s because of the country's strategic importance as a transit route across the isthmus. British settlers seized the port of San Juan del Norte—at the mouth of the Río San Juan on the southern Caribbean coast—and expelled all Nicaraguan officials on January 1, 1848. The following year, Britain forced Nicaragua to sign a treaty recognizing British rights over the Miskito on the Caribbean coast. Britain's control over much of the Caribbean lowlands, which the British called the Mosquito Coast (present-day Costa de Mosquitos), from 1678 until 1894 was a constant irritant to Nicaraguan nationalists. The start of the gold rush in California in 1849 increased United States interests in Central America as a transoceanic route, and Nicaragua at first encouraged a United States presence to counterbalance the British.

The possibility of economic riches in Nicaragua attracted international business development. Afraid of Britain's colonial intentions, Nicaragua held discussions with the United States in 1849, leading to a treaty that gave the United States exclusive rights to a transit route across Nicaragua. In return, the United States promised to protect Nicaragua from other foreign intervention. On June 22, 1849, the first official United States representative, Ephraim George Squier, arrived in Nicaragua. Both liberals and conservatives welcomed the United States diplo-

Colonial architecture in
Granada
Courtesy Nicaraguan
Tourism Institute

mat. A contract between Commodore Cornelius Vanderbilt, a United States businessman, and the Nicaraguan government was signed on August 26, 1849, granting Vanderbilt's company—the Accessory Transit Company—exclusive rights to build a transisthmian canal within twelve years. The contract also gave Vanderbilt exclusive rights, while the canal was being completed, to use a land-and-water transit route across Nicaragua, part of a larger scheme to move passengers from the eastern United States to California. The westbound journey across Nicaragua began by small boat from San Juan del Norte on the Caribbean coast, traveled up the Río San Juan to San Carlos on Lago de Nicaragua, crossed Lago de Nicaragua to La Virgen on the west shore, and then continued by railroad or stagecoach to San Juan del Sur on the Pacific coast. In September 1849, the United States-Nicaragua treaty, along with Vanderbilt's contract, was approved by the Nicaraguan Congress.

British economic interests were threatened by the United States enterprise led by Vanderbilt, and violence erupted in 1850 when the British tried to block the operations of the Accessory Transit Company. As a result, United States and British government officials held diplomatic talks and on April 19, 1850, without consulting the Nicaraguan government, signed the Clayton-Bulwer Treaty, in which both countries agreed that neither would claim exclusive power over a future canal in Central America nor gain exclusive control over any part of the region. Although the Nicaraguan government originally accepted the idea of a transit route because of the economic benefit it would bring Nicaragua, the operation remained under United States and British control. Britain retained control of the Caribbean port of San Juan del Norte, and the United States owned the vessels, hotels, restaurants, and land transportation along the entire transit route.

Continued unrest in the 1850s set the stage for two additional elements in Nicaragua history: frequent United States military interventions in Nicaragua and a propensity for Nicaraguan politicians to call on the United States to settle domestic disputes. In 1853 conservative General Fruto Chamorro had taken over the government and exiled his leading liberal opponents. Aided by the liberal government in neighboring Honduras, an exile army entered Nicaragua on May 5, 1854. The subsequent conflict proved prolonged and bloody; Chamorro declared that his forces would execute all armed rebels who fell into their hands, and the liberal leader, General Máximo Jérez, proclaimed that all government supporters were traitors to the nation.

The liberals enjoyed initial success in the fighting, but the tide turned in 1854 when Guatemala's conservative government invaded Honduras, forcing that nation to end its support of the liberals in Nicaragua. Chamorro's death from natural causes in March 1855 brought little respite to the beleaguered liberals, who began to look abroad for support. They turned to William Walker, a soldier of fortune from Tennessee who had previously invaded Mexico. Through an agent, they offered Walker funds and generous land grants if he would bring a force of United States adventurers to their aid. Walker leaped at the chance—he quickly recruited a force of fifty-six followers and landed with them in Nicaragua on May 4, 1855.

Walker's initial band was soon reinforced by other recruits from the United States. Strengthened by this augmented force, Walker seized Granada, center of conservative power. The stunned conservative government surrendered, and the United States quickly recognized a new puppet liberal government with Patricio Rivas as president. Real power, however, remained with Walker, who had assumed command of the Nicaraguan army.

As Walker's power and the size of his army grew, conservative politicians throughout Central America became increasingly anxious. Encouraged by Britain, the conservative governments of the other four Central American republics agreed to send troops to Nicaragua. In March 1856, Costa Rica declared war on the North American filibuster, but an epidemic of cholera decimated the Costa Rican forces and forced their withdrawal. Encouraged by this victory, Walker began plans to have himself elected president and to encourage colonization of Nicaragua by North Americans. This scheme was too much even for his puppet president Rivas, who broke with Walker and his followers and sent messages to Guatemala and El Salvador requesting their help in expelling the filibusters.

Undeterred, Walker proceeded to hold a farcical election and install himself as president. Making English the country's official language and legalizing slavery, Walker also allied himself with Vanderbilt's rivals in the contest for control of the transit route, hoping that this alliance would provide both funds and transportation for future recruits. His call for Nicaragua's annexation by the United States as a slave state garnered some support from United States proslavery forces.

In the meantime, forces opposing Walker were rapidly gaining the upper hand, leading him to attack his liberal allies, accusing them of half-hearted support. Most Nicaraguans were offended by Walker's proslavery, pro-United States stance; Vanderbilt was determined to destroy him, and the rest of Central America actively sought his demise. The British also encouraged opposition to Walker as a means of curbing United States influence in the region. Even the United States government, fearful that plans to annex Nicaragua as a new slave state would fan the fires of sectional conflict growing within the United States, became opposed to his ambitions.

The struggle to expel Walker and his army from Nicaragua proved to be long and costly. In the process, the colonial city of Granada was burned, and thousands of Central Americans lost their lives.The combined opposition of Vanderbilt, the British Navy, and the forces of all of Central America, however, eventually defeated the filibusters. A key factor in Walker's defeat was the Costa Rican seizure of the transit route; the seizure permitted Walker's opponents to take control of the steamers on Lago de Nicaragua and thereby cut off much of Walker's access to additional recruits and finances. Vanderbilt played a major role in this effort and also supplied funds that enabled the Costa Ricans to offer free return passage to the United States to any of the filibusters who would abandon the cause. Many took advantage of this opportunity, and Walker's forces began to dwindle.

The final battle of what Nicaraguans called the "National War" (1856–57) took place in the spring of 1857 in the town of Rivas, near the Costa Rican border. Walker beat off the attacks of the Central Americans, but the strength and morale of his forces were declining, and it would be only a matter of time until he would be overwhelmed. At this point, Commander Charles H. Davis of the United States Navy, whose ship had been sent to Nicaragua's Pacific coast to protect United States economic interests, arranged a truce. On May 1, 1857, Walker and his remaining followers, escorted by a force of United States marines, evacuated Rivas, marched down to the coast, and took the ships back to the United States.

Walker's forced exile was short-lived, however; he made four more attempts to return to Central America (in 1857, 1858, 1859, and 1860). In 1860 Walker was captured by a British warship as he tried to enter Honduras. The British Navy turned him over to local authorities, and he was executed by a Honduran firing squad. Walker's activities provided Nicaraguans with a long-lasting suspicion of United States activities and designs upon their nation.

Originally a product of interparty strife, the National War ironically served as a catalyst for cooperation between the liberal and conservative parties. The capital was moved to Managua in an effort to dampen interparty conflict, and on September 12, 1856, both parties had signed an agreement to join efforts against Walker. This pact marked the beginning of an era of peaceful coexistence between Nicaragua's political parties, although the onus of the liberals' initial support of Walker allowed the conservatives to rule Nicaragua for the next three decades. After Walker's departure, Patricio Rivas served as president for the third time. He remained in office until June 1857, when liberal General Máximo Jérez and conservative General Tomás Martínez assumed a bipartisan presidency. A Constituent Assembly convened in November of that year and named General Martínez as president (1858–67).

The devastation and instability caused by the war in Nicaragua, as well as the opening of a railroad across Panama, adversely affected the country's transit route. After only a few years of operation in the early 1850s, the transit route was closed for five years from 1857 to 1862, and the entire effort was subsequently abandoned in April 1868. Despite the failure of the transit plan, United States interest in building a canal across Nicaragua persisted throughout most of the nineteenth century. By 1902, however, there was increasing support from the administration of United States president Theodore Roosevelt to build a transisthmian canal in Panama. The opening of the Panama Canal in 1914 effectively ended serious discussion of a canal across Nicaragua.

Conservative and Liberal Regimes, 1858–1909

The Conservative Party (Partido Conservador) ruled in Nicaragua from 1857 to 1893, a period of relative economic progress and prosperity sometimes referred to as the "Thirty Years." A railroad system connecting the western part of Nicaragua with the port of Corinto on the Pacific coast was built, and roads and telegraph lines were extended. Exports of agricultural products also increased during this period. Coffee as an export commodity grew between the 1850s and the 1870s, and by 1890 coffee had become the nation's principal export. Toward the end of the 1800s, Nicaragua experienced dramatic economic growth because of the growing demand for coffee and bananas in the international market. The local economic elites were divided between the established cattle raisers and small growers and the new coffee-producers sector. Disputes about national economic policy arose between these powerful elites. Revealing their sympathies, the ruling conservatives passed laws favoring cheap labor that benefited mostly coffee planters.

The period of relative peace came to an end in 1891 when Roberto Sacasa, who had succeeded to the presidency in 1889 after the death of the elected incumbent, was elected to a term of his own. Although a conservative, Sacasa was from León, not Granada, and his election produced a split within the ruling Conservative Party. When Sacasa attempted to retain power after the March 1893 end of his term, the liberals, led by General José Santos Zelaya, quickly took advantage of the division within conservative ranks.

A revolt began in April 1893 when a coalition of liberals and dissident conservatives ousted Sacasa and installed another conservative in office. An effort was made to share power with the liberals, but this coalition soon proved unworkable. In July, Zelaya's liberal supporters resigned from the government and launched another revolt, which soon proved successful. A constitutional convention was hurriedly called, and a new constitution incorporating anticlerical provisions, limitations on foreigners' rights to claim diplomatic protection, and abolition of the death penalty was adopted. Zelaya was confirmed as president, a post he would retain until 1909.

Zelaya's rule proved to be one of the most controversial periods in Nicaraguan history. Zelaya was a ruthless dictator who managed to stay in power for sixteen years despite foreign and domestic opposition. Nevertheless, he was responsible for the creation of a professional army and the growth of strong nationalist feelings.

Zelaya opened the country to foreign investment, expanded coffee production, and boosted banana exports. His government promoted internal development and modernized Nicaragua's infrastructure. During his tenure, new roads and seaport facilities were constructed, railroad lines were extended, and many government buildings and schools were built. The proliferation of United States companies in Nicaragua grew to the point that, by the early 1900s, United States firms controlled most of the production of coffee, bananas, gold, and lumber.

Zelaya's administration was also responsible for an agreement ending the Nicaraguan dispute with Britain over sovereignty of the Caribbean coast. Aided by the mediation of the United States and strong support from the other Central American republics, control over the Caribbean coast region was finally awarded to Nicaragua in 1894. Sovereignty did not bring the government in Managua control over this region, however; the Caribbean coast remained culturally separate and inaccessible to the western part of the country. Although his reputation was boosted by resolution of the centuries-old dispute with Britain, Zelaya was regarded with suspicion abroad. His imperialistic ambitions in Central America, as well as his vocal rebukes of United States intervention and influence in Central America, won him little support. Zelaya's nationalist anti-United States stance drove him to call upon the Germans and Japanese to compete with the United States for rights to a canal route. Opposition to these schemes from the conservative faction, mostly landowners, led Zelaya to increase repression. In 1903 a major conservative rebellion, led by Emiliano Chamorro Vargas, broke out. Another uprising in 1909, this time aided by British money and the United States marines, was successful in driving Zelaya from power.

The Early Twentieth Century and the Somoza Years, 1909–79

United States Intervention, 1909–33

United States interest in Nicaragua, which had waned during the last half of the 1800s because of isolationist sentiment following the United States Civil War (1861–65), grew again during the final years of the Zelaya administration. Angered by the United States choice of Panama for the site of a transisthmian canal, President Zelaya made concessions to Germany and Japan for a competing canal across Nicaragua. Relations with the United States deteriorated, and civil war erupted in October 1909, when anti-Zelaya liberals joined with a group of conservatives under Juan Estrada to overthrow the government. The United States broke off elations with the Zelaya administration after two United States mercenaries serving with the rebels were captured and executed by government forces. Soon thereafter, 400 United States marines landed on the Caribbean coast. Weakened and pressured by both domestic and external forces, Zelaya resigned on December 17, 1909. His minister of foreign affairs, José Madriz, was appointed president by the Nicaraguan Congress. A liberal from León, Madriz was unable to restore order because of continuing pressure from conservatives and the United States forces, and he resigned on August 20, 1910.

Conservative Estrada, governor of Nicaragua's easternmost department, assumed power after Madriz's resignation. The United States agreed to support Estrada, provided that a Constituent Assembly was elected to write a constitution. After agreeing with this stipulation, a coalition conservative-liberal regime, headed by Estrada, was recognized by the United States on January 1, 1911. Political differences between the two parties soon surfaced, however, and minister of war General Luis Mena forced Estrada to resign. Estrada's vice president, the conservative Adolfo Díaz, then became president. In mid-1912 Mena persuaded a Constituent Assembly to name him successor to Díaz when Díaz's term expired in 1913. When the United States refused to recognize the Constituent Assembly's decision, Mena rebelled against the Díaz government. A force led by liberal Benjamín Zelaydón quickly came to the aid of Mena. Díaz, relying on what was becoming a time-honored tradition, requested assistance from the United States. In August

1912, a force of 2,700 United States marines once again landed at the ports of Corinto and Bluefields. Mena fled the country, and Zelaydón was killed.

The United States kept a contingent force in Nicaragua almost continually from 1912 until 1933. Although reduced to 100 in 1913, the contingent served as a reminder of the willingness of the United States to use force and its desire to keep conservative governments in power. Under United States supervision, national elections were held in 1913, but the liberals refused to participate in the electoral process, and Adolfo Díaz was reelected to a full term. Foreign investment decreased during this period because of the high levels of violence and political instability. Nicaragua and the United States signed but never ratified the Castillo-Knox Treaty in 1914, giving the United States the right to intervene in Nicaragua to protect United States interests. A modified version omitting the intervention clause, the Chamorro-Bryan Treaty, was finally ratified by the United States Senate in 1916. This treaty gave the United States exclusive rights to build an interoceanic canal across Nicaragua. Because the United States had already built the Panama Canal, however, the terms of the Chamorro-Bryan Treaty served the primary purpose of securing United States interests against potential foreign countries—mainly Germany or Japan—building another canal in Central America. The treaty also transformed Nicaragua into a near United States protectorate.

Collaboration with the United States allowed the conservatives to remain in power until 1925. The liberals boycotted the 1916 election, and conservative Emiliano Chamorro was elected with no opposition. The liberals did participate in the 1920 elections, but the backing of the United States and a fraudulent vote count assured the election of Emiliano Chamorro's uncle, Diego Manuel Chamorro.

A moderate conservative, Carlos Solórzano, was elected president in open elections in 1924, with liberal Juan Bautista Sacasa as his vice president. After taking office on January 1, 1925, Solórzano requested that the United States delay the withdrawal of its troops from Nicaragua. Nicaragua and the United States agreed that United States troops would remain while United States military instructors helped build a national military force. In June, Solórzano's government contracted with retired United States Army Major Calvin B. Carter to establish and train the National Guard. The United States marines left Nicaragua in August 1925. However, President Solórzano, who had already purged the liberals from his coalition government, was subsequently forced out of power in November 1925 by a conservative group who proclaimed General Emiliano Chamorro (who had also served as president from 1917 to 1921), as president in January 1926.

Fearing a new round of conservative-liberal violence and worried that a revolution in Nicaragua might result in a leftist victory, which had happened a few years earlier in Mexico, the United States sent marines, who landed on the Caribbean coast in May 1926, ostensibly to protect United States citizens and property. United States authorities in Nicaragua mediated a peace agreement between the liberals and the conservatives in October 1926. Chamorro resigned, and the Nicaraguan Congress elected Adolfo Díaz as president (Díaz had previously served as president, 1911–16). Violence resumed, however, when former vice president Sacasa returned from exile to claim his rights to the presidency. In April 1927, the United States sent Henry L. Stimson to mediate the civil war. Once in Nicaragua, Stimson began conversations with President Díaz as well as with leaders from both political parties. Stimson's meetings with General José María Moncada, the leader of the liberal rebels, led to a peaceful solution of the crisis. On May 20, 1927, Moncada agreed to a plan in which both sides—the government and Moncada's liberal forces—would disarm. In addition, a nonpartisan military force would be established under United States supervision. This accord was known as the Pact of Espino Negro.

As part of the agreement, President Díaz would finish his term, and United States forces would remain in Nicaragua to maintain order and supervise the 1928 elections. A truce between the government and the rebels remained in effect and included the disarmament of both liberal rebels and government troops. Sacasa, who refused to sign the agreement, left the country. United States forces took over the country's military functions and strengthened the Nicaraguan National Guard.

A rebel liberal group under the leadership of Augusto César Sandino also refused to sign the Pact of Espino Negro. An illegitimate son of a wealthy landowner and a mestizo servant, Sandino had left his father's home early in his youth and traveled to Honduras, Guatemala, and Mexico. During his three-year stay in Tampico, Mexico, Sandino had acquired a strong sense of Nicaraguan nationalism and pride in his mestizo heritage. At the urging of his father, Sandino had returned to Nicaragua in 1926 and settled in the department of Nueva Segovia, where he worked at a gold mine owned by a United States company. Sandino, who lectured the mine workers about social inequalities and the need to change the political system, soon organized his own army, consisting mostly of peasants and workers, and joined the liberals fighting against the conservative regime of Chamorro. Highly distrusted by Moncada, Sandino set up hit-and-run operations against conservative forces independently of Moncada's liberal army. After the United States mediated the agreement between liberal forces and the conservative regime, Sandino, calling Moncada a traitor and denouncing United States intervention, reorganized his forces as the Army for the Defense of Nicaraguan Sovereignty (Ejército Defensor de la Soberanía de Nicaragua—EDSN). Sandino then staged an independent guerrilla campaign against the government and United States forces. Although Sandino's original intentions were to restore constitutional government under Sacasa, after the Pact of Espino Negro agreement his objective became the defense of Nicaraguan sovereignty against the United States. Receiving his main support from the rural population, Sandino resumed his battle against United States troops. At the height of his guerrilla campaign, Sandino claimed to have some 3,000 soldiers in his army, although official figures estimated the number at only 300. Sandino's guerrilla war caused significant damage in the Caribbean coast and mining regions. After debating whether to continue direct fighting against Sandino's forces, the United States opted to develop the nonpartisan Nicaraguan National Guard to contain internal violence. The National Guard would soon become the most important power in Nicaraguan politics.

The late 1920s and early 1930s saw the growing power of Anastasio "Tacho" Somoza García, a leader who would create a dynasty that ruled Nicaragua for four and a half decades. Moncada won the presidency in 1928 in one of the most honest elections ever held in Nicaragua. For the 1932 elections, the liberals nominated Juan Bautista Sacasa and the conservatives, Adolfo Díaz. Sacasa won the elections and was installed as president on January 2, 1933. In the United States, popular opposition to the Nicaraguan intervention rose as United States casualty lists grew. Anxious to withdraw from Nicaraguan politics, the United States turned over command of the National

*A poster of Sandino hangs in front of the facade of the
Managua Cathedral.
Courtesy Edmundo Flores*

Guard to the Nicaraguan government, and United States marines left the country soon thereafter. President Sacasa, under pressure from General Moncada, appointed Somoza García as chief director of the National Guard. Somoza García, a close friend of Moncada and nephew of President Sacasa, had supported the liberal revolt in 1926. Somoza García also enjoyed support from the United States government because of his participation at the 1927 peace conference as one of Stimson's interpreters. Having attended school in Philadelphia and been trained by United States marines, Somoza García, who was fluent in English, had developed friends with military, economic, and political influence in the United States.

After United States troops left Nicaragua in January 1933, the Sacasa government and the National Guard still were threatened by Sandino's EDSN. True to his promise to stop fighting after United States marines had left the country, Sandino agreed to discussions with Sacasa. In February 1934, these negotiations began. During their meetings, Sacasa offered Sandino a general amnesty as well as land and safeguards for him and his guerrilla forces. However, Sandino, who regarded the National Guard as unconstitutional because of its ties to the United States military, insisted on the guard's dissolution. His attitude made him very unpopular with Somoza García and his guards. Without consulting the president, Somoza García gave orders for Sandino's assassination, hoping that this action would help him win the loyalty of senior guard officers. On February 21, 1934, while leaving the presidential palace after a dinner with President Sacasa, Sandino and two of his generals were arrested by National Guard officers acting under Somoza García's instructions. They were then taken to an airfield in Managua, executed, and buried in unmarked graves. Despite Sacasa's strong disapproval of Somoza García's action, the Nicaraguan president was too weak to contain the National Guard director. After Sandino's execution, the National Guard launched a ruthless campaign against Sandino's supporters. In less than a month, Sandino's army was totally destroyed.

President Sacasa's popularity decreased as a result of his poor leadership and accusations of fraud in the 1934 congressional elections. Somoza García benefited from Sacasa's diminishing power, while at the same time he brought together the National Guard and the Liberal Party (Partido Liberal—PL) in order to win the presidential elections in 1936. Somoza García also cultivated support from former presidents Moncada and Chamorro while consolidating control within the Liberal Party.

Early in 1936, Somoza García openly confronted President Sacasa by using military force to displace local government officials loyal to the president and replacing them with close associates. Somoza García's increasing military confrontation led to Sacasa's resignation on June 6, 1936. The Congress appointed Carlos Brenes Jarquín, a Somoza García associate, as interim president and postponed presidential elections until December. In November, Somoza García officially resigned as chief director of the National Guard, thus complying with constitutional requirements for eligibility to run for the presidency. The Liberal Nationalist Party (Partido Liberal Nacionalista— PLN) was established with support from a faction of the Conservative Party to support Somoza García's candidacy. Somoza García was elected president in the December election by the remarkable margin of 107,201 votes to 108. On January 1, 1937, Somoza García resumed control of the National Guard, combining the roles of president and chief director of the military. Thus, Somoza García established a military dictatorship, in the shadows of democratic laws, that would last more than four decades.

The Somoza Era, 1936–74

Somoza García controlled political power, directly as president or indirectly through carefully chosen puppet presidents, from 1936 until his assassination in 1956. A cynical and opportunistic individual, Somoza García ruled Nicaragua with a strong arm, deriving his power from three main sources: the ownership or control of large portions of the Nicaraguan economy, the military support of the National Guard, and his acceptance and support from the United States. His excellent command of the English language and understanding of United States culture, combined with a charming personality and considerable political talent and resourcefulness, helped Somoza García win many powerful allies in the United States. Through large investments in land, manufacturing, transport, and real estate, he enriched himself and his close friends.

After Somoza García won in the December 1936 presidential elections, he diligently proceeded to consolidate his power within the National Guard, while at the same time dividing his political opponents. Family members and close associates were given key positions within the government and the military.

The Somoza family also controlled the PLN, which in turn controlled the legislature and judicial system, thus giving Somoza García absolute power over every sphere of Nicaraguan politics. Nominal political opposition was allowed as long as it did not threaten the ruling elite. Somoza García's National Guard repressed serious political opposition and antigovernment demonstrations. The institutional power of the National Guard grew in most government-owned enterprises, until eventually it controlled the national radio and telegraph networks, the postal and immigration services, health services, the internal revenue service, and the national railroads. In less than two years after his election, Somoza García, defying the Conservative Party, declared his intention to stay in power beyond his presidential term. Thus, in 1938 Somoza García named a Constituent Assembly that gave the president extensive power and elected him for another eight-year term.

Somoza García's opportunistic support of the Allies during World War II benefited Nicaragua by injecting desperately needed United States funds into the economy and increasing military capabilities. Nicaragua received relatively large amounts of military aid and enthusiastically integrated its economy into the wartime hemispheric economic plan, providing raw materials in support of the Allied war effort. Exports of timber, gold, and cotton soared. However, because more than 90 percent of all exports went to the United States, the growth in trade also increased the country's economic and political dependence.

Somoza García built an immense fortune for himself and his family during the 1940s through substantial investments in agricultural exports, especially in coffee and cattle. The government also confiscated German properties and then sold them to Somoza García and his family at ridiculously low prices. Among his many industrial enterprises, Somoza García owned textile companies, sugar mills, rum distilleries, the merchant marine lines, the national Nicaraguan Airlines (Líneas Aéreas de Nicaragua—Lanica), and La Salud dairy—the country's only pasteurized milk facility. Somoza García also gained large profits from economic concessions to national and foreign companies, bribes, and illegal exports. By the end of World War II, Somoza García had amassed one of the largest fortunes in the region—an estimated US$60 million.

After World War II, however, widespread domestic and international opposition to the Somoza García dictatorship grew among political parties, labor, business groups, and the United States government. Somoza García's decision to run for reelection in 1944 was opposed by some liberals, who established the Independent Liberal Party (Partido Liberal Independiente—PLI). Somoza García's reelection was also opposed by the United States government. The dictator reacted to growing criticism by creating a puppet government to save his rule. He decided not to run for reelection and had the PLN nominate the elderly Leonardo Argüello, believing he could control Argüello from behind the scenes. Argüello ran against Enoc Aguado, a candidate supported by a coalition of political parties that included the conservatives and the PLI. Despite the large support for the Aguado candidacy, Somoza García subverted the electoral process by using government resources and the National Guard to ensure the electoral victory of his candidate. Argüello was sworn in on May 1, 1947, and Somoza García remained as chief director of the National Guard.

Argüello had no intention of being a puppet, however, and in less than a month, when Argüello's measures began to challenge Somoza García's power, the National Guard chief staged a coup and placed a family associate, Benjamín Lacayo Sacasa, in the presidency. The administration of United States president Harry S. Truman responded by withholding diplomatic recognition from the new Nicaraguan government. In an effort to legitimize the new regime and win United States support, Somoza García named a Constituent Assembly to write a new constitution. The assembly then appointed Somoza García's uncle, Víctor Román Reyes, as president. The constitution of 1947 was carefully crafted with strong anticommunist rhetoric to win United States support. Despite efforts by Somoza García to placate the United States, the United States continued its opposition and refused to recognize the new regime. Under diplomatic pressure from the rest of Latin America, formal diplomatic relations between Managua and Washington were restored in mid-1948.

Despite its anticommunist rhetoric, the government promoted liberal labor policies to gain support from the communist party of Nicaragua, known as the Nicaraguan Socialist Party (Partido Socialista Nicaragüense—PSN), and thwarted the establishment of any independent labor movement. The government approved several progressive laws in 1945 to win government support from labor unions. Concessions and bribes were granted to labor leaders, and antigovernment union leaders were displaced in favor of Somoza García loyalists. However, after placement of pro-Somoza García leaders in labor unions, most labor legislation was ignored. In 1950 Somoza García signed an agreement with conservative general Emiliano Chamorro Vargas that assured the Conservative Party of one-third of the congressional delegates as well as limited representation in the cabinet and in the courts. Somoza García also promised clauses in the new 1950 constitution guaranteeing "commercial liberty." This measure brought back limited support from the traditional elite to the Somoza García regime. The elite benefited from the economic growth of the 1950s and 1960s, especially in the cotton and cattle export sectors. Somoza García again was elected president in general elections held in 1950. In 1955 Congress amended the constitution to allow his reelection for yet another presidential term.

Somoza García had many political enemies, and coups against him were attempted periodically, even within the National Guard. For protection, he constructed a secure compound within his residence and kept personal bodyguards, independent of the National Guard, with him wherever he went. Nevertheless, on September 21, 1956, while attending a PLN party in León to celebrate his nomination for the presidency, Somoza García was fatally wounded by Rigoberto López Pérez, a twenty-seven-year-old Nicaraguan poet who had managed to pass through Somoza García's security. The dictator was flown to the Panama Canal Zone, where he died eight days later.

Somoza García was succeeded as president by his eldest son, Luis Somoza Debayle. A United States-trained engineer, Somoza Debayle was first elected as a PLN delegate in 1950 and by 1956 presided over the Nicaraguan Congress. After his father's death, he assumed the position of interim president, as prescribed in the constitution. His brother Anastasio "Tachito" Somoza Debayle, a West Point graduate, took over leadership of the National Guard. A major political repression campaign followed Somoza García's assassination: many political opponents were tortured and imprisoned by guards under orders from Anastasio Somoza Debayle and the government imposed press censorship and suspended many civil liberties. When the Conservative Party refused to participate in the 1957 elections—in protest against government restrictions on civil liberties—the Somoza brothers created a puppet opposition party, the National Conservative Party (Partido Conservador Nacional—PCN), to give a democratic facade to the political campaign. Luis Somoza Debayle won the presidency in 1957 with little opposition. During his six-year term, from 1957 to 1963, his government provided citizens with some freedoms and raised hopes for political liberalization. In an effort to open up the government, Luis Somoza Debayle restored the constitutional ban on reelection.

In 1960 Nicaragua joined El Salvador, Guatemala, and Honduras (Costa Rica joined later) in the establishment of the Central American Common Market (CACM—see Appendix B). The main objective of the regional economic group was to promote trade among member countries. Under this partnership, trade and manufacturing increased, greatly stimulating economic growth. Furthermore, in the international political sphere, Luis Somoza Debayle's anticommunist stance won government favor and support from the United States. In 1959 Nicaragua was among the first nations to condemn the Cuban Revolution and to accuse Fidel Castro Ruz of attempting to overthrow the Nicaraguan government. The Luis Somoza Debayle government played a leading role in the Bay of Pigs invasion of Cuba in 1961, allowing the Cuban exile brigade to use military bases on the Caribbean coast to launch the failed maneuver.

Trusted friends of the Somoza family held the presidency from 1963 until 1967. In 1963 René Schick Gutiérrez won the presidential election; Somoza García's younger son, Anastasio Somoza Debayle, continued as chief director of the National Guard. Shick, who gave the appearance of following the less repressive programs of Luis Somoza Debayle, died in 1966 and was succeeded by Lorenzo Guerrero Gutiérrez.

When poor health prevented Luis Somoza Debayle from being a candidate, his brother Anastasio ran in the 1967 presidential election. To challenge the candidacy of the younger Somoza Debayle, the conservatives, the PLI, and the Christian Social Party (Partido Social Cristiano—PSC) created the National Opposition Union (Unión Nacional Opositora—UNO). The UNO nominated Fernando Agüero as their candidate. In February 1967, Anastasio Somoza Debayle was elected president amidst a repressive campaign against opposition supporters of Agüero. Two months later, Anastasio's brother Luis died of a heart attack. With his election, Anastasio Somoza Debayle became president as well as the director of the National Guard, giving him absolute political and military control over Nicaragua. Corruption and the use of force intensified, accelerating opposition from populist and business groups.

Although his four-year term was to end in 1971, Somoza Debayle amended the constitution to stay in power until 1972. Increasing pressures from the opposition and his own party, however, led the dictator to negotiate a political agreement, known as the Kupia-Kumi Pact, which installed a three-member junta that would rule from 1972 until 1974. The junta was established in May 1972 amidst opposition led by Pedro Joaquín Chamorro Cardenal and his newspaper *La Prensa.* Popular discontent also grew in response to deteriorating social conditions. Illiteracy, malnourishment, inadequate health services, and lack of proper housing also ignited criticism from the Roman Catholic Church, led by Archbishop Miguel Obando y Bravo. The archbishop began to publish a series of pastoral letters critical of Somoza Debayle's government.

On December 23, 1972, a powerful earthquake shook Nicaragua, destroying most of the capital city. The earthquake left approximately 10,000 dead and some 50,000 families homeless, and destroyed 80 percent of Managua's commercial buildings. Immediately after the earthquake, the National Guard joined the widespread looting of most of the remaining business establishments in Managua. When reconstruction began, the government's illegal appropriation and mismanagement of international relief aid, directed by the Somoza family and members of the National Guard, shocked the international community and produced further unrest in Nicaragua. The president's ability to take advantage of the people's suffering proved enormous. By some estimates, his personal wealth soared to US$400 million in 1974. As a result of his greed, Somoza Debayle's support base within the business sector began to crumble. A revived labor movement increased opposition to the regime and to the deteriorating economic conditions.

Somoza Debayle's intentions to run for another presidential term in 1974 were resisted even within his own PLN. The political opposition, led by Chamorro and former Minister of Education Ramiro Sacasa, established the Democratic Liberation Union (Unión Democrática de Liberación—Udel), an opposition group that included most anti-Somoza elements. The Udel was a broad coalition of business groups whose representation included members from both the traditional elite and labor

*Many buildings in downtown Managua, damaged in the 1972
earthquake, remained unrepaired in 1993.
Courtesy Edmundo Flores*

unions. The party promoted a dialogue with the government to foster political pluralism. The president responded with increasing political repression and further censorship of the media and the press. In September 1974, Somoza Debayle was reelected president.

The Rise of the FSLN

The Sandinista National Liberation Front (Frente Sandinista de Liberación Nacional—FSLN) was formally organized in Nicaragua in 1961. Founded by José Carlos Fonseca Amador, Silvio Mayorga, and Tomás Borge Martínez, the FSLN began in the late 1950s as a group of Marxist, antigovernment student activists at the National Autonomous University of Nicaragua (Universidad Nacional Autónoma de Nicaragua—UNAN) in Managua. Many of the early members were imprisoned. Borge spent several years in jail, and Fonseca spent several years in exile in Mexico, Cuba, and Costa Rica. Beginning with approximately twenty members in the early 1960s, the FSLN continued to struggle and grow in numbers. By the early 1970s, the group had gained enough support from peasants and student groups to launch limited military initiatives.

On December 27, 1974, a group of FSLN guerrillas seized the home of a former government official and took as hostages a handful of leading Nicaraguan officials, many of whom were Somoza relatives. With the mediation of Archbishop Obando y Bravo, the government and the guerrillas reached an agreement on December 30 that humiliated and further debilitated the Somoza regime. The guerrillas received a US$1 million ransom, had a government declaration read over the radio and printed in *La Prensa*, and succeeded in getting fourteen Sandinista prisoners released from jail and flown to Cuba along with the kidnappers. The guerrilla movement's prestige soared because of this successful operation. The act also established the FSLN strategy of revolution as an effective alternative to Udel's policy of promoting change peacefully. The Somoza government responded to the increased opposition with further censorship, intimidation, torture, and murder.

In 1975 Somoza Debayle and the National Guard launched another violent and repressive campaign against the FSLN. The government imposed a state of siege, censoring the press, and threatening all opponents with detention and torture. The National Guard increased its violence against individuals and communities suspected of collaborating with the Sandinistas.

In less than a year, it killed many of the FSLN guerrillas, including Fonseca, one of the group's founders. The rampant violation of human rights brought national and international condemnation of the Somoza regime and added supporters to the Sandinista cause.

In late 1975, the repressive campaign of the National Guard and the growth of the group caused the FSLN to split into three factions. These three factions—Proletarians, Prolonged Popular War, and the Insurrectional Faction, more popularly known as the Third Way—insisted on different paths to carry out the revolution. The Proletarian faction, headed by Jaime Wheelock Román, followed traditional Marxist thought and sought to organize factory workers and people in poor neighborhoods. The Prolonged War faction, led by Tomás Borge and Henry Ruiz after the death of Fonseca, was influenced by the philosophy of Mao Zedong and believed that a revolution would require a long insurrection that included peasants and labor movements. The Third Way faction was more pragmatic and called for ideological pluralism. Its members argued that social conditions in Nicaragua were ripe for an immediate insurrection. Led by Daniel José Ortega Saavedra and his brother Humberto Ortega Saavedra, the Third Way faction supported joint efforts with non-Marxist groups to strengthen and accelerate the insurrection movement against Somoza Debayle. The FSLN's growing success led the factions to gradually coalesce, with the Third Way's political philosophy of pluralism eventually prevailing.

The End of the Somoza Debayle Era

United States support for President Somoza waned after 1977, when the administration of United States president Jimmy Carter made United States military assistance conditional on improvements in human rights. International pressure, especially from the Carter administration, forced President Somoza to lift the state of siege in September 1977. Protests and antigovernment demonstrations resumed, although the National Guard continued to keep the upper hand over the FSLN guerrillas.

During October 1977, a group of prominent Nicaraguan businesspeople and academics, among them Sergio Ramírez Mercado—known as Los Doce (the Group of Twelve)—met in Costa Rica and formed an anti-Somoza alliance. Los Doce strengthened the FSLN by insisting on Sandinista representation in any post-Somoza government. Nevertheless, opposition to the dictatorship remained divided. Capital flight increased, forcing President Somoza to depend on foreign loans, mostly from United States banks, to finance the government's deficit.

The dictatorship's repression of civil liberties and the lack of representative institutions slowly led to the consolidation of the opposition and armed resistance. The Somoza regime continually threatened the press, mostly the newspaper *La Prensa* and the critical editorials of its publisher and Udel leader, Pedro Joaquín Chamorro Cardenal. The final act in the downfall of the Somoza era began on January 10, 1978, when Chamorro was assassinated. Although his assassins were not identified at the time, evidence implicated President Somoza's son and other members of the National Guard. The opposition held the president and his guards responsible for Chamorro's murder, thus provoking mass demonstrations against the regime. The Episcopate of the Nicaraguan Roman Catholic Church issued a pastoral letter highly critical of the government, and opposition parties called for Somoza Debayle's resignation. On January 23, a nationwide strike began, including the public and private sectors; supporters of the strike demanded an end to the dictatorship. The National Guard responded by further increasing repression and using force to contain and intimidate all government opposition. Somoza Debayle, meanwhile, asserted his intention to stay in power until the end of his presidential term in 1981. The general strike paralyzed both private industry and government services for ten days. The political impasse and the costs to the private sector weakened the strike, and in less than two weeks most private enterprises decided to suspend their participation. The FSLN guerrillas launched a series of attacks throughout the country, but the better-equipped National Guard was able to maintain military superiority.

Indiscriminate attacks on the civilian population and abuses of human rights by National Guard members further tarnished the international image of the Somoza government and damaged the economy. In February 1978, the United States government suspended all military assistance, forcing Somoza to buy weapons and equipment on the international market. The Nicaraguan economy continued its decline; the country suffered from increased capital flight, lack of investment, inflation, and unemployment.

Although still fragmented, opposition to the Somoza regime continued to grow during 1978. In March, Alfonso Robelo Callejas, an anti-Somoza businessman, established the Nicaraguan Democratic Movement (Movimiento Democrático Nicaragüense—MDN). In May 1978, the traditional Conservative Party joined Udel, Los Doce, and the MDN in creating the Broad Opposition Front (Frente Amplio de Oposición—FAO) to try to pressure President Somoza into agreeing to a negotiated solution to the crisis. Although the FSLN was not represented in the FAO, the participation of Los Doce in the FAO assured a connection between the FSLN and other opposition groups. The FSLN responded to the FAO in July by establishing a political arm, the United People's Movement (Movimiento del Pueblo Unido—MPU). The MPU included leftist labor groups, student organizations, and communist and socialist parties. The MPU also promoted armed struggle and a nationwide insurrection as the only means of overthrowing the Somoza dictatorship.

The FSLN strengthened its position on August 22, 1978, when members of its Third Way faction, led by Edén Pastora Gómez (also known as Commander Zero—Comandante Cero), took over the National Palace and held almost 2,000 government officials and members of Congress hostage for two days. With mediation from Archbishop Miguel Obando y Bravo, as well as from the Costa Rican and Panamanian ambassadors, the crisis was resolved peacefully. The results of the negotiations favored the insurrection and further tarnished the government's image. President Somoza had no alternative but to meet most of the rebels' demands, including the release of sixty FSLN guerrillas from prison, media dissemination of an FSLN declaration, a US$500,000 ransom, and safe passage for the hostage takers to Panama and Venezuela. The attack electrified the opposition. The humiliation of the dictatorship also affected morale within the National Guard, forcing President Somoza to replace many of its officers to forestall a coup and to launch a recruitment campaign to strengthen its rank and file. Fighting broke out throughout the country, but the National Guard, despite internal divisions, kept recapturing most of the guerrilla-occupied territories.

By the end of 1978, the failure of the FAO to obtain a negotiated solution increased the stature of the insurrection movement. In October, Los Doce withdrew from the negotiation process when the FAO persisted in seeking a negotiated settlement with the dictator, and many FAO members resigned in protest over the negotiations with President Somoza. The insurrection movement, meanwhile, gathered strength and increased the fighting. The Somoza regime was further isolated and discredited when in November the Organization of American States (OAS) Inter-American Commission on Human Rights published a report charging the National Guard with numerous violations of human rights. The report was followed by a United Nations (UN) resolution condemning the Nicaraguan government. In December 1978, the FSLN was further strengthened when Cuban mediation led to an agreement among the three FSLN factions for a united Sandinista front. Formal reunification of the FSLN occurred in March 1979.

The Sandinista Revolution

A mediation process led by the OAS collapsed during January 1979, when President Somoza refused to hold a national plebiscite and insisted on staying in power until 1981. As fighting increased, the Nicaraguan economy faced a severe economic crisis, with a sharp decline in agricultural and industrial production, as well as high levels of unemployment, inflation, defense spending, and capital flight. The government debt also increased mostly as a result of defense expenditures and the gradual suspension of economic support from all international financial institutions.

On February 1, 1979, the Sandinistas established the National Patriotic Front (Frente Patriótico Nacional—FPN), which included Los Doce, the PLI, and the Popular Social Christian Party (Partido Popular Social Cristiano—PPSC). The FPN had broad appeal, including political support from elements of the FAO and the private sector. After the formal unification of the Sandinista guerrillas in March, heavy fighting broke out all over the country. By then the FSLN was better equipped, with weapons flowing from Venezuela, Panama, and Cuba, mostly through Costa Rica. The FSLN launched its final offensive during May, just as the National Guard began to lose control of many areas of the country. In a year's time, bold military and political moves had changed the FSLN from one of many opposition groups to a leader in the anti-Somoza revolt.

On June 18, a provisional Nicaraguan government in exile, consisting of a five-member junta, was organized in Costa Rica. Known as the Puntarenas Pact, an agreement reached by the new government in exile called for the establishment of a

*"Revolutionary Art," murals painted on buildings and walls in
Nicaragua in the 1980s
Courtesy Nina Serafino*

mixed economy, political pluralism, and a nonaligned foreign policy. Free elections were to be held at a later date, and the National Guard was to be replaced by a nonpartisan army. The members of the new junta were Daniel José Ortega Saavedra of the FSLN, Moisés Hassan Morales of the FPN, Sergio Ramírez Mercado of Los Doce, Alfonso Robelo Callejas of the MDN, and Violeta Barrios de Chamorro, the widow of *La Prensa*'s editor. Panama was the first country to recognize the junta. By the end of June, most of Nicaragua was under FSLN control, with the exception of the capital. President Somoza's political and military isolation finally forced him to consider resignation. The provisional government in exile released a government program on July 9 in which it pledged to organize an effective democratic regime, promote political pluralism and universal suffrage, and ban ideological discrimination—except for those promoting the "return of Somoza's rule." By the second week of July, President Somoza had agreed to resign and hand over power to Francisco Maliano Urcuyo, who would in turn transfer the government to the Revolutionary Junta. According to the agreement, a cease-fire would follow, and defense responsibilities would be shared by elements of the National Guard and the FSLN.

On July 17, 1979, Somoza Debayle resigned, handed over power to Urcuyo, and fled to Miami. The former Nicaraguan dictator then established residence in Paraguay, where he lived until September 1980, when he was murdered, reportedly by leftist Argentine guerrillas. After President Somoza left Nicaragua in 1979, many members of the National Guard also fled the country, seeking asylum in neighboring countries, particularly in Honduras and Guatemala. Others turned themselves in to the new authorities after the FSLN took power, on promises of amnesty. They were subsequently tried and many served jail terms. The five-member junta arrived in the city of León on July 18, a day after Somoza's departure from the capital. Urcuyo tried to ignore the agreement transferring power, but in less than two days, domestic and international pressure drove him to exile in Guatemala. On July 19, the FSLN army entered Managua, ending the Nicaraguan revolution. The five-member junta entered the Nicaraguan capital the next day and assumed power, reiterating its pledge to work for political pluralism, a mixed economic system, and a nonaligned foreign policy.

The Sandinista Years, 1979–90

Consolidation of the Revolution, 1979–80

The new government inherited a country in ruins, with a stagnant economy and a debt of about US$1.6 billion. An estimated 50,000 Nicaraguans were dead, 120,000 were exiles in neighboring countries, and 600,000 were homeless. Food and fuel supplies were exhausted, and international relief organizations were trying to deal with disease caused by lack of health supplies. Yet the attitude of the vast majority of Nicaraguans toward the revolution was decidedly hopeful. Most Nicaraguans saw the Sandinista victory as an opportunity to create a system free of the political, social, and economic inequalities of the almost universally hated Somoza regime.

One of the immediate goals of the new government was reconstruction of the national economy. The junta appointed individuals from the private sector to head the government's economic team. They were responsible for renegotiating the foreign debt and channeling foreign economic aid through the state-owned International Reconstruction Fund (Fondo Internacional de Reconstrucción—FIR). The new government received bilateral and multinational financial assistance and also rescheduled the national foreign debt on advantageous terms. Pledging food for the poor, the junta made restructuring the economy its highest priority.

At first the economy experienced positive growth, largely because of renewed inflow of foreign aid and reconstruction after the war (see The Sandinista Era, ch. 3). The new government enacted the Agrarian Reform Law, beginning with the nationalization of all rural properties owned by the Somoza family or people associated with the Somozas, a total of 2,000 farms representing more than 20 percent of Nicaragua's cultivable land. These farms became state property under the new Ministry of Agrarian Reform. Large agroexport farms not owned by the Somozas generally were not affected by the agrarian reform. Financial institutions, all in bankruptcy from the massive capital flight during the war, were also nationalized.

The second goal of the Sandinistas was a change in the old government's pattern of repression and brutality toward the general populace. Many of the Sandinista leaders were victims of torture themselves, and the new minister of interior, Tomás Borge Martínez, tried to keep human rights violations low. Most prisoners accused of injustices under the Somoza regime were given a trial, and the Ministry of Interior forbade cruelty to prisoners. In their first two years in power, Amnesty International and other human rights groups found the human rights situation in Nicaragua greatly improved (see Human Rights, ch. 5).

The third major goal of the country's new leaders was the establishment of new political institutions to consolidate the revolution. On August 22, 1979, the junta proclaimed the Fundamental Statute of the Republic of Nicaragua. This statute abolished the constitution, presidency, Congress, and all courts. The junta ruled by unappealable decree under emergency powers. National government policy, however, was generally made by the nine-member Joint National Directorate (Dirección Nacional Conjunto—DNC), the ruling body of the FSLN, and then transmitted to the junta by Daniel Ortega for the junta's discussion and approval.

The new government established a nonelected corporatist legislature, the Council of State, on May 4, 1980. The council could approve laws submitted to it by the junta or initiate its own legislation. The junta, however, had the right of veto over council-initiated legislation, and the junta retained control over much of the budget. Although its powers were limited, the council was not a rubber stamp and often amended legislation given it by the junta. The establishment of the Council of State and the political makeup of its thirty-three members had been decided in negotiations among the revolutionary groups in 1979. The members were not elected but appointed by various political groups. In the discussions establishing the council, it was agreed that the FSLN could name twelve of the thirty-three members. Soon after its formation, however, the junta added fourteen new members to the Council of State, with twelve of those going to the FSLN. This new configuration gave the FSLN twenty-four of the forty-seven seats, enough to bloc any opposition initiative. Opponents of the FSLN viewed the addition of the new members as a power grab, but the FSLN responded that new groups had been formed since the revolution and that they needed to be represented.

The membership of the junta changed during its early years. Chamorro resigned in early 1980, ostensibly for health reasons, but later asserted that she had become dissatisfied with increased FSLN dominance in the government. Robelo resigned in mid-1980 to protest the expansion of the Council of State. Chamorro and Robelo were replaced by a rancher who belonged to the PDC and a banker, one of the members of Los Doce. In 1983 the junta was reduced to three members, with Daniel Ortega clearly playing the lead role among the remaining three.

Immediately after the revolution, the Sandinistas had the best organized and most experienced military force in the country. To replace the National Guard, the Sandinistas established a new national army, the Sandinista People's Army (Ejército Popular Sandinista—EPS), and a police force, the Sandinista Police (Policía Sandinista—PS; see The Sandinista People's Army, 1979–90; and Police and Law Enforcement, ch. 5). These two groups, contrary to the original Puntarenas Pact, were controlled by the Sandinistas and trained by personnel from Cuba, Eastern Europe, and the Soviet Union. Opposition to the overwhelming FSLN influence in the security forces did not surface until 1980. Meanwhile, the EPS developed, with support from Cuba and the Soviet Union, into the largest and best-equipped military force in Central America. Compulsory military service, introduced during 1983, brought the EPS forces to about 80,000 by the mid-1980s.

Immediately after the revolution, the FSLN also developed mass organizations representing most popular interest groups in Nicaragua. The most significant of these included the Sandinista Workers' Federation (Central Sandinista de Trabajadores—CST) representing labor unions, the Luisa Amanda Espinoza Nicaraguan Women's Association (Asociación de Mujeres Nicaragüenses Luisa Amanda Espinoza—AMNLAE), and in 1982 the National Union of Farmers and Cattlemen (Unión Nacional de Agricultores y Ganaderos—UNAG) composed of small farmers and peasants. The FSLN also created neighborhood surveillance organizations, similar to the Cuban Committees for the Defense of the Revolution, called Sandinista Defense Committees (Comités de Defensa Sandinista—CDSs). The opponents of the Sandinistas made little attempt to develop effective mass organizations that could challenge the well organized and well disciplined Sandinista groups. Thus, the FSLN mass organizations were instrumental in consolidating Sandinista power over political and military institutions. By 1980 Sandinista organizations embraced some 250,000 Nicaraguans. Less than a year after their victory, the Sandinistas controlled the government.

Growth of Opposition, 1981–83

Domestic support for the new Sandinista government was not universal, however. The indigenous people of the Caribbean coast, mostly Miskito, had been neglected by national governments since colonial times and rejected Sandinista efforts to merge them into the national mainstream. Government forces responded by forcibly relocating many of the Miskito. International human rights organizations and government critics charged that the forced relocations involved large-scale systematic violations of human rights by the government. Many Miskito and other indigenous people subsequently joined groups opposing the government.

From late 1979 through 1980, the Carter administration made efforts to work with FSLN policies. Relations began to cool, however, during the last months of the Carter administration, and when President Ronald Reagan took office in January 1981, the United States government launched a campaign to isolate the Sandinista government. Claiming that Nicaragua, with assistance from Cuba and the Soviet Union, was supplying arms to the guerrillas in El Salvador, the Reagan administration suspended all United States aid to Nicaragua on January 23, 1981. The Nicaraguan government denied all United States allegations and charged the United States with leading an international campaign against it. Later that year, the Reagan administration authorized support for groups trying to overthrow the Sandinistas.

Using an initial budget of US$19 million and camps in southern Honduras as a staging area, the United States supported groups of disgruntled former members of the National Guard. These groups became known as the Contras (short for *contrarevolucionarios*—see Glossary). The Contras initially consisted of former members of the National Guard who had fled to Honduras after the fall of President Somoza. By the end of 1981, however, the group's membership had multiplied because peasants from the north and ethnic groups from the Caribbean coast had joined in the counterrevolutionary war. Nevertheless, early Contra leadership was represented mostly by former members of the National Guard; this fact made the movement highly unpopular among most Nicaraguans.

The Contras established operational bases in Honduras from which they launched hit-and-run raids throughout northern Nicaragua. The charismatic Edén Pastora abandoned the Sandinista revolution in July 1981 and formed his own guerrilla group, which operated in the southern part of Nicaragua from bases in Costa Rica (see fig. 3). Collectively known as the Nicaraguan Resistance, the three main Contra groups were the United Nicaraguan Opposition, which operated in the north; the Opposition Block of the South, which operated in the southeast; and the Nicaraguan Coast Indian Unity, which operated in the northeast. Although the Sandinista army was larger and better equipped than the Contras, the antigovernment campaign became a serious threat to the FSLN government, largely through damage to the economy (see The Nicaraguan Resistance, ch. 5).

As the Contra war intensified, the Sandinistas' tolerance of political pluralism waned. The Sandinistas imposed emergency laws to ban criticism and organization of political opposition. Most social programs suffered as a result of the war because the Sandinista regime was forced to increase military spending until half of its budget went for defense (see Social Conditions, ch. 2). Agricultural production also declined sharply as refugees fled areas of conflict.

The bishops of the Roman Catholic Church, although supportive of the anti-Somoza movement during the late 1970s, later opposed the Sandinista regime in the 1980s. The church's hierarchy was hurt during the first years of the revolution by the active role of its radical branch, known as the Popular Church of Liberation Theology, whose philosophy was heavily influenced by liberation theology (see Glossary), as well as by radical priests in the Sandinista government. Ernesto Cardenal Martínez, a Jesuit priest who had joined the Sandinista Revolution, became the minister of culture for the FSLN government. Father Miguel D'Escoto Brockman (also known as Jerónimo) was appointed minister of foreign relations, and Father Edgardo Parrales Castillo was named minister of social welfare. However, Cardinal Miguel Obando y Bravo (the former archbishop of Managua) soon became as critical of the FSLN as he had been of the Somoza dictatorship. The cardinal's opposition brought internal divisions within the Roman Catholic Church, with one side, the hierarchy, rejecting the Marxist philosophy of the Sandinista leadership, and the other, the Popular Church, participating in the "civic struggle of the people." The bishops distrusted the Sandinista revolutionary ideology and its base of support. The Popular Church, however, wanted to play a part in the revolutionary programs of the FSLN government.

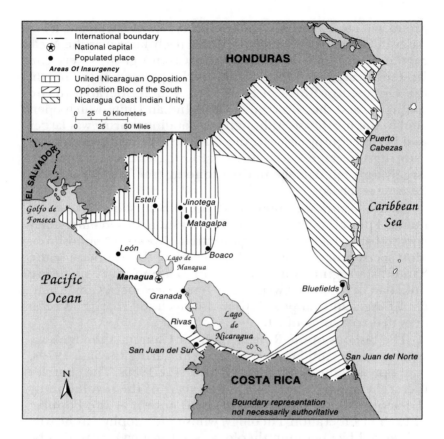

Source: Based on information from Mike Edwards, "Nicaragua, Nation in Conflict,"
National Geographic, 168, No. 6, 1985, 786.

Figure 3. Areas of Insurgency, 1985

Conflict within the Roman Catholic Church broke into the
open when Pope John Paul II visited Nicaragua in March 1983.
Discussions over details of the pontiff's visit had been tense, but
in the end the government provided free transportation for an
estimated half million Nicaraguans to witness the highlight of
the visit, an outdoor mass in Managua. At the mass, the Pope
refused to offer a prayer for the souls of deceased soldiers, and
antigovernment demonstrators began chanting, "We love the
Pope." Their calls were soon drowned out by progovernment
members of the crowd chanting, "We want peace." The entire
mass was disrupted, and the pope angrily asked the crowd for
silence several times. The entire spectacle was broadcast to the

world and was portrayed as a deliberate attempt by the Sandinistas to disrupt the mass. The event proved to be a tremendous public relations debacle for the Sandinistas and a coup for the Nicaraguan church hierarchy.

By 1981 one of the country's most influential papers, *La Prensa*, had joined the growing chorus of dissent against the Sandinista government. Under the state of emergency declared in 1982, the paper was subject to prior censorship. Despite several instances of suspended publication, some mandated by the Ministry of Interior and some in protest by the paper's editor over cut copy, the paper continued to operate. In anticipation of upcoming elections, the government eased censorship in 1983. Increased latitude in what it could publish only increased *La Prensa's* bitter criticism of the government.

Institutionalization of the Revolution, 1984

Discussion over the date and procedures for the first national postrevolutionary election began almost immediately after the revolution. The Fundamental Statue of the Republic of Nicaragua gave the junta the authority to call for elections "whenever the conditions of national reconstruction might permit." In 1983 the Council of State passed an amended Political Parties Law that, among other things, defined a political party as a group "vying for power" (the original version proposed by the FSLN defined a political party as a group already "participating in public administration"). Amendments to the law also promised all parties full access to the media.

In mid-1984, the Electoral Law was passed setting the date and conditions for the election. As was the case with the Political Parties Law, much debate went into the law's drafting. The opposition parties favored the election of a two-year interim president and a six-year legislature that would draft a new constitution. The junta, citing foreign pressure to hold elections early and the added cost of two elections in two years, prevailed with its proposal to simultaneously elect the president and members of the new legislature for six-year terms. The opposition preferred a 1985 date for elections in order to give it time to prepare its campaign, but the FSLN set the elections for November 4, 1984, and the inauguration for January 10, 1985. The law set the voting age at sixteen, which the opposition complained was an attempt to capitalize on the FSLN's popularity with the young. The number of National Assembly seats would vary with each election—ninety seats to be apportioned among each party according to its share of the vote and an additional seat for each losing presidential candidate. The entire electoral process would be the responsibility of a new fourth branch of government, the Supreme Electoral Council. Parties that failed to participate in the election would lose their legal status.

By July 1984, eight parties or coalitions had announced their intention to field candidates: the FSLN with Daniel Ortega as presidential candidate; the Democratic Coordinator (Coordinadora Democrática—CD), a broad coalition of labor unions, business groups, and four centrist parties; and six other parties—the PLI, the PPSC, the Democratic Conservative Party (Partido Conservador Democrático—PCD), the communists, the socialists, and the Marxist-Leninist Popular Action Movement. Claiming that the Sandinistas were manipulating the electoral process, the CD refused to formally file its candidates and urged Nicaraguans to boycott the election. In October, Virgilio Godoy Reyes of the PLI also withdrew his candidacy, although most of the other candidates for the National Assembly and the PLI's vice presidential candidate remained on the ballot. Other parties reportedly also were pressured to withdraw from the election.

On November 4, 1984, about 75 percent of the registered voters went to the polls. The FSLN won 67 percent of the votes, the presidency, and sixty-one of the ninety-six seats in the new National Assembly. The three conservative parties that remained in the election garnered twenty-nine seats in the National Assembly; the three parties on the left won a total of six seats. Foreign observers generally reported that the election was fair. Opposition groups, however, said that FSLN domination of government organs, mass organizations, and much of the media created a climate of intimidation that precluded a truly open election. Inauguration day was January 10, 1985; the date was selected because it was the seventh anniversary of the assassination of newspaper editor Chamorro. Attending Ortega's swearing in as president were the presidents of Yugoslavia and Cuba, the vice presidents of Argentina and the Soviet Union, and four foreign ministers from Latin America.

The Regional Peace Effort and Retrenchment of the Revolution, 1986–90

Daniel Ortega began his six-year presidential term on January 10, 1985. After the United States Congress had turned down continued funding of the Contras in April 1985, the Reagan administration ordered a total embargo on United States trade with Nicaragua the following month, accusing the Sandinista regime of threatening United States security in the region. The FSLN government responded by suspending civil liberties. Both the media and the Roman Catholic bishops were accused of destabilizing the political system. The church's press, as well as the conservative newspaper *La Prensa*, were censored or closed at various periods because of their critical views on the military draft and the government's handling of the civil war. In June 1986, the United States Congress voted to resume aid to the Contras by appropriating US$100 million in military and nonmilitary assistance. The Sandinista government was forced to divert more and more of its economic resources from economic development to defense against the Contras.

Debate in the United States over military aid for the Contras continued until November 1986, when the policy of the Reagan staff toward Nicaragua was shaken by the discovery of an illegal operation in which funds from weapons sold to Iran during 1985 were diverted to the Contras. The Iran-Contra scandal resulted from covert efforts within the Reagan staff to support the Contras in spite of a 1985 United States Congressional ban on military aid. In the aftermath of the Iran-Contra affair, the United States Congress again stopped all military support to the Contras in 1987 except for what was called "nonlethal" aid. The result of the cutoff was a military stalemate; the Contras were unable or unwilling to keep on fighting without full United States support, and the Sandinista government could not afford to continue waging an unpopular war that had already devastated the economy. The conditions for a negotiated solution to the conflict were better than ever, leaving both parties, the Contras and the Sandinistas, with few options other than to negotiate.

After Oscar Arias Sánchez was elected to the presidency of Costa Rica in 1986, he designed a regional plan to bring peace to Central America, following earlier efforts by the Contadora (see Glossary) Group (formed by Mexico, Venezuela, Panama, and Colombia in 1983). The Arias Plan, officially launched in February 1987, was signed by the presidents of five Central American republics (Guatemala, Honduras, El Salvador, Nicaragua, and Costa Rica) at a presidential summit held in Esquipulas, Guatemala, in August 1987. This agreement, also known

47

as Esquipulas II, called for amnesty for persons charged with political crimes, a negotiated cease-fire, national reconciliation for those countries with insurgencies (Guatemala, El Salvador, and Nicaragua), an end to all external aid to insurgencies (United States support to the Contras and Soviet and Cuban support to guerrillas in Guatemala and El Salvador), and democratic reforms leading to free elections in Nicaragua. After the signing of Esquipulas II, the government created a National Reconciliation Commission headed by Cardinal Miguel Obando y Bravo. The United States government responded by encouraging the Contras to negotiate. At the time, there were an estimated 10,000 Contra rebels and as many as 40,000 of their dependents living in Honduras.

An additional step toward the solution of the Nicaraguan conflict was taken at a summit of Central American presidents held on January 15, 1988, when President Daniel Ortega agreed to hold direct talks with the Contras, to lift the state of emergency, and to call for national elections. In March the FSLN government met with representatives of the Contras and signed a cease-fire agreement. The Sandinistas granted a general amnesty to all Contra members and freed former members of the National Guard who were still imprisoned.

By mid-1988, international institutions had demanded that the Sandinistas launch a drastic economic adjustment program as a condition for resumption of aid. This new economic program imposed further hardship on the Nicaraguan people. Government agencies were reorganized, leaving many Nicaraguans unemployed. The Sandinista army also went through a reduction in force. To complicate matters, in October 1988 the country was hit by Hurricane Joan, which left 432 people dead, 230,000 homeless, and damages estimated at US$1 billion. In addition, a severe drought during 1989 ruined agricultural production for 1990.

With the country bankrupt and the loss of economic support from the economically strapped Soviet Union, the Sandinistas decided to move up the date for general elections in order to convince the United States Congress to end all aid to the Contras and to attract potential economic support from Europe and the United States. As a result of Esquipulas II, the Sandinista regime and the Contras successfully concluded direct negotiations on a cease-fire in meetings held at Sapoá, Nicaragua, during June 1988. In February 1989, the five Central American presidents met once again in Costa del Sol, El

Salvador, and agreed on a plan to support the disarming and dissolving of Contra forces in Honduras, as well as their voluntary repatriation into Nicaragua. President Ortega also agreed to move the next national elections, scheduled for the fall of 1990, up to February 1990; to guarantee fair participation for opposition parties; and to allow international observers to monitor the entire electoral process.

The UNO Electoral Victory

As a result of the Esquipulas II peace accords, the FSLN government reinstated political freedoms. At first, the various anti-Sandinista groups were weak and divided and did not have a cohesive government program to challenge the FSLN. The Sandinistas, therefore, felt confident of their success at the polls despite deteriorating socioeconomic conditions in the country. On June 6, 1989, fourteen parties, united only in their opposition to the Sandinistas, formed a coalition called the National Opposition Union (Unión Nacional Opositora—UNO), whose support was drawn from a broad base, including conservative and liberal parties as well as two of Nicaragua's traditional communist factions. Despite its determination to vote the Sandinistas out of power, however, the UNO coalition remained a weak opposition lacking a cohesive program.

The UNO and the Sandinistas began their political campaigns in the summer of 1989. Although sharp divisions within the UNO remained, all fourteen parties finally compromised, and on September 2 the anti-Sandinista coalition nominated Violeta Barrios de Chamorro, publisher of *La Prensa* and former member of the junta, as its candidate for president. Virgilio Godoy Reyes, head of the PLI and former minister of labor under the Sandinistas, was chosen as her running mate. The FSLN nominated Daniel Ortega for the presidency and Sergio Ramírez Mercado as his running mate.

The political campaign was conducted under the close international supervision of the OAS, the UN, and a delegation headed by former United States president Jimmy Carter. The administration of United States president George H.W. Bush provided economic assistance to the Sandinista opposition. Despite some violent incidents, the electoral campaign was carried out in relative peace. The FSLN was better organized than the opposition and used government funds and resources—such as school buses and military trucks—to bring Sandinista supporters from all over the country to their rallies. In an effort to divert attention from the critical economic situation, the Sandinista campaign appealed to nationalism, depicting UNO followers as pro-Somoza instruments of United States foreign policy and enemies of the Nicaraguan revolution. Despite limited resources and poor organization, the UNO coalition under Violeta Chamorro directed a campaign centered around the failing economy and promises of peace. Many Nicaraguans expected the country's economic crisis to deepen and the Contra conflict to continue if the Sandinistas remained in power. Chamorro promised to end the unpopular military draft, bring about democratic reconciliation, and promote economic growth. In the February 25, 1990, elections, Violeta Barrios de Chamorro carried 55 percent of the popular vote against Daniel Ortega's 41 percent. Exhausted by war and poverty, the Nicaraguan people had opted for change.

Although the election results surprised many observers, both sides began conversations to bring about a peaceful transfer of power. In March a transition team headed by Chamorro's son-in-law, Antonio Lacayo Oyanguren, representing the UNO, and General Humberto Ortega, representing the FSLN, began discussions on the transfer of political power. During the two-month lame-duck period, Sandinista bureaucrats systematically ransacked government offices and gave government assets to loyal government supporters, destroyed records, consolidated many of the government agencies (in particular, the Ministry of Interior, whose security forces were incorporated into the EPS), and passed legislation to protect their interests once they were ousted from the government. On May 30, the Sandinista government, along with the UNO transition team and the Contra leadership, signed agreements for a formal cease-fire and the demobilization of the Contras. Despite continued sporadic clashes, the Contras completed their demobilization on June 26, 1990 (see The Chamorro Government Takes Power, ch. 4).

The FSLN accepted its new role of opposition and handed over political power to Chamorro and the UNO coalition on April 25, 1990. President Chamorro pledged her determination to give Nicaragua a democratic government, bring about national reconciliation, and keep a small nonpartisan professional army. Nicaragua underwent yet another sea change as the country stepped out of the Cold War spotlight.

*   *   *

Although the study of Nicaragua dramatically increased among scholars all over the world after the 1979 revolution, a comprehensive history of Nicaragua in English is still not available. The most current references on the subject are part of large volumes on Latin American and Central American history, all of which include chapters on Nicaragua. The best volumes currently available are James Dunkerley's *Power in the Isthmus: Political History of Modern Central America* and *Central America: A Nation Divided*, written by Ralph Lee Woodward Jr. There are, however, many books treating specific periods of Nicaraguan history. Information on Nicaragua's colonial history can be found in Benjamin Keen's *A History of Latin America* as well as in Thomas E. Skidmore and Peter H. Smith's chapter on "Central America: Colonialism, Dictatorship, and Revolution," in their *Modern Latin America*. The six decades of transition from colonial status to incipient nation-state are brilliantly covered by E. Bradford Burns in *Patriarch and Folk: The Emergence of Nicaragua 1798–1858*. A detailed account of British and United States interventions is presented by Neill Macaulay in *The Sandino Affair*. The first half of the twentieth century, including the rise and fall of the Somoza dynasty, is covered in *Politics in Central America* by Thomas P. Anderson. *Somoza and the Legacy of U.S. Involvement in Central America* by Bernard Diederich is a comprehensive look at the Somoza era, and Karl Bermann's *Under the Big Stick: Nicaragua and the United States since 1848* covers United States-Nicaragua relations.

Many works cover the history of the Sandinista period. The most comprehensive analysis of the first half of the Sandinista regime is *Nicaragua: The First Five Years*, edited by Thomas W. Walker. An excellent source for information on the FSLN leaders, as well as the inner workings of the FSLN as a political party, is Dennis L. Gilbert's *Sandinistas: The Party and the Revolution*. Reed Brody's *Contra Terror in Nicaragua* presents the testimony of victims of Contra attacks. *Banana Diplomacy: The Making of American Policy in Nicaragua, 1981–1987* by Roy Gutman provides a full account of United States foreign policy toward Nicaragua during the Reagan administration. (For further information and complete citations, see Bibliography.)

Chapter 2. The Society and Its Environment

Roman Catholic Church in Managua

DEDICATED REVOLUTIONARIES, the Sandinistas (see Glossary) came to power in 1979 determined to transform Nicaraguan society. How well they succeeded in their goal was still being debated in 1993. During their years in power, the Sandinistas nationalized the country's largest fortunes, redistributed much of the rural land, revamped the national education and health care systems to better serve the poor majority, rewrote the laws pertaining to family life, and challenged the ideological authority of the Roman Catholic bishops. But although the Sandinistas were confronting a society that was subject to powerful forces of secular change, this society also had deeply ingrained characteristics. Before and after the Sandinista decade, Nicaraguan society was shaped by the strength of family ties and the relative weakness of other institutions; by rapid population growth and rising urbanization; by male dominance, high fertility rates, and large numbers of female-headed households; by the predominance of nominal Roman Catholicism existing alongside the dynamism of evangelical Protestantism; by steep urban-rural and class inequalities; and by sweeping cultural differences between the Hispanic-mestizo west and the multiethnic society of the Caribbean lowlands.

In 1993 the permanence of the changes made by the Sandinistas was unclear. The relevant social scientific literature was slim, and many basic statistics were unavailable. Furthermore, the forces set in motion by the Sandinista revolution might take decades to play themselves out.

Climate and Terrain

Natural Regions

Nicaragua, approximately the size of New York state, is the largest country in Central America (see Glossary). The country covers a total area of 129,494 square kilometers (120,254 square kilometers of which are land area) and contains a diversity of climates and terrains. The country's physical geography divides it into three major zones: the Pacific lowlands, the central highlands, and the Caribbean lowlands (see fig. 4).

The Pacific lowlands extend about seventy-five kilometers inland from the Pacific coast. Most of the area is flat, except for a line of young volcanoes, many of which are still active, running between the Golfo de Fonseca and the western shore of Lago de Nicaragua. These peaks lie just west of a large crustal fracture or structural rift that forms a long, narrow depression passing southeast across the isthmus from the Golfo de Fonseca to the Río San Juan. The rift is occupied in part by the largest freshwater lakes in Central America: Lago de Managua (fifty-six kilometers long and twenty-four kilometers wide) and Lago de Nicaragua (about 160 kilometers long and seventy-five kilometers wide). These two lakes are joined by the Río Tipitapa, which flows south into Lago de Nicaragua. Lago de Nicaragua drains into the Río San Juan (the boundary between Nicaragua and Costa Rica), which flows through the southern part of the rift lowlands to the Caribbean Sea. The valley of the Río San Juan forms a natural passageway close to sea level across the Nicaraguan isthmus from the Caribbean Sea to Lago de Nicaragua and the rift. From the southwest edge of Lago de Nicaragua, it is only nineteen kilometers to the Pacific Ocean. This route was considered as a possible alternative to the Panama Canal at various times in the past.

Surrounding the lakes and extending northwest of them along the rift valley to the Golfo de Fonseca are fertile lowland plains highly enriched with volcanic ash from nearby volcanoes. These lowlands are densely populated and well cultivated. More directly west of the lake region is a narrow line of ash-covered hills and volcanoes that separate the lakes from the Pacific Ocean. This line is highest in the central portion near León and Managua.

Because western Nicaragua is located where two major tectonic plates collide, it is subject to earthquakes and volcanic eruptions. Although periodic volcanic eruptions have caused agricultural damage from fumes and ash, earthquakes have been by far more destructive to life and property. Hundreds of shocks occur each year, some of which cause severe damage. The capital city of Managua was virtually destroyed in 1931 and again in 1972.

The triangular area known as the central highlands lies northeast and east of the Pacific lowlands. This rugged mountain terrain is composed of ridges 900 to 1,800 meters high and a mixed forest of oak and pine alternating with deep valleys that drain primarily toward the Caribbean. Very few significant streams flow west to the Pacific Ocean; those that do are steep, short, and flow only intermittently. The relatively dry western slopes of the central highlands, protected by the ridges of the

highlands from the moist winds of the Caribbean, have drawn farmers from the Pacific region since colonial times and are now well settled. The eastern slopes of the highlands are covered with rain forests and are lightly populated with pioneer agriculturalists and small communities of indigenous people.

The eastern Caribbean lowlands of Nicaragua form the extensive (occupying more than 50 percent of national territory) and still sparsely settled lowland area known as Costa de Mosquitos. The Caribbean lowlands are sometimes considered synonymous with the former department of Zelaya, which is now divided into the North Atlantic Autonomous Region (Región Autonomista Atlántico Norte) and the South Atlantic Autonomous Region (Región Autonomista Atlántico Sur) and constitutes about 45 percent of Nicaragua's territory. These lowlands are a hot, humid area that includes coastal plains, the eastern spurs of the central highlands, and the lower portion of the Río San Juan basin. The soil is generally leached and infertile. Pine and palm savannas predominate as far south as the Laguna de Perlas. Tropical rain forests are characteristic from the Laguna de Perlas to the Río San Juan, in the interior west of the savannas, and along rivers through the savannas. Fertile soils are found only along the natural levees and narrow floodplains of the numerous rivers, including the Escondido, the Río Grande de Matagalpa, the Prinzapolka, and the Coco, and along the many lesser streams that rise in the central highlands and cross the region en route to the complex of shallow bays, lagoons, and salt marshes of the Caribbean coast.

Climate

Temperature varies little with the seasons in Nicaragua and is largely a function of elevation. The *tierra caliente*, or the "hot land," is characteristic of the foothills and lowlands from sea level to about 750 meters of elevation. Here, daytime temperatures average 30°C to 33°C, and night temperatures drop to 21°C to 24°C most of the year. The *tierra templada*, or the "temperate land," is characteristic of most of the central highlands, where elevations range between 750 and 1,600 meters. Here, daytime temperatures are mild (24°C to 27°C), and nights are cool (15°C to 21°C). *Tierra fría*, the "cold land," at elevations above 1,600 meters, is found only on and near the highest peaks of the central highlands. Daytime averages in this region are 22°C to 24°C, with nighttime lows below 15°C.

Rainfall varies greatly in Nicaragua. The Caribbean lowlands are the wettest section of Central America, receiving between 2,500 and 6,500 millimeters of rain annually. The western slopes of the central highlands and the Pacific lowlands receive considerably less annual rainfall, being protected from moisture-laden Caribbean trade winds by the peaks of the central highlands. Mean annual precipitation for the rift valley and western slopes of the highlands ranges from 1,000 to 1,500 millimeters. Rainfall is seasonal—May through October is the rainy season, and December through April is the driest period.

During the rainy season, eastern Nicaragua is subject to heavy flooding along the upper and middle reaches of all major rivers. Near the coast, where river courses widen and river banks and natural levees are low, floodwaters spill over onto the floodplains until large sections of the lowlands become continuous sheets of water. River bank agricultural plots are often heavily damaged, and considerable numbers of savanna animals die during these floods. The coast is also subject to destructive tropical storms and hurricanes, particularly from July through October. The high winds and floods accompanying these storms often cause considerable destruction of property. In addition, heavy rains (called *papagayo* storms) accompanying the passage of a cold front or a low-pressure area may sweep from the north through both eastern and western Nicaragua (particularly the rift valley) from November through March. Hurricanes or heavy rains in the central highlands, where agriculture has destroyed much of the natural vegetation, also cause considerable crop damage and soil erosion. In 1988 Hurricane Joan forced hundreds of thousands of Nicaraguans to flee their homes and caused more than US$1 billion in damage, most of it along the Caribbean coast.

Demography

Since the 1950s, Nicaragua has had a persistently high rate of population increase and rapid urban growth, both of which are expected to continue into the twenty-first century. The Sandinista revolution had little effect on these demographic trends. The Nicaraguan government has not carried out a national census since 1971, although it continued to register vital statistics and collect demographic data through periodic sample surveys of the population. A United Nations (UN) agency, the Latin American Center for Demography (Centro Latino-Americano de Demografía—Celade), has collaborated with Nicaraguan authorities in developing national population estimates.

In 1990 an estimated 3.87 million people lived in Nicaragua (see table 2, Appendix A). The population had tripled in the preceding twenty-five years and was expected to double again in the following twenty-five (see fig. 5). In the late 1980s, the population was expanding at a rate of 3.4 percent annually, far above the Latin American average of 2.1 percent for the same period.

This extraordinary growth reflects declining mortality and high fertility rates (see fig. 6). Mortality rates have dropped steadily since the 1950s. By 1990 the death rate, which had been high by regional standards, had dropped to 8 per 1,000 inhabitants, close to the Latin American average of 7 per 1,000 inhabitants. Nicaragua's total fertility rate in the 1980s was 5.7, meaning that a typical Nicaraguan woman could expect to have almost six children in the course of her childbearing years, two more than the regional average. Although total fertility and crude birth rates are expected to decline, both, according to demographic projections, should remain above Latin American averages well into the next century.

Continuing high fertility rates, together with a long-term reduction in the infant mortality rate, have produced a very young population. In 1990 nearly half of the population was less than fifteen years old. The broad base and rapidly tapering shape of Nicaragua's age-sex pyramid is typical of high-growth, developing countries. Although the pyramid can be expected to broaden in the middle as the population ages and mortality and fertility rates drop, the pyramid will not assume the almost-diamond shape typical of high-income countries until well into the twenty-first century (see fig. 7).

Life expectancy at birth in Nicaragua advanced from about forty-five in the late 1950s to sixty-two in 1991. There are, nevertheless, considerable variations in these average figures. In general, women can expect to survive three years longer than men. Casual observation in Nicaragua and world experience suggest that city dwellers and more affluent segments of the population live significantly longer lives. The life expectancy of upper-class Nicaraguans was probably closer to the seventy-one-year average found in developed countries in 1988 than to the Nicaraguan national average of sixty-two.

In 1993 Nicaragua was rapidly turning into an urban society. The thickening bands of shantytowns surrounding the larger

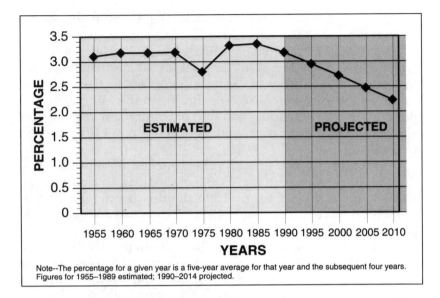

Note--The percentage for a given year is a five-year average for that year and the subsequent four years.
Figures for 1955–1989 estimated; 1990–2014 projected.

Source: Based on information from *Boletín Demográfico/Demographic Bulletin*, Santiago,
Chile, 1990, 45.

Figure 5. Annual Rate of Population Increase, 1955–2014

cities provide ample evidence of the hectic pace of change.
The government defines as urban all cities and towns with
more than 1,000 inhabitants. By this standard, 55 percent of
the population lived in urban areas in 1990. Although birth
rates in the towns and cities are significantly lower than they
are in the countryside, large-scale internal migration to towns
and cities has resulted in the faster growth of the urban population. From 1970 to 1990, the urban population expanded at an
explosive annual rate of 4 percent, whereas the rural population grew at only 2.3 percent.

Much of the urban growth is concentrated in the capital
city. The inhabitants of Managua constituted 7.5 percent of the
national population in 1940, 15 percent in 1960, and 28 percent in 1980. By 1992 Managua's population was estimated at
1.5 million. No other Nicaraguan city was anywhere near that
size. The country's second largest city is León, an important
regional center with a population of roughly 130,000 in 1990.
The other important provincial cities, all with populations that
range from 50,000 to 100,000, are Matagalpa, Masaya, and
Granada. Somewhat smaller are the principal towns on the

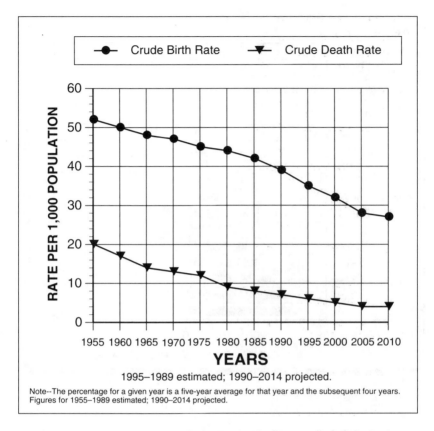

Source: Based on information from *Boletín Demográfico/Demographic Bulletin*, Santiago, Chile, 1990, 45.

Figure 6. Crude Birth and Death Rates, 1955–2014

Caribbean coast, Bluefields and Puerto Cabezas. However, accurate estimates of populations of Nicaraguan cities have not been available since the 1970s.

Explosive population growth and rapid urbanization magnify many of Nicaragua's development problems (see fig. 8). High birth rates strain the country's inadequate health and education systems, and the expanding population takes a heavy toll on the environment. Rapid urbanization requires expensive investment in transportation and sanitation infrastructures. Despite these problems, successive Nicaraguan governments (including the Sandinista administration) have declined to make population control a national priority. Nica-

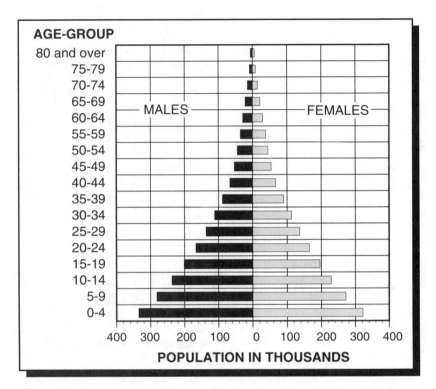

Source: Based on information from Nicaragua, Instituto Nacional de Estadísticas y Censos, *Nicaragua: 10 Años en Cifras*, Managua, 1988, 11

Figure 7. Population by Age and Sex, 1988

raguans are, in fact, divided over the issue. Although some people regard excessive demographic growth as an obstacle to development, others question the notion that their country, with the lowest population density in Central America (32 persons per square kilometer in 1990), should worry about overpopulation. In addition, the hierarchy of the Nicaraguan Roman Catholic Church and other conservative Roman Catholics have repeatedly stated their religious objections to birth control.

Nicaragua's population historically has been unevenly distributed across the country. In pre-Columbian times, the Pacific lowlands, with their fertile soils and relatively benign climate, supported a large, dense population. The central highlands sustained smaller numbers, and the inhospitable

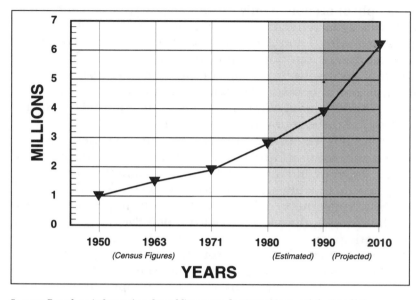

Source: Based on information from Nicaragua, Instituto Nacional de Estadísticas y
Censos, *Nicaragua: 10 Años en Cifras*, Managua, 1988, 11.

Figure 8. Population, 1950–2010

Caribbean lowlands were only sparsely populated. This basic
settlement pattern remains unchanged 500 years later. More
than 60 percent of Nicaraguans live within the narrow confines
of the Pacific lowlands. About half as many live in the central
highlands, but the Caribbean lowlands, covering more than
half of the national territory, hold less than 10 percent of the
population. In 1986 population densities ranged from 137 persons per square kilometer in the Pacific departments to 28 in
the departments of the central highlands and fewer than 10
persons in the two eastern autonomous regions.

Ethnically, Nicaragua is a relatively homogeneous country.
In 1993 some 86 percent of Nicaraguans were ladinos—people
of European or mixed European and indigenous descent, who
share a national Hispanic culture. In the nineteenth century,
there was still a substantial indigenous minority, but this group
largely has been assimilated culturally into the Hispanic mainstream. The country's racial composition is roughly as follows:
mestizo (mixed indigenous-European), 76 percent; European,
10 percent; indigenous, 3 percent; and Creoles (see Glossary),

or people of predominantly African ancestry, 11 percent. Modern Nicaragua generally has been spared the bitter ethnic conflicts that other Latin American countries with large culturally distinct indigenous populations have suffered. In Nicaragua, friction has involved relations between the ladinos, who predominate in the west (the Pacific lowlands and central highlands), and the nonladino minorities (indigenous peoples and Creoles) of the east or Caribbean lowlands.

In social terms, the country is split into two zones: the economic and political heartland of the west, encompassing the Pacific lowlands and the central highlands; and the sparsely settled east or Caribbean lowlands. The west, containing the major urban centers, is populated by Spanish-speaking whites and mestizos, both of whom regard themselves as Nicaraguans and participate, to a greater or lesser extent, in national life. The east, historically remote from the centers of political and economic decision making on the other side of the mountains, includes a sizable indigenous and Creole population that has never identified with the nation or participated in national affairs.

Almost the entire population of the Pacific lowlands and central highlands is either mestizo or white. Although no distinct color line separates these two groups, social prestige and light skin color tend to be correlated, and the white minority is distinctly overrepresented among economic and political elites. Almost no culturally distinct indigenous enclaves remain in the western half of the country. Nicaraguans sometimes refer to the "Indian" barrio of Monimbó in Masaya, to the barrio of Subtiava in León, and to the highly acculturated Matagalpan "Indians" in the central highlands, but the cultural patterns of these populations are almost indistinguishable from others who share their economic position.

Having escaped assimilation into the Hispanic majority, the eastern, or Caribbean, hinterland is culturally heterogeneous. In many ways, it is a completely different country from the Spanish-speaking nation to the west. The Miskito, a mixed Indian-Afro-European people who speak an indigenous language, have traditionally been the largest ethnic group in the region. There are also smaller indigenous communities known as Sumu and Rama, a large group of Creoles, and a rapidly expanding mestizo population fed by migration from the west. In 1990 the Miskito and Sumu composed most of Nicaragua's indigenous population.

Class Structure

Describing the Nicaraguan class structure that existed in the early 1990s is a problematic task. Current data on the distributions of occupation and income are not available. In the wake of a decade of Sandinista rule, certain aspects of the class structure are still in flux. Nonetheless, the general profile of the class structure can be described with data from the recent past (see table 3, Appendix A).

An outline of the Nicaraguan class structure, based on labor force and rural property data from 1980 and reflecting the 1979 seizures of properties held by the Somoza family and other early expropriations under the Sandinistas, revealed a highly stratified society. Less than one-fifth of the population could be described as middle class or higher. Another study from the same period showed that 60 percent of income went to the top 20 percent of households. The data also indicated that although a high proportion of Nicaraguans were self-employed, relatively few held stable, salaried employment. Self-employed workers constituted almost half of the labor force in 1980, and salaried workers made up less than 30 percent.

Land is the traditional basis of wealth in Nicaragua, and in the twentieth century the greatest fortunes have come from land devoted to export production, including coffee, cotton, beef, and sugar. Almost all of the upper class and nearly a quarter of the middle class are substantial landowners. The rapid expansion of agro-export production in the decades after World War II encouraged growth of the urban economy. Planters diversified their investments. Together with an expanding class of urban entrepreneurs, they found opportunities in banking, industry, commerce, construction, and other nonagricultural sectors. Economic growth created jobs for salaried managers and technicians. The impact of this period is reflected in the varied occupations held by the middle class.

The rural lower class is characterized by its relationship to the agro-export sector. Rural workers are dependent on agricultural wage labor, especially in coffee and cotton. Only a minority hold permanent jobs. Most are migrants who follow crops during the harvest period and find whatever work they can during the off-season. The "lower" peasants are typically smallholders without sufficient land to sustain a family; they also join the harvest labor force. The "upper" peasants have enough resources to be economically independent. They produce a substantial surplus, beyond what they can consume directly, for national and even international markets. Studies have shown that peasant farmers supply much of the country's domestic grains, beef, and coffee.

Many, if not most, of the workers in the urban lower class are dependent on the informal sector of the economy. The informal sector consists of small-scale enterprises that employ primitive technologies and operate outside the legal regime of labor protections and taxation to which large modern firms are subject. Workers in the informal sector are self-employed, unsalaried family workers or employees of small enterprises, and they are generally poor. In the past, many economists believed that the informal sector in Latin America was a remnant of past underdevelopment that would disappear with economic modernization. But in Nicaragua, as elsewhere in the region, the informal sector expanded at the same time that modern factories were being built and new technologies were transforming export agriculture.

Nicaragua's informal sector workers include tinsmiths, mattress makers, seamstresses, bakers, shoemakers, and carpenters; people who take in laundry and ironing or prepare food for sale in the streets; and thousands of peddlers, owners of tiny businesses (often operating out of their own homes), and market stall operators. Some work alone, but others labor in the small *talleres* (workshops; sing., *taller*) that are responsible for a large share of the country's industrial production. Because informal sector earnings are generally very low, few families can subsist on one income. A man who works in a *taller* might have a wife at home making tortillas or a child on the street peddling cigarettes.

The Sandinistas attempted to transform the Nicaraguan class structure, most notably by expropriating wealth from the privileged classes. Upon assuming power in 1979, the Sandinista government expropriated the banks and seized the property of the Somoza family and its closest associates. These early measures targeted the interests of the country's most powerful capitalists: the Somoza group and two competing financial groups, each organized around a separate bank. In subsequent years, the government gradually took over other large urban and rural enterprises, until the private sector was reduced to about half of the gross national product (GNP—see Glossary).

In the countryside, where the Sandinista revolution probably has had its most enduring effects, the Agrarian Reform Law transferred nearly a third of the total land under cultivation.

Momotombo Volcano between Managua and León
Courtesy Nicaraguan Tourism Institute

Land expropriations began in 1979 with Somoza's properties, constituting about a fifth of all farmland, and continued under agrarian reform laws passed in 1981 and 1986. Most of the affected land belonged to the richest 5 percent of landowners, who, at the end of the Somoza period, controlled more than half of the land under cultivation. By 1988 the reform had benefited 60 percent of Nicaraguan peasant families: 43 percent received land, typically as members of government cooperatives, and another 17 percent received the land (often located on the agricultural frontier) on which they had been squatters.

The restructuring of land tenure between 1978 and 1988 resulted in a sharp decline in the share of land held by the largest landowners. Expropriated farms generally became state farms or peasant cooperatives. By 1988 the land reform had passed through its most active phase. During the brief lame-duck period following the Sandinistas' electoral defeat in 1990, however, Sandinista authorities granted several thousand new agrarian reform titles, often to land transferred from the state farm sector. Some properties, which later became objects of controversy, went to influential Sandinistas, but the net effect of these actions was to further reduce the concentration of land in the hands of the few.

The government of President Violeta Barrios de Chamorro (president, 1990–) assumed power committed to privatizing the state sector in both urban and rural areas. But the new government also agreed to reserve a 25 percent share of state sector enterprises for their workers and to uphold the rights of the peasant beneficiaries of the agrarian reform. The government faced militant demands for land from ex-fighters on both sides of the civil war. Of roughly 300,000 hectares of state cotton, coffee, and cattle lands privatized by late 1991, former combatants received 38 percent, and farm workers received 32 percent. Far from attempting to reverse the agrarian reform, the Chamorro administration was compelled to extend it.

The enduring effects of the Sandinista revolution on the Nicaraguan class structure may not be known for some time. In the early 1990s, the property situation remained unsettled. It was also uncertain how many of the businesspeople, professionals, and skilled workers who became expatriates in the 1980s would reestablish themselves in the country. The Sandinistas did reduce class inequalities, most notably by eliminating the three major financial groups that once dominated the economy and by redistributing land. They seem also to have altered the perceptions and expectations of the population. The gap between the privileged classes and the poor majority did not appear as proper or as inevitable as it did in the past. However, some key aspects of the class structure that existed before 1979 remained unchanged. During the 1980s, the urban informal sector actually grew in size, and a large part of the rural population continued to depend on seasonal employment. Even before the economic collapse of the late 1980s wiped out the gains of the early Sandinista years, the vast majority of Nicaraguans lacked the resources to satisfy basic needs, according to a government study.

Social Conditions

Nicaragua was one of the poorest countries in the Western Hemisphere in 1992, with a per-capita gross domestic product (GDP—see Glossary) estimated at approximately US$425. In real terms, per-capita income was almost half of what it had

Faces of Nicaragua
Courtesy Robert Buchta,
Larry Simon, Marcelo
Montecino, and
Larry Boyd

been in 1981. The country's low living standards are reflected in nutrition and housing data. In 1989 each Nicaraguan consumed 1,524 calories and forty-four grams of protein a day—well below minimum recommended allowances. Fewer than one in five urban households had sufficient income to purchase a minimum "market basket," as defined by the government. In the mid-1980s, 55 percent of urban houses and 67 percent of rural houses consisted of a single room; nearly half lacked drinking water and plumbing. The national housing deficit, according to a 1990 estimate, was 420,600 units.

A 1985 government study classified 69.4 percent of the population as poor because they were unable to satisfy one or more of their basic needs in housing, sanitary services (water, sewerage, and garbage collection), education, and employment. The defining standards for this study were set quite low. For example, housing was considered substandard if it was constructed of discarded materials with dirt floors or if it was occupied by more than four persons per room. Predictably, the poverty rate was higher in rural areas (85.9 percent) than in urban areas (54.8 percent). Regionally, the highest rate was recorded in the two eastern autonomous regions on the Caribbean coast (94.5 percent) and the lowest in urban Managua (49.6 percent).

Conditions in Nicaragua have fluctuated widely with the economic and political upheavals of recent decades. In the years from 1950 to 1975, real GDP per capita more than doubled, driven by the rapid growth in exports of coffee, cotton, and beef. Capital generated by agro-exports contributed to the development of a thriving industrial sector. In the three decades ending in 1980, the urban population expanded from 35 percent to 53 percent of the total population.

The benefits of this remarkable period of economic expansion have been unevenly distributed, however. Precise data are not available, but local observers have noted that the middle class blossomed and many new fortunes emerged during these growth years. Some benefits did flow to the lower class. For example, in the 1950s and 1960s, primary school enrollment grew 400 percent. Infant mortality, a significant indicator of social well-being, declined from 167 deaths per 1,000 live births in the period from 1950 to 1955 to 100 per 1,000 in the years from 1970 to 1975. Despite these gains, however, Nicaragua's school enrollment and infant mortality statistics remained poor by regional standards. The distribution of income in the 1970s was highly skewed, probably more so than it had been in the past: 30 percent of personal income went to the richest 5 percent of households, but only 15 percent went to the poorest 50 percent. Furthermore, some of the poorest Nicaraguans were the direct victims of economic development. As agro-export production expanded in the Pacific lowlands and the central highlands, thousands of peasants were pushed off their land, many of them to be converted into low-wage, seasonally employed agricultural laborers. Between 1965 and 1975, the GNP and the number of children under five years of age suffering from malnutrition both doubled. Clearly, many Nicaraguans were getting poorer as their country grew richer.

The Sandinista revolution brought a new cycle of upheaval to Nicaraguan society. The 1978–79 insurrection that toppled the Somoza regime left 30,000 to 50,000 people dead, a large population homeless, several cities devastated by government bombing, and extensive damage to the economy, including the destruction of much of Managua's modern industrial district. After they assumed power, the Sandinistas reversed the national priorities established under the Somozas. Their prime policy objective in the early years was to promote the welfare of the poor majority; national economic growth was a secondary concern. Government policy in areas from land reform and nutrition to health and education was strongly redistributive. In the early 1980s, generous spending on social programs was sustained by a relatively healthy economy and high levels of foreign aid from both Western and Soviet bloc countries.

In the late 1980s, however, the resources available for social programs declined as foreign aid dried up, the economy floundered, and war with the Contras (short for *contrarevoluciona-rios*—see Glossary) compelled the government to redirect spending toward national defense. Living standards sank abruptly during this period. By the end of the decade, the average real wage had dropped to less than 10 percent of its 1985 value, nearly half the labor force was unemployed or underemployed, and the poverty rate was rising. Infant mortality, which had declined sharply in the early years of Sandinista rule, began to rise again. The death rate per 1,000 live births was 97 in 1978, the last full year of the Somoza regime; 63 in 1985; and 72 in 1989. For several years, the Contra war disrupted social and economic life across the country, but especially in contested zones like northeastern Nicaragua and the northern central highlands. In such areas, Contra forces targeted both economic and social infrastructure, including agrarian reform farms, schools, and health facilities. More than 20,000 Nicaraguans died in the fighting, and thousands of others were left maimed or crippled.

Conditions improved after fighting largely stopped in 1988. Democratic elections, followed by peaceful transition to a new government in 1990, resulted in the lifting of the United States trade embargo imposed in 1982, renewal of United States aid, and the removal of informal barriers to international credits. The Nicaraguan economy was, however, slow to respond to these changes. GDP continued to decline in 1990, and no growth was recorded in 1991. Despite making deep cuts in military forces, the new government did not have the resources to restore spending on social programs to prewar levels.

Education

When the Sandinistas came to power in 1979, they inherited an education system that was one of the poorest in Latin America. Under the Somozas, limited spending on education and generalized poverty, which forced many adolescents into the labor market, constricted educational opportunities for Nicaraguans. In the late 1970s, only 65 percent of primary school-age children were enrolled in school, and of those who entered first grade only 22 percent completed the full six years of the primary school curriculum (see table 4, Appendix A). Most rural schools offered only one or two years of schooling, and three-quarters of the rural population was illiterate. Few students enrolled in secondary school, in part because most secondary institutions were private and too expensive for the average family. By these standards, the 8 percent of the college-age population enrolled in Nicaraguan universities seemed relatively high. Less surprising was that upper-class families typically sent their children abroad for higher education.

By 1984 the Sandinista government had approximately doubled the proportion of GNP spent on preuniversity education, the number of primary and secondary school teachers, the number of schools, and the total number of students enrolled at all levels of the education system. A 1980 literacy campaign, using secondary school students as volunteer teachers, reduced the illiteracy rate from 50 percent to 23 percent of the total population. (The latter figure exceeds the rate of 13 percent claimed by the literacy campaign, which did not count adults whom the government classified as learning impaired or otherwise unteachable.) In part to consolidate the gains of the liter-

Rural family fetching water from a communal tap
Courtesy Nina Serafino

acy campaign, the Ministry of Education set up a system of informal self-education groups known as Popular Education Cooperatives. Using materials and pedagogical advice provided by the ministry, residents of poor communities met in the evenings to develop basic reading and mathematical skills. Although designed for adults, these self-education groups also served children who worked by day or could not find a place in overcrowded schools.

At the college level, enrollment jumped from 11,142 students in 1978 to 38,570 in 1985. The Sandinistas also reshaped the system of higher education: reordering curricular priorities, closing down redundant institutions and programs and establishing new ones, and increasing lower-class access to higher education. Influenced by Cuban models, the new curricula were oriented toward development needs. Agriculture, medicine, education, and technology grew at the expense of law, the humanities, and the social sciences.

One of the hallmarks of Sandinista education (and favored target of anti-Sandinista criticism) was the ideological orientation of the curriculum. The stated goal of instruction was the development of a "new man," whose virtues were to include patriotism, "internationalism," an orientation toward productive work, and a willingness to sacrifice individual interests to social and national interests. School textbooks were nationalist and prorevolutionary in tone, giving ample coverage to Sandinista heroes. After the 1990 election, the Chamorro government placed education in the hands of critics of Sandinista policy, who imposed more conservative values on the curriculum. A new set of textbooks was produced with support from the United States Agency for International Development (AID), which had provided similar help during the Somoza era.

Despite the Sandinistas' determined efforts to expand the education system in the early 1980s, Nicaragua remained an undereducated society in 1993. Even before the Contra war and the economic crisis that forced spending on education back to the 1970 level, the education system was straining to keep up with the rapidly growing school-age population. Between 1980 and 1990, the number of children between five and fourteen years of age had expanded by 35 percent. At the end of the Sandinista era, the literacy rate had declined from the level attained at the conclusion of the 1980 literacy campaign. Overall school enrollments were larger than they had been in the 1970s, however, and, especially in the countryside, access to education had broadened dramatically. But a substantial minority of primary school-age children and three-quarters of secondary school-age students were still not in school, and the proportion of students who completed their primary education had not advanced beyond the 1979 level. Even by Central American standards, the Nicaraguan education system was performing poorly.

Health

Like education, health care was among the top priorities of the Sandinista government. At the end of the Somoza era, most Nicaraguans had no access or only limited access to modern health care. Widespread malnutrition, inadequate water and sewerage systems, and sporadic application of basic public health measures produced a national health profile typical of impoverished populations. Enteritis and other diarrheal diseases were among the leading causes of death. Pneumonia, tetanus, and measles, largely among children less than five years old, accounted for more than 10 percent of all deaths. Malaria and tuberculosis were endemic.

By the beginning of 1991, twenty-eight persons had tested positive for the human immunodeficiency virus (HIV) that causes acquired immune deficiency syndrome (AIDS), and eight of those individuals had died. These figures were low in comparison with neighboring countries, but health officials regarded them as accurate because the government had conducted an aggressive search for HIV among prostitutes, blood donors, and tuberculosis patients in the late 1980s. The same officials cautioned against complacency toward AIDS. A large number of sexually transmitted diseases was reported in Managua and Bluefields, and if HIV were introduced into groups with multiple sex partners, AIDS cases would rise rapidly.

Nicaraguans depend on a three-tier health system that reflects the fundamental inequalities in Nicaraguan society. The upper class uses private health care, often going abroad for specialized treatment. A relatively privileged minority of salaried workers in government and industry are served by the Nicaraguan Social Security Institute. These workers and their families compose about 8 percent of the population, but the institute devours 40 to 50 percent of the national health care budget. The remainder of the population, approaching 90 percent, is poorly served at public facilities that are typically mismanaged, inadequately staffed, and underequipped. Health care services are concentrated in the larger cities, and rural areas are largely unserved. In fact, the Ministry of Health, which has sole responsibility for rural health care, preventive health care, and small clinics, received only 16 percent of the health budget in 1992, most of which it spent in Managua.

In the early 1980s, the Sandinista government restructured and reoriented the entire health care system. Following a recommendation made by AID in 1976, authorities combined the medical functions of the Ministry of Health, the Nicaraguan Social Security Institute, and some twenty other quasi-autonomous health care agencies from the Somoza era into a unified health care system. Within a few years, spending on health care was substantially increased, access to services was broadened and equalized, and new emphasis was placed on primary and preventive medicine. During this period, the number of students annually entering medical school jumped from 100 to 500, five new hospitals were built (largely with foreign aid), and a national network of 363 primary care health clinics was created. With help from the United Nations Children's Fund (UNICEF), 250 oral rehydration centers were established to treat severe childhood diarrhea, the leading cause of infant deaths, with a simple but effective solution of sugar and salts. The Ministry of Health trained thousands of community health volunteers (health *brigadistas*) and mobilized broad community participation in periodic vaccination and sanitation campaigns.

The expansion of access to health care was reflected in a doubling of the number of medical visits per inhabitant and a reduction from 64 percent to 38 percent in Managua's share of total medical visits between 1977 and 1982. These early years also saw a substantial drop in infant mortality and reductions in the incidence of transmittable diseases such as polio, pertussis, and measles.

In health as in education, some of the ground gained in the early 1980s was lost during the second half of the decade. Health care activities, including vaccination campaigns, had to be curtailed in regions experiencing armed conflict. The health care system was flooded with war victims. Among an increasingly impoverished population, children especially grew more vulnerable to disease. But the steep economic decline and tight budgetary restraints of the period resulted in severe shortages of medicines and basic medical supplies. In addition, deteriorating salaries drove many doctors out of public employment.

Despite the problems of the late 1980s, however, the Sandinista decade left behind an improved health care system. According to a 1991 AID assessment of Nicaraguan development needs, the Chamorro government inherited a health care system that emphasized preventive and primary care; targeted the principal causes of infant, child, and maternal mortality; provided broad coverage; and elicited high levels of community participation. The AID report noted the effectiveness of the oral rehydration centers, the wide coverage of vaccination campaigns, and the key role of the health *brigadistas*, three programs maintained by the new government. The report concluded that the major problem of the health sector was lack of budgetary resources.

Family

In the 1990s, traditional Hispanic kinship patterns, common to most of Latin America, continued to shape family life in Nicaragua. The nuclear family forms the basis of family structure, but relationships with the extended family and godparents are strong and influence many aspects of Nicaraguan

New health clinic in Matagalpa
Courtesy Nina Serafino

life. Because few other institutions in the society have proved as
stable and enduring, family and kinship play a powerful role in
the social, economic, and political relations of Nicaraguans.
Social prestige, economic ties, and political alignments frequently follow kinship lines. Through the *compadrazgo* (see
Glossary) system (the set of relationships between a child's parents and his or her godparents), persons unrelated by blood or
marriage establish bonds of ritual kinship that are also important for the individual in the society at large.

Nicaraguan institutions, from banks to political parties, have
traditionally been weak and more reflective of family loyalties
and personal ties than broader institutional goals and values.
For several decades prior to 1979, the Nicaraguan state was
scarcely differentiated from the Somoza family. Family ties
played a diminished but still critical role in the politics of the
1980s and early 1990s. The Roman Catholic Church, which,
until recently, had little or no presence in the countryside, still
does not touch the lives of most Nicaraguans. To survive in a
country whose history is replete with war, political conflict, and
economic upheaval, Nicaraguans turn to the one institution
they feel they can trust—the family. As a result, individuals are
judged on the basis of family reputations, careers are advanced

79

through family ties, and little stigma is attached to the use of institutional position to advance the interests of relatives. For both men and women, loyalty to blood kin is frequently stronger than loyalty to a spouse.

Most Nicaraguan families are built around conjugal units. Outside of the upper and middle classes, however, relatively few couples formalize their marriages through the church or state. Legislation passed in the 1980s recognized this situation by giving common-law unions the same legal status as civil marriages. Although stable monogamous unions and strong patriarchal authority at home are deeply ingrained cultural ideals, at least a third of Nicaraguan families were headed by women in the 1980s. Among urban households, this proportion is even higher.

Because of high fertility and the presence of relatives beyond the nuclear family, households are large—six to eight people are common. The Nicaraguan household is typically augmented by the presence of a grandparent, an aunt or uncle, an orphaned relative, a poor godchild, or a daughter with children of her own. Newly married couples sometimes take up residence in the home of one of the parental families. In the countryside, peasants feel that a large number of children helps them meet their everyday labor needs and provides for their own security in old age. Families are smaller in the city, but housing shortages and low incomes encourage the urban poor to create expanded households that can share shelter and pool resources.

Both traditional values and practical considerations support the maintenance of strong ties with a large kinship network outside the household. Nicaraguans maintain ties with kin of the same generation, which may extend to fourth or fifth cousins. Peasant patriarchs build rural clans by accumulating small parcels of land near their own land for the families of sons and daughters. City people of all classes look to relatives for jobs and other forms of economic assistance. In times of economic crisis, the survival strategies of the urban poor often center on mutual assistance among kin.

Like other Nicaraguans, members of the upper class maintain relations with extensive numbers of kin. In addition to these "horizontal" ties, however, they place special emphasis on "vertical" descent. Upper-class Nicaraguans are much more likely than their compatriots to be aware of ancestors more than two generations removed from the present. This tendency

Equestrian parade in Managua
Courtesy Nicaraguan Tourism Institute

is supported by shared family fortunes, which have been passed from generation to generation, and by the prominence of historical surnames rooted in the eighteenth and nineteenth centuries.

Through the institution of *compadrazgo*, the attributes of kinship are extended to those not related by blood or marriage. When an infant is baptized, the parents choose a godfather (*padrino*) and godmother (*madrina*) for their child. This practice is common to Roman Catholics around the world, but in Nicaragua and many other Latin American countries, it assumes a broader social significance. *Compadrazgo* establishes relationships similar to those of actual kinship not only between the child and the godparents, but also between the parents and the godparents. The latter relationships are recognized through the use of *compadre* and *comadre* (literally, co-father and co-mother) as reciprocal terms of address between the child's parents and godparents. The godparents are responsible for the baptism ceremony and the festivities afterward. They are also expected to concern themselves with the welfare of the child and his or her family, and come to their aid in times of hardship.

Godparents are typically trusted friends of the parents. However, lower-class families (for whom the *compadrazgo* has the greatest significance) often chose godparents of superior economic, political, or social status, who are in a position to help the child in the future. Large landowners, affluent businesspeople, government officials, and political leaders may become godfathers to the children of social inferiors in order to build up a system of personal loyalties. In such cases, *compadrazgo* becomes the basis of a network of patron-client relationships.

The Lives of Women

Collectively, the lives of Nicaraguan women are shaped by traditional Hispanic values regarding appropriate sex roles and high fertility, the prevalence of female-headed households, and an increasing rate of participation in the labor force. Although the Sandinista revolution drew thousands of women into public life, encouraged females to work outside the home, spawned a national women's movement, and enshrined gender equality in the national constitution, it left largely intact the values, beliefs, and social customs that traditionally had regulated relations between the sexes.

Virility, sexual prowess, independence, protectiveness, assertiveness, and a drive to dominate have traditionally been expected of the male. Dependence, devotion, submissiveness, and faithfulness are attributes that the female ideally reflected. From adolescence, men are encouraged to demonstrate their machismo (masculinity) through acts of sexual conquest. Married men commonly have regular extramarital relations and even maintain more than one household. However, premarital and extramarital relations, more or less expected from men, are stigmatized in women. The ideal female role, glorified in the culture, is that of mother. Her place is in the home, and her duty is to raise her children.

The ideal expectations of the culture do not prevent most Nicaraguan women from becoming sexually active early in life: 38 percent by age sixteen and 73 percent by age nineteen, according to one study. This phenomenon contributes to the high birth rates noted earlier, as does a lack of use of contraceptives. In 1986 the Ministry of Health estimated that, because of lack of knowledge and the limited availability of contraceptives, only 26 percent of sexually active women practiced contraception. An informal poll of 200 Nicaraguan women of diverse educational and class backgrounds revealed that only ten were aware that women are most fertile at the midpoint of the menstrual cycle. The Nicaraguan Roman Catholic Church has publicly condemned contraception other than the rhythm method. Although most Nicaraguans are probably not even aware of the church's position, it appears to have influenced government policy.

In most cases, abortion is illegal but not uncommon in Nicaragua. Although affluent women have access to medical abortions, poorer women generally depend on more dangerous alternatives. During the 1980s, when lax enforcement expanded access to medical abortion, studies conducted at a large maternity hospital in Managua determined that illicit abortions accounted for 45 percent of admissions and were the leading cause of maternal deaths. Relatively few of the victims of botched abortions are single women, and the majority have had pregnancies earlier in life. The most common reasons for seeking abortion are abandonment by the father and strained family budgets.

Many Nicaraguan women spend at least part of their lives as single mothers. Early initiation of sexual activity and limited practice of contraception contribute to this phenomenon, as does the very character of the Nicaraguan economy. The key agro-export sector requires a large migrant labor force. The long months that agricultural workers spend away from home harvesting coffee and cotton greatly disrupt family life and often lead to abandonment.

The steadily growing proportion of women in the labor force results, for the most part, from their being single heads of households. The vast majority of female heads of households work, and they are twice as likely to be employed as married women. Women's share of the labor force rose from 14 percent in 1950 to 29 percent in 1977 and to 45 percent in 1989. By the 1980s, women predominated in petty commerce, personal services, and certain low-wage sectors such as the garment industry. Peasant women traditionally have performed agricultural labor as unpaid family workers; their economic significance thus probably has been underestimated by official labor statistics. By the 1980s, however, they formed a large and growing part of the salaried harvest labor force in cotton and coffee. Because men assume little of the domestic workload, the growth in female labor force participation has meant a double workday for many Nicaraguan women. Middle- and upper-class women have a good chance of escaping this trap as they are much less likely to work outside the home and can depend on domestic help for household duties.

Religion

In the early 1990s, the majority of Nicaraguans were nominally Roman Catholic. Many had little contact with their church, however, and the country's Protestant minority was expanding rapidly. Roman Catholicism came to Nicaragua in the sixteenth century with the Spanish conquest and remained, until 1939, the established faith. The Roman Catholic Church was accorded privileged legal status, and church authorities usually supported the political status quo. Not until the anticlerical General José Santos Zelaya (1893–1909) came to power was the position of the church seriously challenged.

Nicaraguan constitutions have provided for a secular state and guaranteed freedom of religion since 1939, but the Roman Catholic Church has retained a special status in Nicaraguan society. When Nicaraguans speak of "the church," they mean the Roman Catholic Church. The bishops are expected to lend their authority to important state occasions, and their pronouncements on national issues are closely followed. They can also be called upon to mediate between contending parties at moments of political crisis. A large part of the education system, in particular the private institutions that serve most upper- and middle-class students, is controlled by Roman Catholic bodies. Most localities, from the capital to small rural communities, honor patron saints, selected from the Roman Catholic calendar, with annual fiestas. Against this background, it is not surprising that the Sandinista government provided free public transportation so that 500,000 Nicaraguans, a substantial part of the national population, could see Pope John Paul II when he visited Managua in 1983 (see The Growth of Opposition, 1981–83, ch. 1).

Despite the leading position of the Roman Catholic Church, it touches the lives of most Nicaraguans only sporadically at best. The activities and resources of the church are concentrated in the cities. Although the church attempts to reach people in small towns and rural areas, its capacity to do so is limited. In the mid-1980s, there was approximately 1 priest for every 7,000 Roman Catholics, a ratio lower than the Latin American average and considerably lower than the 1 priest per 4,550 Nicaraguan Roman Catholics recorded in 1960.

Urbanites, women, and members of the upper and middle classes are the most likely to be practicing Roman Catholics, that is, those who attend mass, receive the sacraments, and perform special devotions with some degree of regularity. Nicaraguans of the lower classes tend to be deeply religious but not especially observant. Many limit their practice of the sacraments to baptism and funeral rites. Yet they have a strong belief in divine power over human affairs, which is reflected in the use of phrases such as "God willing" or "if it is God's desire" in discussions of future events.

Religious beliefs and practices of the masses, although more or less independent of the institutional church, do not entail the syncretic merger of Roman Catholic and pre-Columbian elements common in some other parts of Latin America. Popular religion revolves around the saints, who are perceived as intermediaries between human beings and God. Prayers are directed to a relevant saint asking for some benefit, such as curing an illness, in exchange for ritual payment, such as carrying a cross in an annual procession. Pictures of saints, called *cuadros*, are commonly displayed in Nicaraguan homes. Set in a corner or on a table and surrounded with candles, flowers, or other decorations, a *cuadro* becomes the centerpiece of a small domestic shrine. In many communities, a rich lore has grown up around the celebrations of patron saints, such as Managua's Saint Dominic (Santo Domingo), honored in August with two colorful, often riotous, day-long processions through the city's lower-class neighborhoods. The high point of Nicaragua's religious calendar for the masses is neither Christmas nor Easter, but *La Purísima*, a week of festivities in early December dedicated to the Immaculate Conception, during which elaborate altars to the Virgin Mary are constructed in homes and workplaces.

Protestantism and other Christian sects came to Nicaragua during the nineteenth century, but only during the twentieth century have Protestant denominations gained large followings in the western half of the country. By 1990 more than 100 non-Roman Catholic faiths had adherents in Nicaragua, of which the largest are the Moravian Church, the Baptist Convention of Nicaragua, and the Assemblies of God. Other denominations include the Church of God, the Church of the Nazarene, the Episcopal Church, the Church of Jesus Christ of Latter-Day Saints (Mormons), Jehovah's Witnesses, and the Seventh Day Adventists. Most of these churches have been established through the efforts of missionaries from the United States and, although now institutionally independent and led by Nicaraguans, retain strong links with members of the same denomination in the United States.

The Moravian Church, established in eastern Nicaragua in the late nineteenth century, is the dominant faith among the non-Hispanic population of the region. Virtually all Miskito are Moravians, as are many Creoles, Sumu, and Rama. Moravian pastors play a prominent leadership role in Miskito communities. The Nicaraguan Baptists are related to the American Baptist Church, which began missionary work in 1917. The Nicaraguan Baptist Church's membership is concentrated in the Pacific region and is heavily middle class.

The Assemblies of God, dating from 1926, is the largest of the rapidly expanding Pentecostal denominations. Known for ecstatic forms of worship, energetic evangelization, and the strict personal morality demanded of members, the Pentecostal faiths are flourishing among the urban and rural poor. By helping recent arrivals from the countryside adjust to city life, they draw many migrants into their congregations. Pentecostalism reportedly has particular appeal to poor women because it elicits sobriety and more responsible family behavior from men. Largely because of the Pentecostals, the long-stagnant Protestant population has accelerated in numbers, going from 3 percent of the national population in 1965 to more than 20 percent in 1990. It could easily surpass 30 percent in the 1990s.

The 1970s and 1980s were years of religious ferment in Nicaragua, often coupled with political conflict. Encouraged by the spirit of liberal renovation then sweeping through Latin American Catholicism, a new generation of Nicaraguan Roman Catholic Church officials and lay activists tried to make the Roman Catholic Church more democratic, more worldly in its concerns, and more sensitive to the plight of the poor majority. Many were inspired by the radical doctrines of liberation theology (see Glossary) and the related idea of consciousness-raising Christian base communities (small groups of people from an urban slum or rural district who met regularly to read the Bible together and reflect on social conditions). In the 1970s, priests, nuns, and lay workers committed to social change organized community development projects, education programs, and Roman Catholic base communities. Especially after 1972, Roman Catholic clergy and lay activists were increasingly drawn into the movement opposed to the regime of Anastasio Somoza

Views of Managua, with Lago de Managua in the background
Courtesy Nina Serafino

Debayle. Many developed links with the Sandinista National Liberation Front (Frente Sandinista de Liberación Nacional—FSLN), which was very receptive to radicalized Roman Catholics and led the insurrection that finally toppled the dictator.

No previous Latin American revolution has had such broad religious support as that of the Sandinistas. Even the Roman Catholic bishops openly backed the anti-Somoza movement in its final phases. In the late 1970s and early 1980s, the Roman Catholic Christian Base Communities (Comunidades Eclesiásticas de Base—CEBs) provided the FSLN with vital political support among the urban poor. Roman Catholics, including several priests, accepted positions in the new government and became members of the Sandinista party. But the close ties between Sandinistas and Roman Catholics generated tensions within the Roman Catholic Church and between the Roman Catholic hierarchy and the FSLN. The bishops, led by Cardinal Miguel Obando y Bravo, accused the Sandinistas and their Roman Catholic supporters of attempting to divide the church by creating a separate Popular Church out of the CEBs. They viewed the Marxist-oriented FSLN as a long-term threat to religion in Nicaragua, despite the professed tolerance of the Sandinistas. An explosive church-state conflict developed, during which the bishops more or less openly allied with the Sandinistas' political enemies and the FSLN struggled vainly to contain the influence of the institutional church. Throughout the 1980s, pro- and anti-Sandinista forces regularly manipulated religious symbols for political effect.

Protestant leaders were less inclined than the Roman Catholic episcopate to become embroiled in conflicts with the Sandinistas. Some, including prominent Baptist ministers and a minority of pastors from other faiths, were sympathetic to the FSLN. At the other extreme, a few Moravian ministers openly identified with Miskito Contra forces operating from Honduras. Most Pentecostal leaders, reflecting the conservative attitudes of the United States denominations with which they were affiliated, were cool toward the Sandinistas but generally adopted a public stance that was apolitical. Suspecting that the United States Central Intelligence Agency (CIA) and Christian conservatives in the United States were promoting evangelical activity in Nicaragua to undercut their government, Sandinista authorities monitored and tried to intimidate certain Pentecostal leaders. They did not, however, attempt to limit the growth of normal religious activity. The expansion of the Protestant population actually accelerated under Sandinista rule. During the first five years of Sandinista government, the number of evangelical churches (largely Pentecostal) doubled to 3,000.

By the time the Sandinistas left power in 1990, church-state relations were considerably smoother than they had been in the early 1980s and mid-1980s, in part because the Contra war, which intensified conflict over religion, was winding down. Some of the radicalized Roman Catholics who had supported the Sandinistas in the years since the 1970s remained loyal to them, but their influence outside the Sandinista movement and a few religious think tanks was limited. The number of active CEBs plunged in the early 1980s and never recovered, in part because the bishops had systematically restricted the church-based activities of pro-Sandinista clergy. The Pentecostal churches continued their rapid growth among the poor, eclipsing the radical branch of Roman Catholicism and challenging the Roman Catholic Church's traditional religious monopoly. By the early 1990s, the Pentecostal minority was large enough to cause some observers, aware of the recent role of Christian conservatives in United States politics, to speculate about the influence of Pentecostals in future Nicaraguan elections.

Caribbean Society

Nicaragua's extensive Caribbean lowlands region, comprising the country's two autonomous regions and the department of Río San Juan, has never been fully incorporated into the nation. This area, known as the Costa de Mosquitos, is isolated from western Nicaragua by rugged mountains and dense tropical rainforest. Communications across these barriers are poor. In 1993 there was still no paved road between the cities of the Pacific region and the Caribbean littoral. *Costeños* (the indigenous peoples and Creoles native to the Caribbean lowlands) are also divided by history and culture from the whites and mestizos of the west, whom they call "the Spanish."

The Caribbean lowlands were never part of the Spanish empire but were, in effect, a British protectorate beginning in the seventeenth century (see Colonial Rule, ch. 1). In the mid-nineteenth century, the United States displaced Britain as the region's protecting power. Not until 1894 did the entire region come under direct Nicaraguan administration. Even then, continuing United States political weight, commercial activity, and missionary interest in the Caribbean lowlands eclipsed the weak influence of western Hispanic Nicaragua until World War II. As a result of this history, *costeños* have not traditionally regarded themselves as Nicaraguans. Rather, they see Nicaraguan rule as an alien imposition and fondly recall the years of semisovereignty and intermittent prosperity they enjoyed under British and American tutelage. *Costeños* are more likely to speak English or an indigenous language at home than Spanish. Most are Protestants, generally Moravians; those who became Roman Catholics did so under the influence of priests from the United States rather than from Nicaragua.

The Caribbean lowlands are home to a multiethnic society. Miskito, Creoles, and mestizos account for most of the population of the region, but there are also small populations of Sumu, Rama, and Garifuna, an Afro-Carib group. The Miskito, the largest of the indigenous groups, themselves reflect the region's diverse ethnic history. Like the Sumu, they are linguistically related to the Chibcha of South America. Their culture reflects adaptations to contacts with Europeans that stretch back to their seventeenth-century collaboration with English, French, and Dutch pirates. Their genetic heritage is from indigenous, European, and African ancestors. During the colonial period, the Miskito, allied with Britain, became the dominant group in the Caribbean lowlands. A Miskito monarchy, established over the region with British support in 1687, endured into the nineteenth century.

The Miskito population is concentrated in northeasternmost Nicaragua, around the interior mining areas of Siuna, Rosita, and Bonanza, and along the banks of several rivers that flow east out of the highlands to the Caribbean. Honduras also has a large Miskito population in territory adjoining Nicaragua. In modern times, the Miskito have survived by alternating subsistence activities with wage labor, often in foreign-controlled extractive enterprises.

The black people of the Caribbean region, known as Creoles, are the descendants of colonial-era slaves, Jamaican merchants, and West Indian laborers who came to work for United States lumber and banana companies. As British influence receded from the Caribbean lowlands in the nineteenth century, the Creoles displaced the Miskito at the top of the region's ethnic hierarchy and became the key colonial intermediary. Concentrated in the coastal cities of Bluefields and Puerto Cabezas, on the Islas del Maíz, and around Laguna de Perlas, the contemporary Creoles are English-speaking, although many speak Miskito or Spanish as a second language. As a group, they are urban, well educated, and amply represented in skilled and white-collar occupations. The Creoles are disdainful of indigenous groups, over whom they maintain a distinct economic advantage. All Caribbean groups, however, share the traditional *costeño* resentment of the western Hispanic elite.

The expanding mestizo population in the Caribbean lowlands is concentrated in the region's western areas, inland from the Caribbean littoral. Many live in mining areas. Since the 1950s, the expansion of export agriculture in the western half of the country has forced many dispossessed peasants to seek new land on the agricultural frontiers. On the Caribbean side of the central highlands, this movement has produced bitter clashes between mestizo pioneers and Miskito and Sumu agriculturalists over what the indigenous people regard as communal lands.

Within contemporary Caribbean lowlands society, a clear ethnic hierarchy exists. The indigenous groups—Miskito, Sumu, and Rama—occupy the bottom ranks. These groups are the most impoverished, least educated, and generally relegated to the least desirable jobs. Above them, at successively higher ranks, are recently arrived poor mestizos, Creoles, and a small stratum of middle-class mestizos. Prior to 1979, Europeans or North Americans, sent to manage foreign-owned enterprises, were at the top of the hierarchy. In the mines, Miskito and Sumu work at the dangerous, low-wage, underground jobs; mestizos and Creoles hold supervisory positions; and foreigners dominate in the top positions. Also prior to 1979, a special niche was occupied by a small group of Chinese immigrants, who dominated the commerce of the main coastal towns.

The demography of the Caribbean lowlands is a subject of speculation and controversy. The last census data are from 1971. Since then, the region has experienced rapid natural increase and heavy migration of mestizos from the west. Traditionally, the Miskito are recognized as the numerically dominant group, but that status has been challenged by the mestizo influx. In the early 1980s, armed conflict in the region drove thousands of Miskito over the Honduran border, but as the violence ebbed in the late 1980s, refugees returned. The most recent government estimates of the ethnic composition of the region are based on data from a 1981 housing survey.

The Sandinista Revolution on the Caribbean Coast

The Sandinista administration, which enjoyed broad popular support in the Pacific region and central highlands during the early 1980s, was a political failure in the Caribbean lowlands from the beginning. In retrospect, this was hardly remarkable. *Costeños*, who were barely reconciled to their incorporation into Nicaragua, were unlikely to respond enthusiastically to bold new initiatives from the west. The Somoza regime had presented a low profile in the Caribbean region, physically limited to a few National Guard outposts, customs offices in the ports, and scattered health and educational facilities; the government allowed designated village leaders to serve as official community contacts. Despite some development policies that threatened local interests, the Somoza government was never despised on the coast the way it was in the west. Accordingly, *costeño* participation in the 1979 Sandinista revolution was minimal.

In the early 1980s, the Caribbean region was feeling the effects of long-term economic decline, especially in the north. The foreign-dominated extractive industries, such as lumber and mining, were shrinking, largely as a result of overexploitation of resources. A few foreign firms departed in the wake of the Sandinista victory or were expropriated by the new government. Subsistence agriculture, the traditional economic refuge of the Miskito when wage work was unavailable, became less secure as a result of growing land pressures. Increasing population, land competition with westerners on the agricultural frontier, and an adverse International Court of Justice (ICJ) decision settling a border dispute with Honduras all reduced the land available to indigenous cultivators in the east. These circumstances left *costeños* convinced that the region's best times had passed.

The Sandinista revolution arrived in the east with a mestizo face. Few *costeños* and, in particular, few indigenous people filled government and party positions in the Caribbean lowlands. The Sandinista cadres sent to the region were generally ignorant of the area's cultures and languages and were unconsciously discriminatory in their attitudes toward *costeños*. Even well-intentioned government initiatives could clash with local sensitivities. For example, the expansion of government-supported social services threatened the Moravian Church's long-established authority in these areas.

Miskito boy harvesting coconuts in eastern Nicaragua
Courtesy Nicaraguan Tourism Institute

Sandinista ideology appealed to class interests and anti-American nationalism, sentiments that had less appeal in the east than on the western side of the country. Although poor mestizos in the west could identify with the "exploited classes," *costeños* were, for very good reasons, more likely to perceive themselves as members of oppressed ethnic communities. Views that the Sandinistas described as "anti-imperialist" made little sense to *costeños*, who historically had depended on the United States and Britain to protect them from Nicaragua, felt an affinity with Anglo-American culture, and appreciated foreign investment, which they identified with the region's most prosperous eras. These attitudes were reinforced by the anti-communist, pro-United States orientation of the Moravian Church.

In early October 1980, Creoles in the southern port city of Bluefields staged large-scale anti-Sandinista protests. A more serious challenge to Sandinista power, however, was brewing in the northeast among the Miskito. Between 1982 and 1984, large numbers of Miskito were in open revolt against the government. Like other Contra forces, the Miskito rebels were armed and encouraged by the United States. As the Sandinistas later acknowledged, however, their own ethnocentric, heavy-handed, and, on occasion, brutal exercise of power on the

Caribbean coast fueled the anger that drove the rebellion. Beyond these contemporary circumstances, the Miskito revolt reflected the *costenos'* resentment of "Spanish" rule, of their own subordination within the ethnic hierarchy of the Caribbean region, and of the economic decline of the region.

By 1985 the Sandinista leadership had altered its policies toward the Caribbean region. Negotiations with rebel groups produced a tense but enduring peace in the region. Broader discussions with *costeño* representatives led to an accord dividing the area into two autonomous regions. The accord also granted the peoples of the region limited rights of self-rule, cultural guarantees, and influence over the use of the region's natural resources, including land. The accord was written into the 1987 constitution and subsequent enabling legislation. How the autonomy framework would function in practice remained to be determined. Historically, the ruling elites of the west have sought to enlarge rather than temper their power over the Caribbean region. However, the Sandinista experience reinforced ethnic consciousness and political militancy among *costeños*. The peoples of the Caribbean region would in all likelihood be quicker to assert their rights in the future.

*   *   *

The Nicaraguan revolution inspired a sudden outpouring of writing about a society that had been largely ignored by students of Latin America. Although these works were overtaken by events, even as they were being published in the late 1980s and early 1990s, many are still worth consulting. Useful overviews include David Close's *Nicaragua: Politics, Economics and Society,* Dennis Gilbert's *Sandinistas: The Party and the Revolution,* Kent Norsworthy's *Nicaragua: A Country Guide,* Carlos Maria Vilas's *The Sandinista Revolution,* Thomas W. Walker's *Nicaragua: The Land of Sandino,* and the collections edited by Walker, especially *Nicaragua: The First Five Years* and *Revolution and Counterrevolution in Nicaragua.*

Rural society and agrarian reform are covered in Eduardo Baumeister's "Agrarian Reform," Laura Enriquez's *Harvesting Change: Labor and Agrarian Reform,* and Joseph Collins's *Nicaragua: What Difference Could a Revolution Make? Food and Farming in the New Nicaragua.* The religious foment of the 1970s and 1980s is the subject of Michael Dodson and Laura Nuzzi O'Shaughnessy's *Nicaragua's Other Revolution, Religious Faith and Political Struggle,* Giulio Giraldi's *Faith and Revolution in Nicaragua,*

Roger N. Lancaster's *Thanks to God and the Revolution: Popular Religion and Class Consciousness in the New Nicaragua*, and David Stoll's *Is Latin America Turning Protestant? The Politics of Evangelical Growth*. On health and education, see John M. Donahue's *The Nicaraguan Revolution in Health*, Richard Garfield and Glen Williams's *Health and Revolution*, and Robert F. Arnove's *Education and Revolution in Nicaragua*. The lives of Nicaraguan women are examined in *Women and Revolution in Nicaragua*, edited by Helen Collinson and Lucinda Broadbent, and Patricia M. Chuchryk's "Women in the Revolution." The Caribbean region and its peoples and conflicts are described in Carlos Vilas's *State, Class, and Ethnicity in Nicaragua*. On the physical and human geography of Nicaragua, see Robert West and John P. Augelli's *Middle America*. Nicaraguan population trends are recorded in the United Nations' *Boletín Demográfico*. For short, fact-laden updates on varied aspects of Nicaragua society, see the English-language monthly *Envío*.

For further reading suggestions, see the exhaustive annotated bibliography, *Sandinista Nicaragua*, by Neil Snarr, particularly the chapters on the social sector, religion, the Caribbean coast, and the economy. (For further information and complete citations, see Bibliography.)

Chapter 3. The Economy

Worker harvesting coffee beans

THE NICARAGUAN ECONOMY has seen no "business as usual" for almost twenty years. From the mid-1940s to the mid-1970s, high rates of growth and investment changed Nicaragua's economy from a traditional agrarian economy dependent on one crop to one with a diversified agricultural sector and a nascent manufacturing component. Beginning in the late 1970s, however, more than a decade and a half of civil war, coupled with a decade of populist economic policies, severely disrupted the Nicaraguan economy. Extraordinary expenses to support the constant fighting, with its incalculable burden upon the population, the environment, and the country's infrastructure, rendered most economic indicators largely meaningless. Add several catastrophic natural disasters—an earthquake in 1972, a hurricane in 1988, and a drought in 1989—and five years of a total trade embargo by the United States to the effects of the fighting, and it becomes clear why Nicaragua in 1993 vied with Haiti and Guyana as the poorest country in the Western Hemisphere.

Finding solutions to address the human costs of Nicaragua's wars is the economic challenge facing the government of President Violeta Barrios de Chamorro. Those human costs are numerous: the diversion of resources from social programs to the military, loss of agricultural and industrial production, increased misery and widespread hunger, destruction of natural resources and infrastructure, the uprooting of families and communities, and demands for land and resources from internal and returning external refugees. Getting Nicaragua's national economy in order may be the easier part of the challenge. Controlling inflation, adjusting exchange rates, and setting new agricultural and industrial prices and priorities are only first steps. The government faces the even larger problems of endemic poverty and widening environmental deterioration.

The February 1990 election of a politically moderate president and the reconciliation of most armed conflict soon after seemed to offer a rare opportunity for Nicaragua to build almost from scratch a better future. However, continued political problems and natural disasters in 1991 and 1992 dimmed the initial optimism. The goal of revitalizing Nicaragua's economy in an era of fragile democracy and increasingly scarce resources remained the country's greatest problem in 1993.

Historical Background

Pre-Columbian and Colonial Era

The first Spanish explorers of Nicaragua found a well-developed agrarian society in the central highlands and Pacific lowlands. The rich volcanic soils produced a wide array of products, including beans, peppers, corn, cocoa, and cassava (manioc). Agricultural land was held communally, and each community had a central marketplace for trading and distributing food.

The arrival of the Spanish in the early 1500s destroyed, for all intents and purposes, the indigenous agricultural system. The early conquistadors were interested primarily in gold; European diseases and forced work in the gold mines decimated the native population. Some small areas continued to be cultivated at the end of the 1500s, but most previously tilled land reverted to jungle. By the early 1600s, cattle raising, cultivation of small amounts of corn and cocoa, and forestry had become the major uses for Nicaragua's land. Beef, hides, and tallow were the colony's principal exports for the next two and a half centuries.

The Coffee Boom, 1840s–1940s

Coffee was the product that would change Nicaragua's economy. Coffee was first grown domestically as a curiosity in the early 1800s. In the late 1840s, however, as coffee's popularity grew in North America and Europe, commercial coffee growing began in the area around Managua. By the early 1850s, passengers crossing Nicaragua en route to California were served large quantities of Nicaraguan coffee. The Central American coffee boom was in full swing in Nicaragua by the 1870s, and large areas in western Nicaragua were cleared and planted with coffee trees.

Unlike traditional cattle raising or subsistence farming, coffee production required significant capital and large pools of labor. Laws were therefore passed to encourage foreign investment and allow easy acquisition of land. The Subsidy Laws of 1879 and 1889 gave planters with large holdings a subsidy of US$0.05 per tree.

By the end of the nineteenth century, the entire economy came to resemble what is often referred to as a "banana republic" economy—one controlled by foreign interests and a small

Woman selling hand-woven baskets at the Managua central market
Courtesy Nina Serafino

domestic elite oriented toward the production of a single agricultural export. Profits from coffee production flowed abroad or to the country's small number of landowners. Taxes on coffee were virtually nonexistent. The economy was also hostage to fluctuations in the price of coffee on the world markets— wide swings in coffee prices meant boom or bust years in Nicaragua.

Diversification and Growth, 1945–77

The period after World War II was a time of economic diversification. The government brought in foreign technocrats to give advice on increasing production of new crops; hectarage in bananas and sugarcane increased, livestock herds grew, and cotton became a new export crop. The demand for cotton during the Korean War (1950–53) caused a rapid increase in cotton production, and by the mid-1950s, cotton was the nation's second largest export-earner, after coffee.

Economic growth continued in the 1960s, largely as a result of industrialization. Under the stimulus of the newly formed Central American Common Market (CACM; see Appendix B), Nicaragua achieved a certain degree of specialization in processed foods, chemicals, and metal manufacturing. By the end of the 1960s, however, import-substitution industrialization

101

(ISI—see Glossary) as a stimulus for economic growth had been exhausted. The 1969 Soccer War between Honduras and El Salvador, two members of the CACM, effectively suspended attempts at regional integration until 1987, when the Esquipulas II agreement was signed. By 1970 the industrial sector was undergoing little additional import substitution, and the collapse of the CACM meant that Nicaragua's economic growth, which had come from the expanding manufacturing sector, halted. Furthermore, the manufacturing firms that had developed under the tariff protection of the CACM were generally high-cost and inefficient; consequently, they were at a disadvantage when exporting outside the region.

Although statistics for the period 1970–77 seemed to show continued economic growth, they reflected fluctuations in demand rather than a continued diversification of the economy. The gross domestic product (GDP—see Glossary) rose 13 percent in 1974, the biggest boom in Nicaragua's economic history. However, these figures largely represented the jump in construction as the country struggled to rebuild after the disastrous 1972 earthquake. Likewise, the positive growth in 1976–77 was merely a reflection of the high world prices for coffee and cotton.

Positive GDP growth rates in the 1970s masked growing structural problems in the economy. The 1972 earthquake destroyed much of Nicaragua's industrial infrastructure, which had been located in Managua. An estimated 10,000 people were killed and 30,000 injured, most of them in the capital area. The earthquake destroyed most government offices, the financial district of Managua, and about 2,500 small shops engaged in manufacturing and commercial activities. About 4 percent of city housing in Managua was left unstable.

Government budget deficits and inflation were the legacies of the earthquake. The government increased expenses to finance rebuilding, which primarily benefited the construction industry, in which the Somoza family had strong financial interests. Because earthquake reconstruction generated few new revenues, except through borrowing, most of the resulting public deficits were covered by foreign loans. In the late 1970s, Nicaragua had the highest level of foreign indebtedness in Central America (see Glossary).

Most of the benefits of the three decades of growth after World War II were concentrated in a few hands. Several groups of influential firms and families, most notably the Somoza family, controlled most of the nation's production. The Banamérica Group, an offshoot of the conservative elite of Granada, had powerful interests in sugar, rum, cattle, coffee, and retailing. The Banic Group, so-called because of its ties to the Nicaraguan Bank of Industry and Commerce (Banco Nicaragüense de Industria y Comercio—Banic), had its roots in the liberal families of León and had ties to the cotton, coffee, beer, lumber, construction, and fishing industries.

The third interest controlling the nation's production was the Somoza family, which had wide holdings in almost every segment of Nicaraguan society. Financial dealings for the Somozas were handled by the Central Bank of Nicaragua (Banco Central de Nicaragua), which the Somozas treated as if it were a commercial bank. The Central Bank made frequent personal loans, which often went unpaid, to the Somozas. Although the other financial groups used financial means primarily to further their interests, the Somozas protected their financial interests by controlling the government and its institutions. The Somoza family owned an estimated 10 percent to 20 percent of the country's arable land, was heavily involved in the food processing industry, and controlled import-export licenses. The Somozas also controlled the transportation industry by owning outright, or at least having controlling interest in, the country's main seaports, the national airline, and Nicaragua's maritime fleet. Much of the profit from these enterprises was then reinvested in real estate holdings throughout the United States and Latin America. Some analysts estimated that by the mid-1970s, the Somozas owned or controlled 60 percent of the nation's economic activity. When Anastasio Somoza Debayle (president, 1967–72, 1974–79) fled Nicaragua in 1979, the family's worth was estimated to be between US$500 million and US$1.5 billion (see The End of the Anastasio Debayle Somoza Era, ch. 1).

Legacy of the Sandinista Revolution, 1977–79

By the mid-1970s, the government's economic and dictatorial political policies had alienated nearly all sectors of society. Armed opposition to the Somoza regimes, which had started as a small rural insurrection in the early 1960s, had grown by 1977 to a full-scale civil war. The fighting caused foreign investment to drop sharply and the private sector to cut investment plans. Many government expenditures were shifted to the military budget. As fighting in the cities increased, destruction and looting caused a large loss in inventories and operating stock. Foreign investment, which before 1977 had been a significant factor in the economy's growth, almost stopped. As the fighting intensified further, most liquid assets flowed out of the country.

Although the anti-Somoza forces finally won their struggle in July 1979, the human and physical cost of the revolution was tremendous. As many as 50,000 people lost their lives in the fighting, 100,000 were wounded, and 40,000 children were left orphans. About US$500 million in physical plants, equipment, and materials was destroyed; housing, hospitals, transportation, and communications incurred damages of US$80 million. The GDP shrank an estimated 25 percent in 1979 alone.

The Sandinista Era, 1979–90

The new government, formed in 1979 and dominated by the Sandinistas (see Glossary), resulted in a new model of economic development. The new leadership was conscious of the social inequities produced during the previous thirty years of unrestricted economic growth and was determined to make the country's workers and peasants, the "economically underprivileged," the prime beneficiaries of the new society. Consequently, in 1980 and 1981, unbridled incentives to private investment gave way to institutions designed to redistribute wealth and income. Private property would continue to be allowed, but all land belonging to the Somozas was confiscated.

However, the ideology of the Sandinistas put the future of the private sector and of private ownership of the means of production in doubt. Even though under the new government both public and private ownership were accepted, government spokespersons occasionally referred to a reconstruction phase in the country's development, in which property owners and the professional class would be tapped for their managerial and technical expertise. After reconstruction and recovery, the private sector would give way to expanded public ownership in most areas of the economy. Despite such ideas, which represented the point of view of a faction of the government, the Sandinista government remained officially committed to a mixed economy.

Economic growth was uneven in the 1980s (see table 5, Appendix A). Restructuring of the economy and the rebuilding immediately following the end of the civil war caused the GDP to jump about 5 percent in 1980 and 1981. Each year from 1984 to 1990, however, showed a drop in the GDP. Reasons for the contraction included the reluctance of foreign banks to offer new loans, the diversion of funds to fight the new insurrection against the government, and, after 1985, the total embargo on trade with the United States, formerly Nicaragua's largest trading partner. After 1985 the government chose to fill the gap between decreasing revenues and mushrooming military expenditures by printing large amounts of paper money. Inflation skyrocketed, peaking in 1988 at more than 14,000 percent annually.

Measures taken by the government to lower inflation were largely wiped out by natural disaster. In early 1988, the administration of Daniel José Ortega Saavedra (Sandinista junta coordinator, 1979–85; president, 1985–90) established an austerity program to lower inflation. Price controls were tightened, and a new currency was introduced. As a result, by August 1988 inflation had dropped to an annual rate of 240 percent. The following month, however, Hurricane Joan cut a devastating path directly across the center of the country. Damage was extensive, and the government's program of massive spending to repair the infrastructure destroyed its anti-inflation measures.

In its eleven years in power, the Sandinista government never overcame most of the economic inequalities that it inherited from the Somoza era. Years of war, policy missteps, natural disasters, and the effects of the United States trade embargo all hindered economic development. The early economic gains of the Sandinistas were wiped out by seven years of sometimes precipitous economic decline, and in 1990, by most standards, Nicaragua and most Nicaraguans were considerably poorer than they were in the 1970s.

The Chamorro Era, 1990–

The economic policies of Violeta Barrios de Chamorro (president, 1990–) were a radical change from those of the previous administration. The president proposed to revitalize the economy by reactivating the private sector and stimulating the export of agricultural products (see fig. 9). However, the administration's political base was shaky. The president's political coalition, the National Opposition Union (Unión Nacional Opositora—UNO), was a group of fourteen parties ranging from the far right to the far left. Furthermore, 43 percent of the voting electorate had voted for the Sandinistas, reflecting

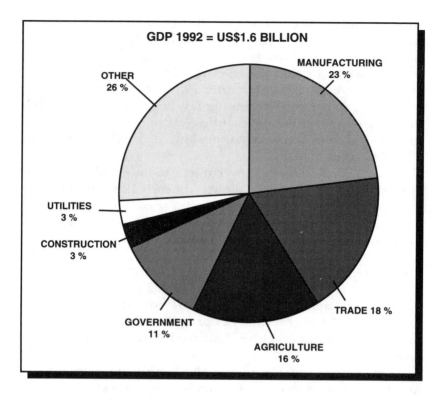

GDP 1992 = US$1.6 BILLION

MANUFACTURING 23 %

OTHER 26 %

UTILITIES 3 %

CONSTRUCTION 3 %

GOVERNMENT 11 %

AGRICULTURE 16 %

TRADE 18 %

Source: Based on information from Economist Intelligence Unit, *Country Profile: Nicaragua, Costa Rica, Panama, 1991–1992*, London, 1992, 14.

Figure 9. Gross Domestic Product (GDP) by Sector of Origin, 1992

support for the overall goals of the former administration although not necessarily the results.

The Chamorro government's initial economic package embraced a standard International Monetary Fund (IMF—see Glossary) and World Bank (see Glossary) set of policy prescriptions. The IMF demands included instituting measures aimed at halting spiraling inflation, lowering the fiscal deficit by downsizing the public-sector work force and the military and reducing spending for social programs, stabilizing the national currency, attracting foreign investment, and encouraging exports. This course was an economic path mostly untraveled by Nicaragua, still heavily dependent on traditional agro-industrial exports, exploitation of natural resources, and continued foreign assistance.

Inspired by the IMF, Minister of Finance Francisco Mayoraga quickly put together an economic "Plan of 100 Days." This plan, also called the "Mayoraga Plan," cut the deficit and helped to lower inflation. Loss of jobs and higher prices under the plan, however, also resulted in crippling public- and private-sector strikes throughout the country. Mayoraga's tenure in office barely exceeded the 100 days of his economic plan. By the end of 1990, the government was forced to abandon most of its free-market reforms.

A series of political problems and natural disasters continued to plague the economy in 1991 and 1992. The need to accommodate left- and right-wing views within its ruling coalition and attempts to work with the Sandinista opposition effectively prevented the implementation of unpopular economic measures. The government was unable to lower government expenditures or to hold the value of the newly introduced gold córdoba (C$o—for value, see Glossary) stable against the United States dollar. A severe drought in 1992 decimated the principal export crops. In September 1992, a tidal wave struck western Nicaragua, leaving thousands homeless. Furthermore, foreign aid and investment, on which the Nicaraguan economy had depended heavily for growth in the years preceding the Sandinista administration, never returned in significant amounts.

Nationalization and the Private Sector

Nationalization under the Sandinistas

Despite initial fears that the Sandinista government would nationalize the economy as was done in Cuba after the revolution, the Sandinista administration pledged to maintain a mixed (privately and publicly owned) economy. All property and businesses owned by the Somoza family or their associates were immediately taken over by the government. Farm workers were encouraged to organize under cooperatives on appropriated land. However, private businesses not previously owned by the Somozas were allowed to continue operations, although under stringent new government regulations.

The Sandinista administration held the right to further nationalize any industry or land that it deemed was underutilized or vital to national interests. Exercising this right, the government made a few "showcase" nationalizations, such as the takeover of the Club Terraza, a nightclub in Managua. In gen-

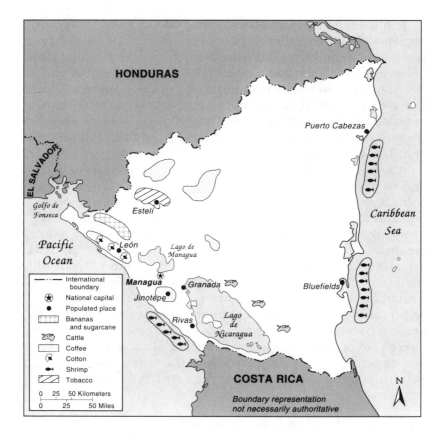

Figure 10. Economic Activity, 1993

eral, however, nationalization was concentrated in the banking, insurance, mining, transportation, and agricultural sectors. During the eleven-year tenure of the Sandinistas, the private sector's contribution to the GDP remained fairly constant, ranging from 50 percent to 60 percent.

Privatization and the Private Sector

To win the February 1990 election, Violeta Barrios de Chamorro promised to represent all sectors of Nicaraguan society, including the small but powerful private sector with which she was closely identified. Nicaragua's private sector, mostly organized under the Superior Council of Private Enterprise (Consejo Superior de la Empresa Privada—Cosep), was instrumental in President Ortega's electoral defeat. Private industry had suffered heavy losses during the struggle to overthrow the Somoza regime and then fared even worse during the decade-long administration of the Sandinistas.

Nicaragua's private sector also was gravely affected by the five-year United States trade embargo directed at destabilizing the government of President Ortega. One year after the trade embargo began in 1986, the government had already shifted much of its economy away from dependence on trade with the United States. The private sector, which in 1985 produced 56 percent of the GDP and 62 percent of Nicaragua's most important exports, suffered from diminished credit and from cost increases and delays for essential supplies.

The private sector had led the political and military opposition to the Sandinista government. By election day 1990, the Nicaraguan private sector held high expectations that it would benefit from a change in government and that it would be compensated for the injustices it felt it had suffered during the Sandinista years. Privately owned factories and land had been confiscated, abandoned, or shuttered or had suffered war damage during the Sandinista era. Private industry looked to exercise the political and economic power it had enjoyed under the Somoza administrations. The private sector also hoped for a return of nationalized property and privatization of government assets still dominated by representatives of the Sandinista government.

In some cases, rehabilitation of the factories and firms required only reactivation of idle capacity; other assets, however, including both agricultural and industrial machinery, had frequently deteriorated beyond repair. In some cases, assets had been deliberately destroyed or sold. Much of the Nicaraguan private sector remained on the sidelines in 1990, waiting for the government to lure it with promises of security for its investments and of repair of private property at public expense. The Nicaraguan industrial sector showed only a mild 3 percent recovery by the end of 1990, mostly as the result of renewed access to overseas markets (see fig. 10). Threats of urban labor unrest, renewed hostilities in the countryside, poor infrastructure, political tensions, and delays in passage of property laws returning private property to previous owners continued to discourage most investment. A leery and still belligerent private sector stood ready to turn its political struggle against the new Chamorro government and to do battle with labor unions and other groups identified with the Sandinista revolution.

In 1990 the government initiated a privatization effort to transfer more than 100 of Nicaragua's 350 state-owned companies to private ownership. The process included the outright sale, devolution, or liquidation of assets. The government holding company established to privatize state-owned assets initially identified forty companies to be sold within six months and an additional fifty to be returned to their previous owners or liquidated at a later date. Industrial workers would later negotiate retaining 25 percent ownership of enterprises sold, based on a claim of value added, or "sweat equity," during the Sandinista period.

State-owned enterprises contributed about 40 percent of the gross national product (GNP—see Glossary) in 1991. Most state-owned enterprises were former Somoza properties, although some had been confiscated under agrarian reform from absentee owners or from the Contras (short for *contrarevolucionarios*—see Glossary). The government also agreed to give back 50,000 hectares of fifty-six rural properties provided that owners pay for improvements made during the revolution. Another 70,000 hectares went to workers, former army officers, and demobilized Contras.

By mid-1992, the government of Nicaragua had also returned two slaughterhouses to their previous owners and sold a third. The government privatization company tendered bids for the administration of two of the largest shrimp processing plants in the country, one located in Corn Island and the other in Bluefields. A bid was also sought for the sale of a ship manufacturing and maintenance plant in Bluefields.

The Issue of Land Ownership

The expropriation of lands owned by the Somozas in 1979 left the new Sandinista administration holding about 20 percent of the country's arable lands. At first, these holdings were turned into state farms. In 1981 the administration passed the Agrarian Reform Law defining the process of nationalization and stating what could be done with expropriated land. The law guaranteed property rights to those who continued to use their property, but land that was underdeveloped or abandoned was subject to expropriation. Land could also be declared necessary for agrarian reform and purchased from its owners at a price set by the government. The Agrarian Reform

Law gave free title to land, mostly in eastern Nicaragua, that was occupied by homesteaders. Bank foreclosures in the event of default on a bank loan were prohibited.

Farmland that had been bought or expropriated could be turned over to agricultural cooperatives. The farmers who constituted a cooperative were then given title to the land. These "agrarian reform" titles could be inherited, but the title or any part of the land could not be sold. The process of turning state farms into cooperatives with the transfer of title began slowly at first. The process picked up steam in 1984 when rumors began circulating that the government would use a lack of clear title on state farms as an excuse to remove farmers from state farms. In 1985 it was estimated that 120,000 families were farming lands redistributed by the Agrarian Reform Law, half on state farms and half in cooperatives.

In its last months in office, the Ortega government awarded additional land to Sandinista supporters as payment for government service. Nicknamed the Piñata, after a children's game in which a hollow papier-mâché animal filled with candy is broken open and the candy falls out, the property giveaway consisted of more than 5,000 houses and hundreds of thousands of hectares of land.

The new administration of President Chamorro promised to compensate the large landowners whose land had been taken over by the Sandinista government. President Chamorro also issued two controversial land decrees: one provided for temporary rental of idle state farmland to those willing to work the land for a year, and another established a commission to adjudicate more than 1,600 claims on land confiscated by the former government. Bank foreclosures were allowed again, and the government indicated that it favored changing the titling provision of the Agrarian Reform Law to allow for sale of property.

Combined opposition forces would soon force the Chamorro administration to ease some of its new policies. The critical issue of land ownership would, in fact, prove to be the most contentious issue confronting the new government. The Sandinista-led opposition derided the rental decree, which primarily benefited former Contras, as a return of land to supporters of the Somoza family. Threatened by a major strike, President Chamorro agreed to suspend the rental land decree. Former President Ortega called the revocation of the decree a major victory, while critics assailed it as an abrogation of power.

Because Chamorro's plan did not take back property given away in the Piñata, the powerful private-sector umbrella group, Cosep, refused to participate in her economic plan. Henceforth, Nicaragua's private sector would prove to be an intractable opponent.

Finance

Banking

Prior to 1979, Nicaragua's banking system consisted of the Central Bank of Nicaragua and several domestic- and foreign-owned commercial banks. One of the first acts of the Sandinista government in 1979 was to nationalize the domestic banks. Foreign banks were allowed to continue their operations but could no longer accept local deposits. In 1985 a new decree loosened state control of the banking system by allowing the establishment of privately owned local exchange houses.

In 1990 the National Assembly passed legislation permitting private banks to resume operations. In 1992 the largest state-owned commercial bank was the National Development Bank (Banco Nacional de Desarrollo—BND), originally established by Chase National Bank. Other state-owned commercial banks were the Bank of America (Banco de América—Bamer) and the Nicaraguan Bank of Industry and Commerce (Banco Nicaragüense de Industria y Comercio—Banic). The People's Bank (Banco Popular) specialized in business loans, and the Real Estate Bank (Banco Inmobilario—Bin) provided loans for housing. Three foreign banks continued operations: Bank of America, Citibank, and Lloyds Bank.

The Inter-American Development Bank (IDB) was instrumental in restructuring Nicaragua's technically bankrupt banking sector. In December 1991, the IDB approved a US$3 million technical cooperation grant to restructure the Central Bank, and in March 1992 it approved a US$3 million loan to a new commercial bank, the Mercantile Bank (Banco Mercantil). The Mercantile Bank program was expected to make loans available to small- and medium-sized private-sector enterprises and to finance investments to bolster fixed assets and create permanent working capital. The Mercantile Bank was the first private bank to be established in Nicaragua since 1979. Three additional new commercial banks were scheduled to open in 1992.

Restructuring of the National Financial System (Sistema Financiero Nacional—SFN) was one of the key elements of the government's economic reform program. According to an agreement between President Chamorro and the World Bank, Banic was to be merged with Bin. The BND would handle only rural credit operations, and the People's Bank was to take over all credit operations for small- and medium-sized industry. International operations, which had been managed exclusively by the Central Bank since 1984, were transferred to the BND and Banic. The Central Bank would continue to handle operations pertaining to the central government, while the newly merged banks would be responsible for letters of credit, imports, transfers, and dollar checking accounts.

The Central Bank also auctioned off one of the government's largest exchange houses. This exchange house had been established in 1988 under the direction of the Financial Corporation of Nicaragua (Corporación Financiera de Nicaragua—Corfin). In 1989 the Central Bank authorized the exchange house to operate a foreign money exchange office as an agent of the bank. In May 1991, Corfin voted to turn over its shares in the exchange house to the Central Bank so that the exchange house could be sold.

Opponents charged that this sale was unconstitutional. They argued that the exchange house was the property of the Central Bank and could not be transferred. The Federation of Bank Workers also charged that the new government banking policy was weakening the state bank while giving the advantage to the private banks.

Currency

From 1912 to 1988, the córdoba was the basic unit of currency. Relatively stable during most of that period, the value of the córdoba was pegged to the United States dollar. One of the last economic decisions by the Somoza administration was a devaluation in April 1979 of the córdoba from US$1 = C$7 to US$1 = C$10, a value it held until 1985.

In 1985 mounting economic problems, especially the imposition of the trade embargo by the United States, forced the Ortega administration to opt for a multitiered exchange rate, with one rate for petroleum imports, one for agricultural goods, one for capital goods, and another used at government exchange houses. Amid this confusion, a black market sprang up offering significantly more córdobas per dollar than any of the official government rates. As inflation increased from 1985 through 1988, the value of the córdoba plummeted, and by mid-1988 the government exchange houses offered US$1 = C$20,000, while a United States dollar on the black market fetched 60,000 córdobas.

To curb hyperinflation, the government introduced its economic shock program in February 1988. Currency stabilization was an integral part of this package, and a new currency, the new córdoba (C$n—for value, see Glossary), was introduced. Each new córdoba equaled 1,000 old córdobas, and the new currency's exchange rate was set at US$1 = C$n10. By the end of 1988, however, the rate at government exchange houses had dropped to US$1 = C$n920.

Devaluation accelerated in 1989 and 1990. Immediately after the 1990 elections, the currency lost four-fifths of its value. By the end of 1990, it took 3.2 million new córdobas to buy a United States dollar on the black market. The government was unable to print money in large enough denominations to make simple transactions convenient.

To help control inflation, the Chamorro government introduced a third currency, the gold córdoba (C$o), in mid-1990. At first used only as an accounting device, this new currency was introduced gradually to the general populace, and for six months both currencies were legal tender, with a conversion rate of 5 million new córdobas to one gold córdoba. After April 31, 1991, the gold córdoba became the sole legal currency and was pegged to the United States dollar at a rate of US$1 = C$o5, a rate it maintained throughout 1992. By July 1993, the exchange rate had slipped only slightly, to US$1 = C$o6.15.

Inflation

In the first half of the 1980s, the annual inflation rate averaged 30 percent. After the United States imposed a trade embargo in 1985, Nicaragua's inflation rate rose dramatically. The 1985 annual rate of 220 percent tripled the following year and skyrocketed to more than 14,000 percent in 1988, the highest rate for any country in the Western Hemisphere in that year. An economic austerity plan introduced in late 1988 caused the 1989 figure to drop somewhat, but inflation jumped again in 1990 to more than 12,000 percent. President Chamorro's economic plan and the resumption of trade with the United States had a positive effect on the country's inflation. Despite the abandonment of many of the points of the economic plan, the annual inflation rate dropped to 400 percent in 1991, and was estimated to be only 10 percent in 1992.

Tax Reform

The Chamorro government instituted tax reform in July 1990. New measures included lower tariff rates, lower income tax, and payment of tax in gold córdobas. The reform reduced top tariff rates from 61 percent to 20 percent and top income tax from 60 percent to 38.5 percent. Collection of tax may have increased because of reduced evasion, but tax revenues, reported to be 23.5 percent of GDP in 1989, fell to only 15 percent by 1990.

To encourage investment, the government eliminated a 2 percent export tax on coffee and cotton and lowered the general sales tax from 15 percent to 10 percent. The government also granted tax incentives for exporters of nontraditional products under a new export-promotion act. Like previous governments, the Chamorro administration announced it would extend preferential long-term credit for agro-industrial development.

Deficits

Nicaragua's budget deficits were low in the decades of economic growth following World War II. This situation changed dramatically in the late 1970s when the Somoza government had to borrow large amounts of capital to finance military expenditures in the civil war. Deficits also increased during the Sandinista years because large sums of money were diverted to social programs even as income from traditional export crops decreased. The deficit in the final years of the Sandinista administration showed an eerie parallel to the final Somoza years because the government had to increase finances for the military in order to prevent the government's overthrow.

In 1990, despite a new administration, all sources of government revenue declined. Even without the drain of war, the Central Bank of Nicaragua projected in early 1990 that the fiscal deficit for 1990 would average US$13 million per month. Shortly after the inauguration of President Chamorro in 1990, the government's monthly deficit fell from more than US$30 million to about US$8 million. The improvement in finances was temporary, however, as the government was forced to abandon tight budgetary restraints later in 1990 when it paid large sums in severance pay to reduce the number of military and public-sector employees. Former members of the military, Contras, and public-sector workers were offered "golden parachutes" in return for retirement. Altogether, the Chamorro government spent approximately US$5 million to disarm 17,000 former combatants. The average payoff was US$200 per person and US$1,000 for each weapon that was turned over to the government. A few former military leaders from both sides of the conflict may have received as much as US$150,000 each, according to stories reported in the international press. These former leaders also received promises of land, credit, houses, and vehicles.

External Sector

Foreign Trade and the Balance of Payments

In 1992 Nicaragua's foreign trade consisted almost entirely of agricultural exports (mostly coffee, cotton, bananas, sugar, and beef) and imports of petroleum, consumer goods, and machinery. Although the country's major trading partners have changed in response to the political orientation of the administration in power and the trade balance has fluctuated with the world price for agricultural products, Nicaragua's basic pattern of imports and exports has remained unchanged throughout the twentieth century.

The late 1970s and 1980s saw the country's trading partners shift dramatically (see table 6, Appendix A). Prior to the outbreak of large-scale fighting in 1977, the country's main trading partner was the United States. The period of widespread hostilities from 1977 to 1979, along with dwindling worldwide support for the Somoza administration, halted almost all foreign trade. When peace returned in 1979, the new Sandinista government encouraged trade with the Soviet Union, Cuba, and Eastern Europe. This shift in trading partners gathered momentum in the 1980s when the United States trade embargo forced the Sandinista administration to strengthen ties with socialist countries. Nicaraguan exports to Soviet bloc countries went from nil in 1979 to 31 percent in 1987; in the same time period, imports from socialist nations rose from less than 1 percent to more than 44 percent.

As trade with the socialist countries increased, trade with the United States and neighboring Central American countries decreased. The growth of the Contra insurgency in border areas made overland trade to Nicaragua's neighbors difficult.

The disruption of trade routes, along with political opposition to the Sandinista government by the other Central American republics, caused trade between Nicaragua and the rest of Central America to decline 75 percent from 1982 to 1985. Trade with the United States in the 1980s also fell. In 1983 the United States lowered the sugar import quota from Nicaragua, and sugar exports from Nicaragua to the United States declined 90 percent. The 1985 United States embargo on trade with Nicaragua ended what exchange was left between the two nations; the United States accounted for 23 percent of Nicaraguan exports and 31 percent of Nicaraguan imports in 1980; trade between the two was practically nonexistent after 1985.

The change of administrations in Nicaragua in 1990, along with the overthrow of communism in Eastern Europe and the Soviet Union and the collapse of the Cuban economy, caused Nicaraguan trade patterns to shift yet again. Trade with Cuba, Russia, and Eastern Europe plummeted. The end of the United States trade embargo in 1990 resulted in 16.4 percent of Nicaragua's exports going to the United States and 21.3 percent of Nicaragua's total foreign purchases coming from the United States in the following year.

Nicaragua's balance of trade has shown a sizable deficit every year since 1980. Export income declined in the 1980s because of poor harvests, low prices for agriculture exports, difficulty in obtaining foreign credits and foreign exchange, the decline of the Central American Common Market (CACM) as a trading bloc, and the loss of United States markets. Despite a decrease in export earnings, imports of petroleum and consumer goods continued at roughly the same pace throughout the 1980s. The yearly trade balance for that decade ranged from US$230 million to US$562 million (in constant 1980 United States dollars), and the negative trade balances were paid for by a rapid increase in the country's external debt. Ironically, resumption of trade with the United States exacerbated the balance of payments situation because imports of consumer goods and machinery from the United States increased much faster than exports of agricultural products.

Foreign Aid

Having won the 1990 elections and made significant steps toward peace, the new Chamorro government expected that Western nations and financial institutions would rally to its support. The United States, however, made resumption of economic assistance conditional on steadfast adherence to privatization of government-controlled resources, cuts in the military, and cancellation of Nicaragua's 1985 damage suit against the United States in the International Court of Justice (ICJ). Additional requirements for trade and tariff liberalization quickly followed the more general conditions that the United States placed on resumption of foreign assistance.

To enable Nicaragua to meet eligibility requirements for borrowing from international financial institutions, the United States government promised Nicaragua approximately US$300 million in 1990. These funds were designated primarily for debt repayment and petroleum imports (the country's petroleum bill in 1989 was US$90 million). A smaller portion was earmarked for employment generation. However, these promised funds would prove slow to come. Two hundred days after the inauguration of President Chamorro, only US$160 million of the US$300 million pledged by the United States had been delivered.

Conditions for new loans were also placed by international banking organizations. In 1991 the IMF approved a US$55.7 million standby credit over an eighteen-month period to support President Chamorro's economic program. Requirements for the money, however, were similar to those imposed by the United States government and included accelerated privatization.

In July 1991, President Chamorro signed a US$420 million loan with the World Bank and the IDB. Beginning in 1992, US$220 million was disbursed for investment in coffee, cotton, and cattle and for improvement of damaged and worn infrastructure. The remainder was to be used to pay off a bridge loan from Colombia, Spain, Venezuela, and Mexico, money those countries had loaned Nicaragua to pay a US$360 million debt to the World Bank and the IDB. Arrears payments to the international financial institutions were a standard condition for eligibility for new loans. Nicaragua also received additional aid from seventeen other countries to pay off arrears.

External Debt

After the Sandinista revolution, first under the provisional junta and later under President Ortega, Nicaragua moved from a historically high dependence on financing from Western nations to financial dependence on the Soviet Union and Eastern Europe. By 1990 and the election of President Chamorro,

Nicaragua was the most indebted country in Central America, owing close to US$4 billion to the Soviet Union and another US$6 billion to US$8 billion to Western nations and international lending institutions.

As the result of a de facto moratorium on Somoza-contracted debt by the Sandinista government, Nicaragua faced US$350 million in debt arrears in 1990. This debt was owed mostly to international financial institutions, including the World Bank, the IMF, and the IDB. New borrowing was precluded by the old debt and accumulated arrears.

The need to overcome the burden of a growing foreign debt, estimated at US$10.6 billion, drove the Chamorro government's economic program in the 1990s. The Nicaraguan debt, which was owed mostly to governments and the multilateral lending institutions, was still the highest per capita debt in the region. Despite some debt forgiveness since the inauguration of President Chamorro, significant additional debt relief remained an absolute necessity for economic recovery.

Labor

Composition of the Labor Force

In 1989 the total labor force consisted of approximately 1,277,000 persons. Almost one-third of the labor force is made up of women, and about one-third of all working-age women hold jobs. In general, members of the labor force are relatively unskilled and have a high degree of mobility, frequently changing jobs or moving to other areas of the country to obtain work. Agriculture accounts for more than 30 percent of all employment, and workers outside of agriculture are more likely to be self-employed in small family-owned enterprises than salaried employees of larger concerns.

Approximately 40,000 new people enter the Nicaraguan labor force each year. Throughout the 1980s, many Nicaraguan workers were diverted from productive economic activities to the war effort. The 1990 demobilization of the military, however, added 50,000 persons to the work force.

Nicaragua entered the 1980s with a severe scarcity of skilled labor, especially technicians and other professionals. A "brain drain"—more than half a million professionals moved out of the country during the Sandinista era—further robbed the country of the expertise needed to staff its institutions. As many as 70 percent of Nicaraguan graduates with a master's degree in business administration were estimated to be in self-imposed exile in 1990.

Employment Conditions

Conditions of work are covered by several labor laws and are also spelled out by articles in the 1987 Nicaraguan constitution. The constitution specifies no more than an eight-hour workday in a forty-eight-hour (six-day) work week, with an hour of rest each day. Health and safety standards are also provided for by the constitution, and forced labor is prohibited.

The Labor Code of 1945, patterned after Mexican labor laws, was Nicaragua's first major labor legislation. Provisions of the code prohibited more than three hours of overtime, three times a week. Workers were entitled to fifteen days of vacation annually (eight national holidays and seven saint's days). The Nicaraguan social security program, passed in 1957, enumerates workers' benefits, including maternity, medical, death, and survivors' benefits; pensions; and workers' compensation for disability.

The constitution provides for the right to bargain collectively. In addition, the Labor Code of 1945 was amended in 1962 to allow for sympathy strikes, time off with pay when a worker has been given notice of an impending layoff, and the right to claim unused vacation pay when terminated. The minimum age for employment is fourteen, but the Ministry of Labor, which has the responsibility of enforcing labor laws, rarely prosecutes violations of the minimum-age regulation; young street vendors or windshield cleaners are a common sight in Managua, and children frequently work on family farms at a young age.

A National Minimum Wage Commission establishes minimum wages for different sectors of the economy. Enforcement of the minimum wage is lax, however, and many workers are paid less than the law allows. Labor groups have argued that the minimum wage is inadequate to feed a family of four, and in 1992 the country's largest umbrella group of unions issued a statement demanding that the government index the minimum wage to the cost of living.

Organized Labor

All public- and private-sector workers, except the military and the police, are entitled to join a union. The estimate of the number of workers in unions varies considerably, but some

Much of the labor force ekes out an existence in the informal sector.
Market scene, Managua
Courtesy Nina Serafino

labor leaders place the number as high as 50 percent. Unions are required to register with the Ministry of Labor and must be granted legal status before they can bargain collectively; however, some labor groups complain of intentional delays in this legalization process. Unions are allowed to associate freely with each other or with international labor organizations.

The country's two largest unions, the Sandinista Workers' Federation (Central Sandinista de Trabajadores—CST) and the Association of Agricultural Workers (Asociación de Trabajadores del Campo—ATC), are associated with the Sandinista political party and are also a part of the umbrella group for all Sandinista unions, the National Workers' Front (Frente Nacional de Trabajadores—FNT). Three smaller unions, the General Confederation of Workers-Independent (Confederación General de Trabajadores Independiente—CGT-I), the Federation for Trade Union Action and Unity (Central de Acción y Unidad Sindical—CAUS), and the Workers' Front (Frente Obrero—FO), are affiliated with leftist political parties. The Social Christian Workers' Front (Frente de Trabajadores Socialcristianos—FTS) has ties with the Nicaraguan Social Christian Party (Partido Social Cristiano Nicaragüense—PSCN). Workers in various sectors of the economy, including health care, transportation, coffee, livestock, and agriculture, have their own unions.

Unemployment and Underemployment

Reliable labor statistics are difficult to obtain, but nearly half of Nicaragua's work force was estimated to be unemployed or underemployed in 1990. Many Nicaraguan workers eke out speculative incomes in the burgeoning informal sector, which encompasses about 55 percent of the economically active population. After several years of hyperinflation in the late 1980s had eroded conventional salaries, thousands of Nicaraguans chose to cast their lot as black marketeers, street vendors, taxicab drivers, and other persons earning their livings on the streets. Almost everyone sought some means to augment or replace inflation-ruined salaries.

Wages

As fixed salaries became increasingly meaningless in the late 1980s, high annual turnover, as much as 100 percent for urban industrial workers, was also typical of the Nicaraguan labor force. By 1988 real wages in Nicaragua were less than one-tenth of those in 1980, reflecting the impoverishment of the middle class as well as increasing numbers of the poor. Nonwage incentives instituted by the Sandinista government in the early 1980s for public-sector workers were abandoned during the period of extreme economic adjustment of the late 1980s. By inauguration day 1990, it was not uncommon for skilled office workers to earn the equivalent of US$10 per month, augmented in some cases by dollar-denominated bonuses for workers in the private sector.

Labor Unrest

By 1990 labor unrest was rampant. Urban workers vied with their rural counterparts to protest deteriorating economic conditions. The workers' protests, however, were soon drowned out by demands by the business class for government trade subsidies, preferential investment, and credit, particularly in the historically dominant agricultural sector. Drought in several food-producing areas in 1990 decreased the amount of food available, increased prices, and exacerbated already severe poverty. In addition, as many as 500,000 refugees returned to Nicaragua, including thousands of former Contras. They, along with thousands of former private- and public-sector workers, further swelled the ranks of the unemployed and underemployed, and increased the burden of grievances with which the new government had to deal.

One of the most troublesome problems for the Chamorro government was ongoing support for the Sandinista revolutionary ideals from a large segment of the population and high expectations for government help to address the needy. The Sandinista administration had permanently altered the "psyche" of the Nicaraguan poor. From inauguration day onward, President Chamorro was confronted by a strike-ready labor force motivated by pressing needs and a suspicious, foot-dragging private sector.

Industry

Historically, Nicaragua's small industrial sector has consisted primarily of food processing. Except for one cement plant and one petroleum refinery, agro-processing industries (slaughterhouses, meat packing plants, food processing plants, cooking oil plants, and dairy facilities) and the manufacture of animal by-products (candles, soap, and leather) have been the backbone of Nicaragua's urban industry. The 1960s were a period of rapid growth of the industrial sector, as new external tariffs established by the CACM allowed the growth of import-substitution plants in Nicaragua. Formation of new import-substitution plants slowed in the 1970s, however, and the percentage of GDP derived from industry dropped to only 23 percent in 1978.

Political and economic problems caused the industrial sector to shrink in the years after 1978. The civil war caused manufacturing output to decrease by one-quarter in 1979 alone. In the agro-industries, which represented 75 percent of the total industrial output, idle capacity became a serious problem after the Sandinista victory in 1979. In the early 1980s, food processing plants were operating at only 50 percent capacity; sugar mills, 49 percent capacity; animal feed processing plants, 70 percent capacity; fruit canning plants, 94 percent capacity; and vegetable oil refineries, 42 percent capacity. The Sandinista government maintained a monopoly on beef processing facilities, but here, too, idle capacity rose from 30 percent in the period between 1977 and 1979 to 85 percent by 1981. Idle capacity in the beef cattle industry averaged 60 percent in subsequent years. This phenomenon resulted mainly from clandestine slaughterhouses, an illegal network of beef distributors, and the withholding of food products by producers.

Although the government-controlled distribution system created shortages, a black market thrived for milk, cheese, chicken, and eggs, as well as livestock by-products such as soap and shoes. In the mid-1980s, Black-market prices soared, and essentials became next to impossible to obtain through legitimate channels. As basic grains and other food became scarcer, beef consumption in Nicaragua rose to the highest level in Central America. Unable to buy corn, Nicaraguans ate beef. Immediately before the imposition of the United States trade embargo in 1985, many ranchers instituted the wholesale slaughter of beef and dairy cows that they were unable to shift across the borders to Costa Rica or Honduras.

The industrial sector, which had grown only sporadically in the early 1980s, declined in the mid- to late 1980s as the Contra war escalated and United States markets dried up. Industrial production dropped an average of 5 percent each year from 1984 to 1989. By 1989 the industrial sector contributed only 19 percent to the nation's GDP, and construction accounted for only 4 percent.

*Worker harvesting
tomatoes
Courtesy Nicaraguan
Tourism Institute*

By President Chamorro's inauguration in 1990, only about 10 percent of the pre-Sandinista era work force was still employed in the skeletal industrial sector. A few larger-scale industries, including a cement production plant, a chemical plant, a metals processing plant, and a petroleum refinery, were geared toward domestic consumption. Even these suffered badly from shortages of essential imports and the lack of skilled labor, however.

Agriculture

Ironies abound in Nicaragua's historically dominant agricultural sector. The country's relatively low population density and its wealth of land resources have both held the promise of solutions to poverty and been a major cause of it. The importance of one or two crops has meant that the country's entire economy has undergone boom-or-bust cycles determined primarily by worldwide prices for agricultural exports.

Coffee became the country's principal crop in the 1870s, a position it still held in 1992 despite the growing importance of other crops. Cotton gained importance in the late 1940s, and in 1992 was the second biggest export earner. In the early 1900s, Nicaraguan governments were reluctant to give concessions to the large United States banana companies, and

125

bananas have never been as important a crop for Nicaragua as they have been for Nicaragua's Central American neighbors; bananas are grown in the country, however, and were generally the third largest export earner in the post-World War II period. Beef and animal by-products, the most important agricultural export for the three centuries before the coffee boom of the late 1800s, were still important commodities in 1992 (see table 7, Appendix A).

From the end of World War II to the early 1960s, the growth and diversification of the agricultural sector drove the nation's economic expansion. From the early 1960s until the increased fighting in 1977 caused by the Sandinista revolution, agriculture remained a robust and significant part of the economy, although its growth slowed somewhat in comparison with the previous postwar decades. Statistics for the next fifteen years, however, show stagnation and then a drop in agricultural production.

The agricultural sector declined precipitously in the 1980s. Until the late 1970s, Nicaragua's agricultural export system generated 40 percent of the country's GDP, 60 percent of national employment, and 80 percent of foreign exchange earnings. Throughout the 1980s, the Contras destroyed or disrupted coffee harvests as well as other key income-generating crops. Private industry stopped investing in agriculture because of uncertain returns. Land was taken out of production of export crops to expand plantings of basic grain. Many coffee plants succumbed to disease.

In 1989, the fifth successive year of decline, farm production declined by roughly 7 percent in comparison with the previous year. Production of basic grains fell as a result of Hurricane Joan in 1988 and a drought in 1989. By 1990 agricultural exports had declined to less than half the level of 1978. The only bright spot was the production of nontraditional export crops such as sesame, tobacco, and African palm oil.

Agricultural Policy

In 1979 the new Sandinista administration quickly identified food as a national priority so that the country's chronically malnourished rural population could be fed. The government planned to increase production to attain self-sufficiency in grains by 1990. Self-sufficiency in other dietary necessities was planned for the year 2000. For a variety of reasons, however, including the private sector's retention of 60 percent of arable land, the Sandinista government continued to import food and grow cash crops. In 1993 the goal of self-sufficiency in food production was still far from being achieved.

To generate essential foreign exchange, the Ortega administration continued to support an upscale, high-tech agroexport sector, but returns on its investment diminished. By 1990 only one-quarter of the pre-1979 hectarage planted in cotton, one of the leading foreign exchange earners in the 1970s, was still under cultivation. Despite an established priority for food production, food imports to Nicaragua grew enormously from the mid-1970s to the mid-1980s.

In general, the Sandinistas made little progress in reducing economic dependence on traditional export crops (see table 8, Appendix A). To the contrary, faced with the need for food self-sufficiency versus the need for essential foreign exchange earnings, the Ortega administration, demonstrating scant economic expertise, continued to prop up the country's traditional agro-industrial export system. They did so despite expensive foreign imports, diminished export markets, and a powerful opposing private sector. However, revenues from traditional export crops continued their rapid decline throughout the 1980s. Despite this drop, agriculture accounted for 29 percent of the GDP in 1989 and an estimated 24 percent in 1991. Agriculture still employed about 45 percent of the work force in 1991.

Crops

Coffee

Large-scale coffee growing began in Nicaragua in the 1850s, and by 1870 coffee was the principal export crop, a position it held for the next century. Coffee is a demanding crop, however. Coffee trees require several years to produce a harvest, and the entire production process requires a greater commitment of capital, labor, and land than do many other crops. Coffee also grows only in the rich volcanic soil found on mountainous terrain, making transportation of the crop to market difficult.

In 1992 more land was planted in coffee than in any other crop. The actual amount of land devoted to coffee varies somewhat from year to year, but averaged 210,000 hectares in the 1980s. Production is centered in the northern part of the central highlands north and east of Estelí, and also in the hilly volcanic region around Jinotepe. Although production of coffee dropped somewhat in the late 1980s, the 1989 crop was still 42,000 tons. Nicaragua's poor transportation system and ecological concerns over the amount of land devoted to growing crops on volcanic slopes in the Pacific region limit further expansion of coffee cultivation. These limitations have led growers to explore planting other crops in undeveloped areas of the country.

Cotton

Cotton was Nicaragua's second biggest export earner in the 1980s. A latecomer to Nicaraguan agriculture, cotton became feasible as an export crop only in the 1950s, when pesticides were developed that permitted high yields in tropical climates. Cotton soon became the crop of choice for large landowners along the central Pacific coast. As the amount of land under cultivation grew, however, erosion and pollution from the heavy use of pesticides became serious problems. Lack of credit for planting, a drop in world cotton prices, and competition from Chile discouraged cotton production in the mid-1980s. Production of cotton dropped significantly in the 1980s, and the 1989 crop of 22,000 tons was less than a third of that produced in 1985.

Bananas

Unlike in other Central American countries, political squabbles over who would control the plantations and shipment of the crop prevented bananas from becoming the major export earner in Nicaragua. Bananas, a native fruit of tropical Asia, were introduced to Nicaragua early in the colonial period. Initially, until a market for them appeared in the United States in the 1860s, bananas, like other fruit, were destined mostly for local consumption. Small plots of the Gros Michael variety of banana were planted for export, but political turmoil and difficulties in establishing secure transportation routes hampered export. Because United States companies developed banana production in neighboring countries, Nicaragua's large potential for this crop remained underdeveloped.

Politics and outbreaks of disease in the 1900s kept banana production low. During their time in power, the Somoza family, who had discovered that coffee and cattle were more profitable than bananas, refused to give United States banana companies the free rein that they enjoyed throughout the rest of Central

A farmer's cooperative in Estelí
Courtesy Nina Serafino
Rice being harvested mechanically
Courtesy Eugene Robertson

America. In addition, an outbreak of Panama disease, a fungus that kills the plant's underground stem, wiped out most of the banana plantations in the early 1900s. New plants of the Valery and Giant Cavendish variety were planted, but constant use of fungicides was required to control black sigatoka disease. Although Cavendish bananas yield three times the harvest of the older Gros Michael type, Cavendish bananas are more difficult to harvest and transport, Cavendish bananas, for example, bruise easily and must be picked at an earlier stage and crated in the fields for transport. Most banana production is in the Pacific lowlands, in a region extending north from Lago de Managua to the Golfo de Fonseca. In 1989 banana production amounted to 132,000 tons.

Other Crops

Although much of lowland Nicaragua has a climate conducive to growing sugarcane, poor transportation has limited production to roughly the same area in northwest Nicaragua where bananas are grown. Most sugarcane is processed into whitish centrifugal sugar, the raw sugar of international commerce. Some plants further process the sugarcane into refined granulated sugar. Demand for sugar remained comparatively low until the United States-imposed embargo on Cuban sugar began in 1960. Demand then soared, and sugar production tripled over in the next two decades. Like all other agricultural products, sugar production was severely hit by the United States trade embargo on Nicaraguan products from 1985 to 1990. Production of raw sugarcane stood at 2,300 tons in 1989.

In the early 1990s, the government attempted to diversify agriculture, but had limited results. Tobacco and sesame are both produced for export. The first African palm oil plantations, which were established in the Caribbean lowlands, began production in 1990. Beans, corn, rice, and sorghum continue to be widely grown and consumed domestically.

Livestock

The first cattle were brought to Nicaragua by the Spanish in the 1500s, and livestock raising was a mainstay of the early colony. Drier areas on the western slopes of the central highlands are ideal for cattle raising, and by the mid-1700s, a wealthy elite, whose income was based on livestock raising, controlled León, Nicaragua's colonial capital. In the late 1900s, as was true in the late 1500s, cattle raising has been concentrated in the areas east of Lago de Managua. Most beef animals are improved zebu strains. Smaller herds of dairy cattle—mostly Jersey, Guernsey, or Holstein breeds—are found near population centers. From 1979 to 1989, the total number of cattle dropped by a third because of widespread smuggling to Honduras and Costa Rica and illegal slaughter of the animals for sale of meat on the black market.

Natural Resources and Conservation

Fishing and Forestry

Although fishing has long been a source of food for the domestic market in Nicaragua, the rich fishing grounds of the Caribbean began to be exploited for export of shrimp and lobster only in the 1980s. A 1987 loan by the IDB allowed the country to double the size of its fishing fleet to ninety boats. However, damage by Hurricane Joan in 1988 to the two processing plants and the United States trade embargo in 1985 kept production levels far below the potential catch. Restoration of trade with the United States in 1990 did produce a surge in exports, and the government hoped that fishing would provide a significant share of export earnings in the 1990s.

Nicaragua has extensive forests, and despite the large-scale clearing for agricultural use, about one-third of the land, or approximately 4 million hectares, was still forested in 1993. Most of the forests consist of the tropical rain forests of the Caribbean lowlands, where surface transportation is practically nonexistent. Hardwoods abound in this region, but the stands are mixed with other wood, making exploitation difficult. However, some logging of mahogany, cedar, rosewood, and logwood for dyes takes place. In addition, the large stands of pine in the northeast support logging and a small plywood industry.

Mining

Mining is not an important sector of the Nicaraguan economy, although the small amounts of gold and silver that are extracted provide much-needed export income. The country's two principal gold and silver mines are the Bonanza and the Siuna mines, located in northeast Nicaragua about 100 kilometers west of Puerto Cabezas. A small gold mine, the El Limón mine, operates north of León. All mines were nationalized by the government in 1979, and state control, combined with the fact that the two largest mines are in areas where the Contras operated, caused production of gold and silver to drop in the 1980s. The 1988 production figures of 875 kilograms of gold and 500 kilograms of silver were less than half the 1983 production figures. Small amounts of copper, lead, and tungsten have been mined in the past, and the country has unexploited reserves of antimony, tungsten, molybdenum, and phosphate.

Conservation and the Environment

Destruction of the Nicaraguan environment stopped briefly during the 1980s. The Ortega administration generally did not emulate the governments of El Salvador and Guatemala, where a scorched-earth policy was used to fight insurgency. In addition, the Contras were usually based across the Honduran and Costa Rican borders and did not hold significant territory in Nicaragua. The Sandinistas moved 200,000 people out of the combat zones, creating huge land tracts where hunting, fishing, and farming seldom took place. Abandoned agricultural lands returned to their natural states, animal life prospered, and some forests remained uncut. Hunting was minimal because carrying a gun invited disaster. For a short time at least, the Contra war had the accidental effect of stopping the aggressive exploitation of Nicaragua's natural resources.

The Sandinista government established the Nicaraguan Institute for Natural Resources and Environment (Instituto de Recursos Naturales—Irena) in the 1980s to direct environmental conservation on a national scale. Irena created Bosawas, a 1.4-million hectare nature reserve and Central America's largest protected natural area. The institute also attempted management of watersheds, conservation of rainforests, and the establishment of windbreaks. In addition, Irena created a peace park on the border with Costa Rica. This combination of accidental and intentional environmental conservation in the early 1980s temporarily delayed the destruction of land associated with expanding export agriculture.

These conservation measures were not permanent, however. Like many social programs in health and education, environmental programs established in the early years of the Sandinista government soon fell victim to the Contra war. As public-sector spending after 1985 increasingly shifted away from social programs to defense, early environmental efforts were mostly ignored. Hundreds of state farms created by agrarian reform began to imitate their larger predecessors, expand-

Fishing boats and small launches at Bluefields on the Caribbean coast
Courtesy Nicaraguan Tourism Institute

ing agricultural development into previously undeveloped, rain forest areas. As poverty increased because of the weakening economy, rural dwellers turned more and more to forests for fuel wood and supplemental food, thus depleting previously abundant stocks. Although in the 1990s Nicaragua's tropical forests were less than 1 percent the size of the Amazon rain forest in Brazil, Nicaraguan rain forests were disappearing at a rate ten times faster than were rain forests in the Amazon. If that rate continues, the Nicaraguan rain forest will have disappeared by 2010.

Much of the government's hope for economic recovery has remained pinned on exploiting Nicaragua's abundant forest resources, casting serious doubt on any success for the country's future environmental efforts. In 1991 Equipe de Nicaragua, a Nicaraguan branch of a large Taiwanese firm, was granted a logging concession on 375,000 hectares in the Caribbean lowlands. The firm agreed to invest more than US$100 million in a modern plywood manufacturing facility. As part of the deal, the Taiwanese firm offered to help the Nicaraguan government in its reforestation efforts in other parts of the country. In 1992 the government signed an agreement with Equipe de Nicaragua for a large wood-processing plant.

Mostly as the result of environmentalist opposition to a Taiwanese-inspired forestry project, Irena created a new national forest institute to regulate and control the use of the forests. The institute received initial financing and support from foreign governments and international organizations for the conservation of the biological reserve named Indio-Maíz. This reserve, encompassing 4,500 square kilometers, is located in southeast Nicaragua between the Río San Juan and Río Punta Gorda. Together with the previously existing Bosawas reserve, they make up the largest forest reserves in Central America.

Services

Most of Nicaragua's physical infrastructure was not developed until the 1950s. The Somoza dynasty built roads, railroads, and telecommunications in order to support the growing needs of exporters and of the related urban agro-industries in the Pacific lowlands. Although the Sandinista government improved the road system, much of the central highlands and Caribbean lowlands still remained inaccessible in the early 1990s.

Transportation

In 1993 Nicaragua had 26,000 kilometers of roads; 4,000 kilometers were paved, 2,200 kilometers were gravel, and the rest were earthen (see fig. 11). The Pan American Highway, heavily damaged during the civil war, runs north to south for 369 kilometers through western Nicaragua, linking Managua with Honduras and Costa Rica. A modest system of paved and gravel roads connects the populated areas of the Pacific lowlands and also smaller cities in the central highlands. In 1993, however, eastern Nicaragua remained almost without roads, and the primary road to the region from the west stopped at Rama short of the Caribbean coast. During the strife of the 1970s and 1980s, many of the country's bridges and roads deteriorated even further because of fighting and lack of routine maintenance.

Most of Nicaragua's government-owned railroads are only nominally operational. Rail travel is possible from Managua north to León or south to Granada. The existing system consists of 373 kilometers of 1.067-meter narrow gauge in the Pacific region and an isolated three kilometers of 1.435-meter standard-gauge line at Puerto Cabezas in the northeast. Several trains a day carry passengers south from Managua to Granada, or north from the capital to León. The León-to-Corinto section has been out of service since 1982, when floods damaged the tracks. The government has plans to construct a new standard-gauge line from Corinto through Managua to San Juan del Norte on the Caribbean, but lack of funding has delayed construction.

The country has 2,220 kilometers of inland waterways, including two large lakes, Lago de Managua and Lago de Nicaragua, and five significant ports, two on the Pacific Coast and three on the Caribbean coast. Corinto and Puerto Sandino are Nicaragua's principal ports on the Pacific Coast; the smaller Caribbean coast ports are Puerto Cabezas, Bluefields, and El Bluff. Rama is a river port where goods or travelers from western Nicaragua change to river boats to continue their journey to Bluefields. The country's principal port, Corinto, is a deep-water port with alongside berthing facilities and is suitable for general import and export cargo. Puerto Sandino, the second largest Pacific coast port, handles petroleum products through an offshore buoy and pipeline; it is not suitable for deep-water berthing. Although mined by the United States in the 1980s, neither harbor suffered permanent damage. The Caribbean

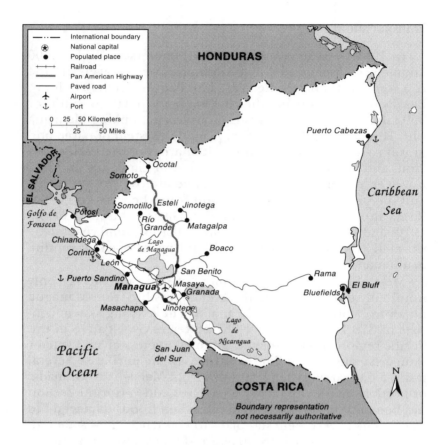

Figure 11. Transportation System, 1993

coast ports are hampered by a lack of rail or road connections with western or central Nicaragua, where most economic activity for the country takes place. Bluefields and Puerto Cabezas are used primarily for fish and lumber exports; El Bluff is a military port.

Augusto C. Sandino International Airport, twelve kilometers outside of Managua, is the country's principal airport. Although ten other cities have paved airfields, none have scheduled airline service.

Telecommunications

Nicaragua's telecommunications system, like the rest of its infrastructure, is outdated and suffers from lack of maintenance. The backbone of the telecommunications system is the Central American Microwave System (CAMS), a 960-channel radio-relay system that extends from Mexico to Panama. Low-capacity radio-relay and wire lines branch off the CAMS to provide service to smaller towns. In 1993 there were approximately 60,000 telephones, only 1.5 per 100 inhabitants. Although the number of telephones increased by about 10 percent per year during the 1970s, that increased number did not begin to meet demand. Few telephones have been installed since 1979.

When the CAMS was installed in the 1970s, planners envisioned that all international telecommunications would travel along the CAMS to satellite ground stations in Guatemala and Panama. However, planners of the system failed to take political realities into account. Whenever disputes arose among the countries of Central America, a common tactic was for one government to shut down the CAMS "for maintenance," effectively isolating the other countries on the isthmus from the outside world. Each country in Central America then built its own satellite ground station in the 1980s to assure continuous communications. In 1993 Nicaragua had two satellite ground stations, one operating with the International Telecommunications Satellite Corporation's (Intelsat) Atlantic Ocean satellite and the other a part of the former Soviet Union's Intersputnik system.

Radio broadcast services reach all parts of the country and include forty-five mostly privately owned amplitude modulation (AM) medium-wave stations and three AM shortwave stations for broadcasts to remote areas in the Caribbean lowlands. Managua also has eleven frequency modulation (FM) radio stations. Eight towns have television stations. In 1993 there were approximately 880,000 radio receivers and 210,000 television sets.

Electric Power and Energy

Nicaraguan electric power capacity expanded rapidly from 1950 to 1970, increasing about sixfold during that period. The system did not receive much attention throughout the Sandinista era, however, and power lines and transformers were frequently a focus of Contra attacks. The major centers of population and industry in the Pacific lowlands are served by an integrated power system. As late as 1993, the Caribbean region remained without an interconnected power grid. In the last nationwide survey in 1975, only 41 percent of the total

Oil refinery near Managua
Courtesy Nicaraguan Tourism Institute

number of dwellings and just 7 percent in rural areas had electricity.

In the early 1990s, Nicaragua obtained half of its 423-megawatt electric generating capacity from thermal generating plants. One geothermal electric plant operates on the slopes of the Momotobo volcano. A Soviet-financed hydroelectric plant was completed at Asturias in 1989, and in 1993 a large 400-megawatt hydroelectric plant was under construction at Copalar on the Río Grande.

Roughly half of Nicaragua's energy needs are satisfied by imported petroleum. The country's only refinery, located in Managua, is operated by Esso (Standard Oil) and has a capacity of 16,000 barrels per day. From 1979 to 1982, most of Nicaragua's oil came from Mexico and Venezuela through terms of the San José Accord (see Glossary), under which Mexico and Venezuela agreed to supply Nicaragua with oil. Both countries stopped supplies, however, when Nicaragua became delinquent on payments. The Sandinista government then turned to Cuba, Eastern Europe, and the Soviet Union for oil. The turmoil in Eastern Europe and the Soviet Union in 1989 resulted in deliveries dropping far short of demand. Electric power generation plummeted to 20 percent of capacity, and blackouts of up to ten hours a day were common. The new government of President Chamorro negotiated Nicaragua's outstanding debts with Mexico and Venezuela, and in 1991 these countries began delivering oil again.

Prospects

After almost four years in office, President Chamorro has made little headway in overcoming the substantial obstacles facing her. She has yet to win the support, or investments, of a reluctant private sector. Significant political realignments during her term have allowed her to move closer to reconciliation with representatives of the Sandinista labor forces. However, in late 1993, Nicaragua continued to face large trade and fiscal deficits, and it had yet to capture the confidence of either domestic or international investors. The government continues to pin its hopes for economic recovery on the potential of its forests and on agricultural exports.

*   *   *

In 1993 analysis of all things Nicaraguan, including the economy, continued to be colored by political orientation. Specialized regional newsletters, particularly *Latin American Newsletter* [London], *Central America Report*, *This Week in Central America*, *Latin American Monitor*, and *Business Latin America*, provide useful data. Brizio N. Biondi-Morr's *Hungry Dreams* is particularly useful, as is Anthony Lake's edited volume, *After the Wars*, for its analysis of the effects of the regional conflicts. Sheldon Annis's data on the new nature of poverty in Central America in *Poverty, Natural Resources, and Public Policy in Central America* are also helpful. (For further information and complete citations, see Bibliography.)

Chapter 4. Government and Politics

President Daniel Ortega congratulating Violeta Chamorro on her electoral victory, February 25, 1990

ON FEBRUARY 25, 1990, Nicaragua's voters elected Violeta Barrios de Chamorro as president, ending almost eleven years of government by the Sandinista National Liberation Front (Frente Sandinista de Liberación Nacional—FSLN). The choice was a dramatic one because voters hoped that the new government of the newly formed National Opposition Union (Unión Nacional Opositora—UNO) would bring an end to more than a decade of civil conflict and the harsh sectarianism of the Sandinista (see Glossary) years and improve the rapidly deteriorating economy. In her predawn acceptance speech the morning after her election, President-elect Chamorro tried to establish a climate of reconciliation, stating that there were neither victors nor vanquished in the election. Soon after, recognizing the FSLN "as the second political force of the nation," she stated her commitment to respect the will of the 40 percent of the people who had voted for the FSLN. The losing candidate, President Daniel José Ortega Saavedra, about two hours later foreswore the FSLN's self-image as a "vanguard party" and delineated the FSLN's future role as a strong, but loyal, opposition party. Rhetorically, at least, the stage seemed set for the cooperation between the two camps needed to bring about economic recovery.

Almost four years later, however, efforts to move the country toward peace and prosperity seemed stalled. Although the Chamorro government continued to stress that it intended to achieve reconciliation, President Chamorro has had the full cooperation of neither the Sandinistas nor her own coalition. Instead, in early 1993 the government faced the dilemma of dealing with a Sandinista opposition that viewed reconciliation as a means of protecting its rights to confiscated property and a powerful element of the UNO coalition that viewed those property rights as ill-gotten gains and urged strong action against the Sandinistas to recover that property.

Whether the new government is consolidating democracy or reverting to the traditional authoritarian and elitist style of Nicaraguan politics is a central issue. President Chamorro's cooperation with the Sandinistas, particularly her decision to retain Humberto Ortega Saavedra as head of the army, has led her supporters to accuse her of capitulating and establishing a "co-government" with the defeated Sandinistas, rather than reforming the political system in cooperation with her electoral partners. Her government also has been accused by members of the UNO coalition of excessively concentrating power in the hands of a small group of members of her extended family, promoting the same brand of government practiced under the Somoza family dynasty: centralizing power in a small group instead of expanding it in a democratic fashion. Finally, the UNO has been criticized for failing to promote the concept of democracy at a grassroots level. Nevertheless, the distribution of power for the first time to the municipal level through the 1990 elections has created a new class of political officials who are struggling to assert power at a grassroots level. The Sandinistas also have continued the grassroots organizing efforts that originally brought them to power. Both phenomena hold promise, as well as dangers, for the future of democracy in Nicaragua.

The Chamorro Government Takes Power

The Chamorro victory in the 1990 elections surprised most of the participants and many observers, both domestic and international. Many Nicaraguans did not view Chamorro as a politician and found her unprepared for a leadership role. The election date had been advanced nine months by the Sandinistas from the constitutionally set month of November 1990. This decision was taken in response to the meeting of representatives of the Nicaraguan government with the Nicaraguan Resistance (commonly referred to as Contras—short for *contrarevolucionarios*—see Glossary) at Sapoá. The talks represented a Sandinista effort to secure a definitive end to United States assistance to the Contras and an end to the civil conflict that was debilitating the economy and eroding the Sandinistas' base of support. The talks seemed designed to project the Sandinistas' image as peacemakers, and the Sandinista leadership was confident of winning the upcoming election.

From the moment on election night that the UNO victory was evident, there was widespread fear that the Sandinistas would block the Chamorro government from taking power. In hopes of securing a stable transition, Chamorro took a conciliatory approach toward the defeated Sandinistas. The three most influential international groups that came to observe the elections became a crucial element in ensuring a peaceful transition. Nevertheless, the negotiated transition created problems

*President Violeta Barrios de
Chamorro
Courtesy Embassy of
Nicaragua, Washington*

that would haunt the Chamorro government through at least
the early years of its existence.

Negotiations on the transition began on February 27, 1990,
in Managua. A meeting between the FSLN and UNO leaders
took place in the presence of former United States president
Jimmy Carter, Organization of American States (OAS) Secretary General João Baena Soares, and the head of the United
Nations (UN) electoral mission, former United States attorney
general Elliott Richardson. The Nicaraguan parties agreed to
continue negotiations on important transition issues and
named two chief negotiators: Antonio Lacayo Oyanguren, Chamorro's son-in-law and campaign manager, for the UNO; and
Humberto Ortega Saavedra, minister of defense and President
Ortega's brother, for the FSLN.

Negotiations between UNO and the Sandinistas led to a
series of arrangements on amnesty, property, and media laws,
as well as a Protocol on Procedures for the Transfer of Presidential Powers, signed by representatives of the UNO and the
FSLN on March 27, one month after the elections. The agreement gave the Sandinistas guarantees that the changes they
had instituted in their eleven years in power would not be over-
turned. The protocol pledged to carry out efforts toward reconciliation "on the basis of a national understanding that will

take into account the achievements and transformations implemented thus far for the people's benefit, and all must be based on full respect for rights, Nicaragua's Constitution, and the laws of the Republic."

Specific guarantees were given on property rights: the protocol provided "tranquility and legal security to the Nicaraguan families who have benefited from grants of urban and rural properties by the state before 25 February 1990, harmonizing such grants with the legitimate legal rights of Nicaraguans whose property was affected, for which purpose actions must be taken according to law. Methods to provide adequate compensation to those who may be affected will be established." The protocol also provided guarantees of job stability to government officials and employees "on the basis of their efficiency, administrative honesty, and years of service. . . ."

On paper at least, the Chamorro government secured guarantees that the military would submit to civilian rule, that it would be amenable to restructuring and downsizing, and that it would be nonpartisan because members on active duty would not be allowed to hold leadership posts in political parties. The Sandinistas, however, obtained guarantees of their continued control of the military because the protocol provided for respect "for the integrity and professionalism of the Sandinista People's Army (Ejército Popular Sandinista—EPS) and of the forces of public order as well as for their ranks [hierarchy and], promotion roster, and . . . [command structure] in accordance with the Constitution and the laws of the Republic . . . ." These guarantees were confirmed on inauguration day, April 25, 1990, by President Chamorro's decision to retain the Sandinista minister of defense, General Humberto Ortega Saavedra, as army chief.

These transition agreements formed the basis for the relationship between the outgoing Sandinista and the incoming Chamorro governments. They facilitated a peaceful transfer of power. Along with the follow-up "transition" laws that the lame-duck Sandinista-dominated National Assembly passed in the interregnum before Chamorro's inauguration, the transition agreements became part of the legal structure under which the Chamorro government would operate. In the first months of the Chamorro regime, the transition agreements provided the basis for Sandinista challenges on the scope and interpretation of laws. They also created a rift between the Chamorro government and most of the leaders of the coalition that had supported it, who charged that the Chamorro team had made unnecessary and detrimental concessions to the FSLN. The Chamorro government, however, argued that its options were limited. It had inherited a Sandinista-constructed constitutional and legal system and owed its existence to the Sandinista revolutionary process; its existence was not the result of a military victory that would have enabled construction of a new political system that may have been more to its constituents' liking.

Constitutional Background

The Nicaraguan constitution promulgated on January 1, 1987, provided the final step in the institutionalization of the Sandinista regime and the framework under which the Chamorro government would take office. It was the ninth constitution in Nicaraguan history. The Sandinistas' revolutionary mythology and aspirations were glorified in the preamble, and the Nicaraguan army was constitutionally named the Sandinista People's Army. Yet, even though drafted and approved by a Sandinista-dominated assembly, the constitution was not a revolutionary document. It established a democratic system of government with a mixed economy based on a separation of powers that could guarantee civil liberties (see fig. 12). There was some discontent with parts of the new system. Early objections were raised that the executive branch was too strong, that property rights were not adequately protected, and that some of the language was vague and subject to widely differing interpretations. These objections continued to be an issue under the Chamorro government.

The Executive

The constitution provides for a strong executive branch, although the legislative and judicial branches retain significant powers of their own. Under the constitution, the president has broader powers than does the president of the United States. The president is commander in chief of the military, has the power to appoint all ministers and vice ministers of his or her cabinet, and proposes a national budget. The executive shares legislative powers that allow him or her to enact executive decrees with the force of law in fiscal and administrative matters, as well as to promulgate regulations to implement the laws. The president assumes legislative powers when the

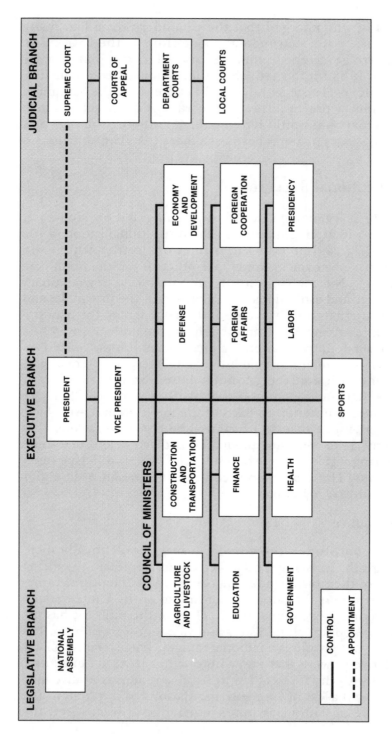

Figure 12. Organization of the Government, 1993

National Assembly is in recess. He or she has extraordinary powers during national emergencies, including the powers to suspend basic civil liberties and to prepare and approve the national budget.

The president's term was set at six years by a decree promulgated in January 1984, during the period when the country had no constitution. Elections held under that decree resulted in Daniel José Ortega Saavedra's beginning a term as president on January 10, 1985. The 1987 constitution reaffirmed a six-year term for the president. Esquipulas II, the international peace accord that ended the Contra insurgency, however, set February 25, 1990, as the date for the next election. Violeta Chamorro assumed the post of president on April 25, 1990, more than eight months before the constitutionally mandated date of January 10, 1991. It was understood that Chamorro would serve for the additional eight-month period created by the advanced elections, as well as for the full six-year term from January 10, 1991 to January 10, 1997. The next elections are scheduled for late 1996, although pressure has been mounting for these elections to be advanced also.

The Legislature

The 1987 constitution replaced the bicameral Congress, which had existed under previous constitutions, with a unicameral National Assembly. The makeup of the National Assembly, first established under the 1984 decree and confirmed by the 1987 constitution, consists of ninety members directly elected by a system of proportional representation plus any unelected presidential or vice presidential candidates who receive a certain percentage of the vote. In 1985 the National Assembly had ninety-six members and in 1990, ninety-two (see table 9, Appendix A). Terms are for six years, to run concurrently with the president's term.

The National Assembly has significant powers, and its cooperation is essential for the smooth functioning of the government. Under the constitution, representatives to the National Assembly propose legislation, which is made law by a simple majority of the representatives present if the National Assembly has a quorum (a quorum is half the total number of representatives, plus one) The National Assembly can override a presidential veto by a simple majority vote if a quorum is present. The constitution also gives the National Assembly the power "to consider, discuss and approve" the budget presented by the

149

president. The National Assembly chooses the seven members of the Supreme Court from lists provided by the president and has the authority to "officially interpret the laws," a prerogative that gives the National Assembly judicial powers.

The Chamorro administration has faced a legislature that, despite its division between the Sandinista members and the members of the UNO coalition, has proved a formidable power in its own right—and one with which the executive branch is often in conflict. In the 1990 elections, of the ninety-two seats in the National Assembly, the UNO won fifty-one and the FSLN gained thirty-nine. The FSLN won thirty-eight seats in assembly races, and President Ortega was given a seat under the provision granting a seat to each losing presidential candidate who earns a certain percentage of the vote. Two other parties of the ten on the ballot gained single seats. One was won by the Christian Social Party (Partido Social Cristiano—PSC) in a legislative race; another was awarded to the losing presidential candidate of the Revolutionary Unity Movement (Movimiento de Unidad Revolucionaria—MUR), a breakaway faction of the FSLN. The only significant brake on the UNO's power was that its majority of 55 percent fell short of the 60 percent needed to amend the Sandinista-approved constitution, a goal of some members of the UNO coalition. The slim UNO majority also presented practical problems for the UNO president because it was possible for relatively few defections from the UNO coalition to undermine the UNO government's programs and initiatives.

The Judiciary

Under the 1987 constitution, the Supreme Court is an independent branch of government, whose members are selected for six-year terms by the National Assembly from lists submitted by the president. From among those members, the president selects the head of the Supreme Court. The constitution also provides that the Supreme Court justices appoint judges to the lower courts. Supreme Court justices can only be removed constitutionally "for reasons determined by law."

In National Assembly-approved 1990 reforms to the Organic Law of Tribunals, the Chamorro government enlarged the Supreme Court's membership from the constitutionally mandated seven justices to nine, as a way of breaking what was perceived as Sandinista domination of the court. Those seven members had been appointed to their six-year terms in December 1987, and their terms were to expire in

*Former National Palace,
renamed the Palace of the
Heroes of the Revolution
Courtesy Edmundo Flores*

1993. In 1990 President Chamorro also dismissed the court's Sandinista-appointed head and replaced him with one of her own choosing. The evaluation of this act depended on one's political point of view. According to Nicaraguan analysts, the nine-member court decided that it would take decisions only on the basis of consensus, a procedure some saw as guaranteeing Sandinista influence on the court, others saw as neutralizing Sandinista influence, and still others saw as effectively paralyzing the operations of the court.

Local Government

Municipal governments have introduced a new element to Nicaraguan politics that promises to substantially decentralize political power and influence. Established by the Law on Municipalities adopted by the Sandinista National Assembly in August 1988, the first municipal governments were selected in 1990. The municipal government structure with basic governing authority is the Municipal Council (Consejo Municipal). Under the provisions of the law, citizens vote directly for council members; the number of these depends on the size of the cities. Once elected, council members select their own leader, the mayor, who serves with their approval.

Administratively, Nicaragua is divided into nine regions, which are subdivided into seventeen departments (fifteen full

151

departments and two autonomous regions in the Caribbean lowlands that are treated as departments). In 1992 the country had 143 municipal units of varying sizes. Of the municipal units, fifteen are cities with populations estimated at more than 50,000; Managua, the capital city, is the largest, with an estimated 1.5 million inhabitants. Of the remaining municipal units, thirty are cities with populations estimated between 20,000 and 50,000, twenty-three are towns of 10,000 to 20,000 inhabitants, and seventy-two have fewer than 10,000 inhabitants. The number of council members is based on the number of inhabitants; in 1992 Managua had the most, with twenty council members. Cities that are department capitals or have 20,000 or more in population have ten council members; towns with fewer than 20,000 inhabitants have five.

The responsibilities and powers of the municipal governments and their method of conduct are based on constitutional provisions and on the 1988 Law on Municipalities. Article 176 of the constitution provides that the municipality is the "basic unit" of the administrative political divisions of the country. Article 177 provides that municipal authorities "enjoy autonomy without detriment to the faculties of the central government." The Law on Municipalities enumerates the responsibilities of the municipal government, specifies its taxing powers, and establishes rules for its functioning. Among the responsibilities are control of urban development; use of the land, sanitation, rainwater drainage, and environmental protection; construction and maintenance of roads, parks, sidewalks, plazas, bridges, recreational areas, and cemeteries; verification of weights and measures; and establishment of museums, libraries, and other cultural activities. As is true in the United States, the primary taxing power of municipal governments is assessment of property, including houses and vehicles.

Public Administration

Nicaragua's public employees are not perceived as civil servants; new appointments are usually made on the basis of political patronage rather than through a selection system based on merit. Nevertheless, both the Sandinista government and the Chamorro government have respected the positions of those whom they found occupying public administration posts when each successive government took power. The primary motive of the Sandinista government, which took power after a revolution, may have been expediency, as it needed at least a core of persons who had occupied posts under the previous Somoza administration to instruct it in the workings of the government. In the case of the Chamorro government, the position of public employees was guaranteed by the transition pacts and was protected by law.

Public employee ranks include not only office workers but also medical and other professional personnel hired by the Sandinista government to work in public programs and state-owned businesses. Soon after the Chamorro government took power, the number of public employees was estimated in newspaper accounts at 150,000, most of whom were Sandinistas. Efforts to restructure the laws to eliminate some public employees led to a strike in May 1990 (see Interest Groups, this ch.). When the Chamorro government sought in early 1991 to cut the number of public employees, it had to offer incentives for workers who volunteered to leave, as well as additional incentives for businesses to hire former government workers or for the workers themselves to set up private enterprises. By the time the severance program expired in April 1992, some 23,000 workers had resigned to take advantage of the plan, and some 20,000 soldiers and police officers had been dismissed.

Political Dynamics

Conflict Between the Executive and Legislative Branches

Almost from the day it took power, the Chamorro government was a stepchild. All groups recognized the necessity of a relationship with the Chamorro government, but even though Violeta Barrios de Chamorro personified the Nicaraguan people's desire for peace, neither the UNO nor the FSLN recognized the government as the legitimate representative of its political, social, and economic aspirations for Nicaragua. The strong constitutional powers of the executive branch theoretically should have given the president adequate control over the political and economic systems, but the transition agreements left the Sandinistas with control over the military and the police, thus curtailing the executive branch's power of coercion. The Sandinistas also continued to control the strongest labor unions, which became a powerful political bloc on the issue of economic reforms. Although increasingly divided, the Sandinistas provided, as Daniel Ortega had warned in his concession speech, a critical opposition that limited the government's range of action.

The president was further weakened by her estrangement from the political and economic coalition that had supported her during the election. Distrust initially was sparked by the transition agreements, which much of the UNO viewed as too accommodating to a political movement that had lost an election and would lose further support when no longer in power. The political parties composing the UNO coalition were quick to establish their own bases of support within the legislature and the municipalities. Although few of the parties reached for grassroots support, whatever was developed was done so by legislators and municipal officials to enhance their personal power bases or for their own parties, not for the central government or the UNO coalition. From the beginning of the Chamorro administration, UNO leaders were critical of the tight family networks that controlled the executive branch. They began to accuse the president of nepotism and to criticize the government for using its prerogatives for private gain.

Other influential voices on all sides also opposed the Chamorro government. Most of the media and the university leadership were joined with opposition forces of either the UNO coalition or the Sandinistas. The hierarchy of the Roman Catholic Church, which had forcefully contested the Sandinista government, also began strongly criticizing the Chamorro administration. Groups of businesspeople and farmers, the unemployed (including former Contras and dismissed Sandinista soldiers), and the unions all entered, sometimes violently, the contest over the future shape of the economy, property ownership, and the redistribution of wealth and land.

Although in stable, democratic countries such political conflict would appear to be no more than the normal cacophony of competing voices, in Nicaragua the stakes were high. At issue was the government's ability to stimulate a war-torn, depressed economy in which nearly half of the working-age population was unemployed or underemployed by early 1992. Also at issue was the government's capacity to institutionalize democratic attitudes and procedures. Different political parties, interest groups, and other influential voices all had their own visions of what form the economy and a democratic government should take and what each group's share and role in both should be. Rather than leading the country, the Chamorro government was compelled to act as a broker among competing interests in

Office of the Ministry of Interior in Managua
Casa del Gobierno in Managua
Courtesy James Rudolph

resolving the two central issues of her early administration: the resolution of property issues and the establishment of peace through the demobilization and resettlement of the Contras and the Sandinista military.

Dispute over Property Rights

The dominant political issue in Nicaragua during the early years of the Chamorro government became the Piñata—the massive transfer and titling of confiscated and expropriated property, including homes, agricultural plots, and businesses, which the Sandinista government conducted during the interim lame-duck period between the February 1990 election and Chamorro's inauguration in April 1990. Named after the candy-stuffed papier-mâché figures that are hung for children to strike with sticks and break open, the Piñata created divisions and resentments throughout the political order. Within the Sandinista movement, rancor arose as the Piñata created new classes of "haves" and "have-nots." Within the UNO, it progressively became one of the more divisive issues as the executive branch of the Chamorro administration sought to protect the titles of the transfer and UNO groups within the National Assembly sought to invalidate them.

Law 85 and Law 86, the two Piñata laws passed by the Sandinista-dominated National Assembly during the transition period, not only guaranteed the rights of squatters and tens of thousands of small farmers given land under the Sandinista agrarian reform, but also allowed Sandinistas to appropriate much other state-owned property. Estimates of the amount of property transferred ranged between US$300 million and US$2 billion. The property reportedly included thousands of "good to luxury homes," including beach houses, that were titled to Sandinistas at a small fraction of their value. Also given away were large state-owned properties such as cattle ranches, warehouses, and office buildings; state-owned businesses; and smaller items such as cars, taxis, trucks, machinery, office furniture, and equipment, including radio and television transmission towers. In what one Nicaraguan referred to as a private Piñata, the Central Bank of Nicaragua (Banco Central de Nicaragua) transferred to Daniel Ortega and his close associates some US$24 million during the last three weeks of the Sandinista government. The result was the instant creation of a propertied and entrepreneurial class of Sandinistas and resentment from the poorer and mid-level Sandinistas who got little or nothing.

The issue of dealing with the Piñata became a political battlefront in 1991, when conservative members of the National Assembly sponsored a proposal to revoke the Piñata laws. In June 1991, the National Assembly voted to pass the matter to the Economic Commission for study, a move that sparked debate and protest from the executive branch because deciding the issue in a legislative commission would preempt negotiation among farmers, trade unions, and businesses over the resolution of property issues. The move also marked the emergence of National Assembly president Alfredo César Aguirre, one of the primary architects of the reconciliation policy toward the Sandinistas, as the leader of the legislative challenge to the executive branch's position.

As a result of reconciliation negotiations, President Chamorro decreed two laws that would allow residents to keep homes awarded them in the Piñata if they owned no others. They also would have to pay market value for the houses if they chose to sell them or convert them to rental property. In response to the president's action, the next day the National Assembly passed an alternative plan, Law 133, by a vote of fifty-two to thirty-nine. Law 133 confirmed transfer of small homes and agrarian properties but required those who had received homes worth more than US$11,600 and farms larger than thirty-four hectares to pay market value for them within three months. The action by the National Assembly nullified the president's decrees of the previous day. The assembly vote in favor of Law 133 was composed of all fifty-one UNO deputies and one independent; the thirty-nine votes against it were from the entire Sandinista delegation in the first parliamentary session they had attended since the property law was introduced in June.

On September 11, 1991, President Chamorro vetoed as unconstitutional twenty-one of thirty-two clauses in the new property law. On December 10, a group of nine deputies from the UNO and the Sandinista delegation, calling itself the "Center Group," (Grupo de Centro—GC) demanded a vote on the veto. When the vote was held four days later, several of the UNO deputies of that group and the delegation of thirty-nine Sandinistas voted to support the presidential veto, touching off accusations that the executive branch had bought the UNO votes.

157

The conflict was defined by principal players as an important step in the process of establishing a state of law. National Assembly president Alfredo César Aguirre viewed invalidating the property title transfer as essential for preserving respect for written agreements because he felt the Sandinistas had abused the transition period by passing laws that contravened the transition agreements. Minister of the Presidency Antonio Lacayo countered that the government was bound to respect the laws transferring title passed by the Sandinista assembly because that assembly had the legal authority to pass those laws, despite its lame-duck status. To revoke those titles, he argued, would be to approve ex-post-facto laws and undermine respect for proper law passage.

More important, however, was how the land-transfer issue catalyzed change in both the Sandinista movement and the UNO coalition. The Piñata was pointed to as one of the major causes of the vocal demands for democratization within the Sandinista movement and one of the principal reasons for the disaffection of mid-level and lower-ranking Sandinistas who sought new political alternatives. The Piñata also appeared to be one of the major causes of the solidification of the UNO bloc in the National Assembly, which became a significant source of power and a weighty counterpoint to the Chamorro government.

The threat to the Sandinistas was multifold, both materially and politically. Reflecting the seriousness of the problem, when the legislation to repeal the land transfer was introduced, former president Daniel Ortega warned that war could return and voiced what was widely interpreted as a death threat against UNO National Assembly deputies. Protesting the repeal bill, Sandinista demonstrators occupied six city halls, including the city hall of Managua, and three radio stations. Besides depriving top Sandinistas of their homes and new livelihoods, the repeal attempt also underscored the gap between the Sandinista elite and the poor.

The government's inability to resolve property issues was also blamed for the stagnation and the subsequent deterioration of the nation's economy. The lack of substantial domestic and foreign investment was viewed as a vote of no confidence in the government's handling of private property issues and its commitment to impartial treatment of private investment. Despite mechanisms subsequently developed by the government to consider property claims on a case-by-case basis, the Piñata remained a volatile issue.

Political Parties

The National Opposition Union (UNO) Coalition

A loose coalition of political parties, UNO traces its origins back to the Nicaraguan Democratic Coordinating Group (Coordinadora Democrática Nicaragüense—CDN), which was formed in 1982 by opposition groups that had protested actions of the Sandinista government as early as November 1980. In 1980 these groups had temporarily withdrawn their members from the corporatist legislature set up by the Sandinista government, the Council of State, to protest the imposition of three emergency decrees that restricted civil liberties and to call for municipal elections that the Sandinistas had stated would be held soon after the revolution. The CDN coalition consisted of three political parties and two factions of a fourth; two labor unions, the Confederation of Nicaraguan Workers (Confederación de Trabajadores Nicaragüenses—CTN) and the Confederation for Trade Union Unity (Confederación de Unificación Sindical—CUS); and the Superior Council of Private Enterprise (Consejo Superior de la Empresa Privada—Cosep), an umbrella organization uniting producer and commercial business groups along the lines of the United States Chamber of Commerce. These groups all formed the earliest opposition to the Sandinista government.

In the mid-1980s, as a result of Nicaragua's 1984 presidential and legislative elections, the opposition broadened with the incorporation of three political parties, which up to that point had cooperated closely with the government: the Independent Liberal Party (Partido Liberal Independiente—PLI), the Popular Social Christian Party (Partido Popular Social Cristiano—PPSC), and the Democratic Conservative Party (Partido Conservador Demócrata—PCD). In the late 1980s, while the CDN parties remained outside the legislative arena, the three other parties, which had run candidates in the elections, became known as the "parliamentary opposition." From inside and outside the legislature, opposition groups became increasingly vocal against the Sandinista government.

Their opposition to the Sandinistas did not forge these groups into a firm coalition, however. Instead, the parties were known for personal rivalries and factionalism. There were animosities and distrust among the leaders of each of the groups, stemming from the degree of cooperation and confrontation each had taken toward the Sandinista government. The groups also held conflicting and ambivalent attitudes toward the United States-supported Contra forces that had carried out a war against the Sandinista government since early 1982.

Nevertheless, during the later years of the Contra war, the "civic opposition," as these political parties, unions, and business organizations came to be called, became of great interest to the international community, which was interested in seeking a negotiated solution to the Contra war through the Central American peace process. The political parties gained the support of international groups such as the Christian Democratic International, the Conservative International, and the Liberal International organizations. Esquipulas II, the Central American peace agreement signed by the presidents of five countries in Central America (see Glossary) on August 7, 1987, gave a major role to the Roman Catholic Church and the opposition political parties in negotiating the terms for national reconciliation and democratization in Nicaragua. Although the arrangements specified in this agreement were never implemented as planned, the accord itself was a major factor in stimulating the Sandinistas to lift various constraints on the civic opposition, creating the opportunity for greater political activity. The accord also played a part in the Sandinista decision to advance the election from November to February 1990 and to allow an extensive system of United Nations (UN) and Organization of American States (OAS) monitors to observe the entire electoral process, beginning several months before the election.

By the time the various political parties coalesced into an electoral coalition in September 1989, the fourteen political parties that had evolved from the earlier opposition parties were committed enough to the goal of opposing the Sandinista government that they united around a single candidate. Violeta Barrios de Chamorro, who had largely stayed outside party politics during the 1980s, was chosen after two bitter rounds of voting eliminated the two other popular candidates: Virgilio Reyes Godoy (who became vice president) and Enrique Bolanos Geyer of Cosep. Both had been active in internal politics throughout the 1980s. At the time of the elections, of the UNO coalition's fourteen political parties, four were considered conservative, seven fell under a broad definition of centrist parties, and three had traditionally been on the far left of the political spectrum (see table 10, Appendix A).

Of all the parties, the largest of the centrist group were the Democratic Party of National Confidence (Partido Demócrata de Confianza Nacional—PDCN), which was one of several breakaway factions of the Nicaraguan Social Christian Party (Partido Social Cristiano Nicaragüense—PSCN), and the PLI of Virgilio Godoy. Among the conservative factions, viewed as the most important was the Conservative Popular Alliance (Alianza Popular Conservadora—APC) of Míriam Argüello Morales, a leading figure in conservative politics since the 1970s. All the other parties were seen as small groups. In the centrist camp, these were the Liberal Party (Partido Liberal—PL), the National Action Party (Partido de Acción Nacional—PAN), the Popular Social Christian Party (Partido Popular Social Cristiano—PPSC, another faction of the PSCN), and the Nicaraguan Democratic Movement (Movimiento Democrático Nicaragüense—MDN). In the conservative arena, the smaller groups were the Conservative National Action Party (Partido de Acción Nacional Conservadora—PANC), the Liberal Constitutionalist Party (Partido Liberal Constitucionalista—PLC), and the National Conservative Party (Partido Conservador Nacional—PCN).

Two years after the inauguration, however, the UNO was still viewed as having a narrow political base. Only three of the fourteen parties, among them the PLI, whose leader was Vice President Virgilio Godoy Reyes, had done local-level political organizing across the country. Although some trade union organizations supported the UNO coalition, the UNO parties did not have the type of widespread organizations of labor, peasant, and women's groups that had provided support for the FSLN.

Friction between the executive branch circle, named the Las Palmas group after the neighborhood in which President Chamorro lived, and the UNO legislators was first apparent in the contest for the presidency of the National Assembly. Held days before the president's inauguration, the struggle for leadership of the National Assembly was one of the first tests of power between the Political Council, composed of the leaders of the fourteen political parties, and Chamorro's advisers, whom many of the traditional political party leaders viewed as interlopers. One of Chamorro's closest advisers, Alfredo César Aguirre, was defeated for an UNO position by the Political

Council's candidate, Míriam Argüello Morales, a leader of the APC. During this and subsequent debates, Vice President Godoy sided with the Political Council. Frictions between the Las Palmas group and the UNO were further exacerbated by President Chamorro's cabinet selections. All were members of her inner circle; none was a leader of a traditional political party.

The dynamic changed slightly with a shift of characters when César was elected leader of the National Assembly for the 1992 legislative session. Within months of his election, however, he had taken a leadership role on the volatile issues of Sandinista property rights and presence in government, this time against the government. The UNO bloc in the assembly seemed to be reuniting on the same issues, but this time under a younger generation of leaders.

Despite the importance of the National Assembly in shaping national policy, much of the nation's future was increasingly shaped by the evolving politics of the municipalities. The 1990 elections established a new class of political leaders. The UNO parties were weak in organization at the grassroots level, and the creation of new political posts at the municipal level offered opportunities and incentives for the development of a broad base of popular support for the UNO. Because of the UNO parties' weaknesses at the national level, however, the leading UNO mayors viewed themselves as enjoying a far greater level of popular support and legitimacy than the national UNO authorities. The local UNO officials, who had power in about 100 of the country's municipal governments, have at times taken united stands challenging the Chamorro government. In general, the UNO municipal authorities, the most visible of whom is Managua's mayor, Arnoldo Alemán, are more conservative than the Las Palmas group and have taken positions similar to that of the Godoy group and later the César group, at the national level.

Small Non-UNO Parties

Several important political groups that opposed the Sandinistas during the 1980s but did not run with the UNO coalition in 1990 had almost disappeared from the national political scene by 1993. These parties were factions of the PCD, considered one of the larger opposition parties during the 1980s; leaders of these factions were Clemete Guido, Eduardo Molina Palacios, and Rafael Cordova Rivas. Other smaller non-UNO

Political slogans painted on walls in Managua
Courtesy Nina Serafino

parties were breakaway factions of parties in the UNO coalition: Mauricio Díaz Dávila's faction of the PPSC; Erick Ramírez Benevente's PCSN, a breakaway from the PSC; and Rodolfo Robelo's Independent Liberal Party of National Unity (Partido Liberal Independiente de Unidad Nacional—PLIUN), a splinter group from the PLI (see table 11, Appendix A). The only member of these parties to gain a seat in the National Assembly was Moisés Hassan Morales of the MUR, a breakaway faction of the FSLN; Hassan automatically gained a seat as a defeated presidential candidate.

Sandinista National Liberation Front

The FSLN has maintained the cohesion needed to continue as a potent force in Nicaraguan politics despite an internal crisis touched off by its electoral defeat. From the moment that Daniel Ortega publicly conceded defeat, he launched an initiative to preserve the gains that the Sandinista government claimed to have secured for the Nicaraguan people and the property that the movement had acquired. However, the performance of the FSLN leadership before and after the elections regarding the social welfare issue became a topic of dispute among the leaders of the groups and between the leadership and the local members. The dispute was so severe that it threatened to destroy the cohesive party apparatus and discipline that the movement had created over almost three decades of struggle and power.

In his concession speech, President Ortega in essence foreswore the FSLN's identity as a "vanguard party" and called on the FSLN to play a role as a strong but loyal opposition party. In subsequent speeches, Ortega made clear that the FSLN, with 40 percent of the vote, still considered itself the largest single political force in Nicaragua. Although this new definition provided the basis for the FSLN's continued role in government, the tension between its two roles—its role as the country's largest political party and as a force in opposition to the government—proved problematic for the FSLN in the early years of adjustment to the Chamorro regime.

Despite the FSLN's success in maintaining a position for the party and benefits for its members in the postelectoral period, the electoral loss intensified preexisting political tensions within the FSLN, opened new ideological divisions, and brought a host of practical problems that posed great difficulties for continuing party activity. The short-term result within the first two years after the FSLN's electoral defeat was the creation of new power bases and elites. In addition, there were contradictory indications about the future of the party: one was that it might begin reconstituting itself along more traditional political party lines, and the other was that it would modernize, but not at the expense of its revolutionary social principles.

The most pressing practical problems were continued financing of the party apparatus and continued employment for party members. By the end of the Sandinista government, the organizational structure of the party coincided with the administrative structure of the state, including the military and security forces. Thus, according to one analyst, the loss of the government meant the loss of party structures and, in effect, the dispersal of the membership when the new government's economic program separated thousands from their work. For the FSLN, this change meant that its political apparatus shrank from several thousand persons to a few hundred after the election; for many members, it meant that holding on to their old jobs or obtaining new ones became the central focus of life. The Piñata was in part a result of the need to secure new means of support: ownership of property and companies established a financial base from which FSLN members could earn personal livelihoods and produce profits for continued party activities.

The ideological and political debate that took place after the election was an outgrowth of ideas that had circulated but never had been formally raised before the election. These ideas acquired new urgency as the Sandinistas sought to understand the causes of their defeat. Positions were formulated in preparation for postelection party activities. The ruling body during the postelectoral years continued to be the National Directorate, which had been in place since 1979, minus two members. Missing were Humberto Ortega, who, under the terms of the transition agreement, had been obliged to give up his place in order to remain at the head of the army, and Carlos Núñez Téllez, who died in October 1990. The new seven-member National Directorate continued to meet regularly and drafted the guidelines for the document analyzing the electoral defeat that was to be discussed in the first postelection Sandinista Assembly in June 1990. That first meeting made clear the extent of the internal differences within the FSLN.

The three-day June 1990 Sandinista Assembly meeting held in El Crucero was attended by a large number of FSLN members. The membership consisted of all FSLN National Assembly members, department coordinators, mass organization leaders, and representatives of the National Workers' Front (Frente Nacional de Trabajadores—FNT). The open debate that characterized this meeting and the resulting statement that eventually was circulated were viewed as central in opening the party to candid public criticism. In addition, the Sandinista Assembly created an Ethics Commission to examine the activities of party members from the top leadership down and called for the FSLN's first national party congress. Party activities for the next year were geared toward preparation for the congress, held in July 1991.

Although calls for the democratization of the party did not produce changes in the top leadership, they had their effect at lower levels. In August and September 1990, for the first time, almost 600 executive committees and coordinators were elected, rather than appointed, at the municipal and departmental levels. These elections were seen as significant because they resulted in the election of people who would not have been selected under the previous rules. The elections were less than a fully democratic enterprise, however, because campaigning was not permitted, forestalling any uncontrolled discussion of the future of the party. The elections also led to debate about the membership of the party. The Sandinistas opted not to follow the model of standard parties by creating an open membership. They did establish, however, in addition to the categories of militants and aspirants, who numbered 18,000 and 17,300, respectively, in August 1990, a third category of membership—affiliates, numbering 60,400 that month. The party leadership also held about 200 local meetings in the summer of 1990 to discuss a draft statement on programs, principles, and a proposal for new bylaws that would be presented to the FSLN's National Congress. More than 3,000 elected delegates attended eighteen departmental meetings in mid-June 1991 to debate the issues and choose 501 representatives to the National Congress.

The democratization process did not reach to the very top of the FSLN leadership, however. Early expectations that the 501 National Congress delegates would elect individual members to the National Directorate were quashed when the National Directorate proposed that the National Congress vote on the candidates as a group. The departmental congresses ratified this proposal and another giving the nonelected members of the Sandinista Assembly voting rights in the National Congress. In July 1991, nine candidates for the National Director-ate ran unopposed as a slate. The slate consisted of the seven current members plus the former vice president and current head of the Sandinista bloc in the National Assembly, Sergio Ramírez Mercado, and the National Directorate secretary, René Núñez Téllez. Humberto Ortega was on the slate but declined a seat because of his army position. Daniel Ortega was elected secretary general of the party. Thus, some congress del-egates' hopes of removing individual members were dashed, and the slate was elected by a 95 percent vote.

Nevertheless, the National Congress did adopt significant liberalization measures. It elected ninety-eight members to a new 120-member Sandinista Assembly. The National Congress also decided that future national congresses, to be held every four years, would elect the members of the Sandinista Assem-bly, the Ethics Commission, and the National Directorate indi-vidually by a secret and direct vote. This change was hailed as progress, although not the democratization that a significant but minority elite desired.

The National Congress also brought to the fore the ideolog-ical debate between two FSLN factions. On the one side were the pragmatists who sought accommodation with the Chamorro forces and professed a new, more social democratic orientation. On the other side were the "principled" or radical forces, who sought a continuation of the old revolutionary model and saw progress as dependent on establishing a clear confrontational position against the Chamorro government. The National Congress also aired the FSLN leadership's self-criticism of the party, attributing the electoral loss to several of the party's own failings. Still, ideologically, the congress's result was indeterminate, preserving many of the party's revolution-ary aspirations and anti-imperialist, anticapitalist principles but also urging modernization and adaptation to the current glo-bal situation.

Differences within the FSLN led to new forces within the party. Three factions have emerged, united on ideals and ends but not necessarily on means, according to analyst Aldo Díaz Lacayo. One faction, headed by Humberto Ortega, stresses the need for an alliance with the Chamorro government's "pro-gressive bourgeoisie." The second faction, composed of those holding positions in state structures such as the National Assembly and headed by Sergio Ramírez, calls for uncondi-tional democratization. The third, headed by Daniel Ortega, is the party's union sector and is often viewed as the most traditionally Sandinista in style and ideology.

Interest Groups

The Ex-Contras and Recontras

The Nicaraguan Resistance was unable to establish itself as a political presence in Nicaragua after the 1990 elections, despite its part in bringing them about. The Chamorro government found little place in its government, outside of national-level organizations set up to deal with the Contras' resettlement, for the fighters and leaders of the principal Contra group that had fought in northern Nicaragua. Part of the reason for this exclusion was that prominent individuals within the new government, such as Alfredo César Aguirre, had served as part of a rival Contra group known as the Southern Front, which disintegrated in the mid-1980s after the United States Central Intelligence Agency (CIA) withdrew its aid. The expulsion of the Contras also has been attributed to social factors because the Chamorro government is largely made up of Nicaragua's old elite and the Contra leaders are from the middle and lower classes. In addition, the restriction of the Contras was a political move: incorporating ex-Contras into the government would alienate many Sandinistas and make more difficult the reconciliation envisioned by Chamorro's government. Whatever the underlying reasons, the rationale stated by supporters of the Chamorro government is that even though the Contras were important to the electoral outcome, the victory was not a military one but an electoral one, and those who waged the electoral battle are those who are entitled to govern. A year after the election, former Contras who felt abandoned by the new government and unable to influence it within the system began rearming.

Obstacles to the establishment of a Contra political presence in Managua began with arrangements for demobilizing and resettling the Contras set forth in transition agreements signed shortly before and after the Chamorro government took power. The first of the documents was the March 27, 1990, Toncontín Accord between the Nicaraguan Resistance and members of the UNO government-elect signed in Honduras. The Contras committed themselves to the concept of demobilizing and promised that all Contras remaining in Nicaragua would hand in their weapons by April 20, 1990. The definitive peace accord between the outgoing Sandinista government and the Nicaraguan Resistance was signed on April 18, 1990, and took effect at noon the following day. The agreement provided that all Nicaraguan Resistance forces would immediately begin to move into security enclaves under the protection of the UN Central American Observer Group, a UN peacekeeping force. The government was to withdraw all military, paramilitary, and security forces to a point at least twenty kilometers from the enclave borders by April 21.

These agreements seemed to be in trouble just hours after the Chamorro inauguration. Contra leaders, protesting President Chamorro's decision to retain General Humberto Ortega as chief of the army, stated that there would be no national reconciliation and that none of their troops would disarm as long as General Ortega remained in that post. Shortly thereafter, however, the Chamorro government and the resistance issued a joint Managua Declaration stating that the Contras would begin the process of turning in their weapons on May 8 and complete the process by June 10. In turn, the government announced on June 10 its plans to reduce the size of the army and to guarantee the Contras' safety.

The subsequent disarmament process was again halted in May when Sandinista unions went on strike and resistance leaders stated that the strike confirmed the Chamorro government's lack of control. Nevertheless, most of the rebels had surrendered their arms by the June 10 Toncontín deadline. Under separate arrangements, the remaining rebels agreed to hand in their weapons—the Yatama Contra forces by June 21 and the Southern Front rebels by July 25, 1990. Demobilized Contras received a change of civilian clothes, farm tools, a US$50 cash grant, rations of rice and beans, and a promise of land.

Within months, however, these agreements had broken down, and violence resumed as the ex-Contras were unable to settle on the land they had been promised in development areas, saw their economic prospects evaporate as the economy worsened, and felt their security threatened by the continued Sandinista presence in the military and in the police. The first incident occurred in July 1990, when some fifteen to twenty armed Contras, led by Commander Rubén (Oscar Manuel Sobalvarro García), briefly occupied the central bus terminal in Managua and exchanged fire with Sandinista labor union strikers.

A dozen members of the UN peacekeeping force negotiated the Contras' withdrawal. However, this incident was followed in 1990 by ex-Contra attempts to seize land held in Sandinista cooperatives and by their blockage, together with local peasants, of the Managua-Rama road, the country's major east-west highway, for eighteen days.

Incidents increased in 1991 as conflict between ex-Contras and Sandinista police and army officials continued. About the time the ex-Contras formally announced that they were taking up arms again (and were promptly dubbed the Recontras), the OAS cease-fire monitoring forces had documented the murders of some thirty-five former Contras. For some Contras, the February 16, 1991, murder of former Contra leader Enrique Bermúdez Varela in a Managua hotel parking lot underscored the state of insecurity and exacerbated their distrust of the Sandinista police. Bermúdez, who had taken up residence in Miami after the war, had been visiting Managua to conduct personal business and to urge the government to treat the ex-Contras better. The police allegedly handled investigations in a manner suggesting negligence, ineptitude, and a cover-up, although Sandinistas countered that Bermúdez may have been killed by disaffected Contras.

The Bermúdez murder came just as ex-Contras, as well as other peasants, were increasing pressure for access to land before the May planting season. Thousands of the some 18,000 to 20,000 Contras who had turned in their weapons had not received the land promised them under the demobilization agreement, and many others found they could not farm the land they had received because of a lack of promised tools and infrastructure. In early April, Commander Dimas (Tomás Laguna Rayo), one of several rearming commanders, claimed that the hills around Estelí concealed 200 newly rearmed Contras, who intended to take over territory to use as leverage to make demands on the government. Incidents between Recontras and Sandinista officials continued throughout the year with no major clashes. Estimates of Recontra strength increased from a few hundred to an estimated 1,000 personnel with assault rifles. By the end of the first year of demobilization, the OAS had verified fifty-two slayings, often of Recontras, about half attributed to Sandinista military or police.

The Recontras' first major action occurred in late July 1991, when eighty Recontras attacked a local police station in Quilalí and battled for six hours under the leadership of Commander

Indomable (José Angel Morán Flores). In August 1991, Minister of Interior Carlos Hurtado Cabrera met with Indomable and Dimas to discuss Recontra demands: the disarming of Sandinista farm cooperatives, the removal of army bases from areas of Recontra activity, removal of police and army officials known to violate human rights, investigation of the killings of ex-Contras, and indemnification of ex-Contra families.

For several months thereafter, although the Recontra activities centered on disruptive rather than violent activities and there were few major battles, the Nicaraguan countryside threatened to return to violence. However, by early 1992 the government seemed to be gaining control of the situation. The uncertainty created by the Recontras was exacerbated in late 1991 by the formation of Recompas, rearmed former Sandinista soldiers. The Recompas, many of them junior officers, acted to bring attention to their demands for land and to respond to Recontra activities, including the assassination of a Sandinista police chief and his secretary. Eventually, there were reports of both groups working together on behalf of one basic demand: land and the equipment to work it. The government countered by ordering the Sandinista People's Army not to engage in combat and retaliatory actions and by offering to meet some Recontra demands. The OAS observer group played an important role in mediating disputes and calming tempers. In early 1992, the government offered Recontra leaders money to retire, offered both Recontras and Recompas from US$100 to US$200 for each weapon turned in, and promised both groups houses and land. That offer led to a surprising 20,000 weapons being turned in under OAS supervision, although estimates were that some 30,000 to 80,000 weapons were still held by civilians.

Labor Organizations

The Sandinista unions played a major role in the politics of the Chamorro government's first years. The change of government sparked a competition in union organizing and activities that posed serious challenges to the new government. One challenge for the new Chamorro government was to create and maintain political bases by organizing workers; the other was to maintain political and economic stability when confronted by strikes led by Sandinista unions.

The first challenge resulted from a new freedom for unions to organize, created by a law the National Assembly had passed in the interregnum. This law changed the labor code to allow workplaces to have more than one union. The law was adopted because the lame-duck Sandinista majority feared that the government would replace the Sandinista unions with UNO unions while maintaining a closed shop. After the new law took effect, the unions that had supported the UNO moved to break the Sandinista monopoly on organizing in the public sector by organizing groups of the required twenty-five members to form a new bargaining unit. In some places, such as the San Antonio sugar mill, which with 5,000 workers was the largest union in the country, workers decided to retain the old union but voted out the board of directors who had been Sandinista supporters.

A greater challenge was posed by strikes initiated by the strongest unions—those affiliated with the FSLN. These unions were no longer bound by ties to a leadership in power to support austerity policies that had adversely affected the workers. Within a month after the Chamorro government took office, the Sandinista unions became a political and economic force with which to reckon.

Despite the election of a government supported by the UNO-affiliated unions, the Sandinista unions are widely believed to remain the largest and most powerful organized labor sector, despite diminishing power and membership. Although there is a law requiring the registration of new unions, the exact number of unions is not known because there is no legal provision to account for those unions that had merged or ceased to exist. At the top of the labor-organizing hierarchy are four confederations: one affiliated with the Sandinistas, two with the UNO, and one with a Trotskyite orientation. The Sandinista-affiliated confederation, FNT, organized in mid-1990, claimed to have 400,000 members among its seven member organizations during the early Chamorro years, although most observers believe that it has lost considerable strength. The members of the FNT include the Sandinista Workers' Federation (Central Sandinista de Trabajadores—CST), a confederation of labor unions; the Association of Agricultural Workers (Asociación de Trabajadores del Campo—ATC); the National Employees Union (Unión Nacional de Empleados—UNE), composed of white-collar workers; the Federation of Health Workers (Federación de Trabajadores de Salud—Fetsalud); the National Association of Nicaraguan Teachers (Asociación Nacional de Educadores de Nicaragua—ANDEN); the Union of Nicaraguan Journalists (Unión de

Periodistas de Nicaragua—UPN); and the Heroes and Martyrs-National Confederation of Professional Associations (Confederación Nacional de Asociaciones Profesionales-Héroes y Mártires—Conapro-Héroes y Mártires).

The UNO-affiliated unions are grouped in two confederations. One is the CTN, headed by Carlos Huembes Trejos. Formed during the 1960s, it is affiliated with the Christian Democratic regional labor group, the Confederation of Latin American Workers (Central Latinoamericana de Trabajadores—Clat), and the Christian Democratic international labor organization, the World Confederation of Labor. The CTN has an estimated 40,000 members. The other UNO union is the Permanent Congress of Workers (Congreso Permanente de Trabajadores—CPT) umbrella group, organized in the late 1980s, which includes five organizations. Most prominent of these is the Confederation for Trade Union Unity (Confederación de Unificación Sindical—CUS), formed in 1968 with the support of the Inter-American Regional Organization of Workers and the Confederation of Nicaraguan Workers (autonomous) (Confederación de Trabajadores Nicaragüenses [autónoma]—CTN[a]) of Agustín Jarquín Anaya, a break-away faction from the CTN. The CPT also includes the Federation for Trade Union Action and Unity (Central de Acción de Unificación Sindical—CAUS) of the Communist Party, the General Confederation of Workers-Independent (Confederación General de Trabajadores-Independiente—CGT-I) of the Nicaraguan Socialist Party (Partido Socialista Nicaragüense—PSN), and the National Teachers' Confederation of Nicaragua (Confederación Nacional de Maestros Nicaragüenses—CNMN).

If the numbers of members given by labor organizations are accurate, some 650,000 of an estimated total active labor force of 1.1 to 1.2 million persons are affiliated with a union. Some analysts believe that number, which is more than 50 percent of the labor force, is very high. Whatever the size of their membership, at least the Sandinista unions have had a major influence in shaping the direction and pace of the Chamorro government's economic policy.

The potential of the Sandinista unions to disrupt the government was demonstrated within two weeks of the Chamorro government's inauguration. Estimates are that 30,000 to 60,000 out of some 150,000 government workers impeded work in government offices, schools, banks, public transportation, and telephone and airport operations in mid-May 1990. The strike began as a result of the Chamorro government's decisions to reexamine the lame-duck legislation passed by the outgoing Sandinista Assembly as well as other government actions during the transition period. In labor matters, the Chamorro government annulled the lame-duck collective bargaining arrangements and suspended the civil service law giving job security and increased benefits to public employees. President Chamorro also announced that tenants would be allowed to cultivate unused expropriated farmlands while property claims were being settled, and she established a commission to review claims to confiscated lands. Other measures taken early in the Chamorro government included the National Assembly's passage of an amnesty law pardoning all political crimes as of the effective date of the legislation and annulment of a March law giving amnesty to Sandinista government officials for crimes committed in the course of performing official duties.

The Sandinista-affiliated UNE called first for a work stoppage of selected workers and then for a general strike. Formally, workers demanded a 200 percent pay increase and restitution of the civil service law, but calls in the streets encompassed a variety of political demands, including President Chamorro's resignation. At first the government declared the strike illegal, threatened to fire striking workers, and refused to meet with Sandinista union leaders. When the strike persisted, the government decided not to test the loyalty of police and military forces by ordering the use of force to dislodge strikers from occupied buildings and instead negotiated with leaders of the public workers' union.

The strike resulted in the Sandinistas gaining some but not all that they had asked for: a 25 percent wage increase on top of the 16 percent that the government had already promised, the right for unions to take part in drafting regulations to implement the civil service law that had been revised by the UNO National Assembly, and the rehiring of workers fired after March 19, 1990. Some analysts viewed the strike as actually hurting the Sandinista unions. Politically, however, the Sandinista unions had demonstrated their power to force the government to reconsider its actions. The strike also strengthened Sandinista demands for national dialogue on the property issue. Many viewed the strike as a fulfillment of Daniel Ortega's promise during the election aftermath that the Sandinistas would rule from below. The FSLN's leadership denied, however, that the FSLN had orchestrated the strike.

The next large-scale strike of 85,000 to 100,000 workers was called on June 27, 1990, by the newly formed FNT. It began in earnest on July 2 and ended on July 11 only after several people had died and hundreds more had been injured. The FNT's initial seven demands, subsequently expanded, encompassed a grab bag of issues, including a higher minimum wage, reenactment of the Sandinista civil service law, suspension of two decrees on property restitution, and measures for public support of construction, basic services, health, and education. The unions were widely viewed as the winners when an agreement was finally reached to end the strike. This agreement provided for increased wages; benefits for dismissed workers; guarantees for continued transportation subsidies; suspension of the program renting unused and disputed land to previous owners; FNT participation in plans for reactivation programs and programs to maintain jobs, including subsidies to failing textile and construction companies; and talks on a minimum wage law. The government's economic concessions were broad and backtracked on its economic reform and adjustment program.

Economically, the May and July strikes cost the government an estimated US$270 million, according to one source. Politically, the July 1990 strikes and settlement pact also dealt several blows to the Chamorro government. First, the tensions between Chamorro's UNO backers and her small executive team over reconciliation gestures toward the Sandinistas widened into an open rupture as the Chamorro government bent to the Sandinista unions. Vice President Godoy announced that he was forming a Committee of National Salvation to deal with the strike and received the backing of Cosep, UNO leaders in the National Assembly, and UNO-affiliated union leaders. Thus, the Chamorro government's short-lived truce with its UNO backers was over. Second, the Sandinista unions demonstrated the destabilizing possibilities of their "rule from below" strategy. Although the Sandinista military and police had dismantled street barricades put up by the strikers and had not been openly disloyal to the government during the strike, the government still appeared unwilling to test their loyalty and did not order the military and police to use force against or arrest the strikers. These events foreshadowed a situation in which the price of social peace would be either substantial concessions from the government or actions by the Sandinista leadership to back up statements of support for the government's economic plan by exercising control over their affiliated unions. The relationship between the Sandinista directorate and the unions became a source of controversy, with members of the directorate denying that they had encouraged the union protests. Critics doubted, however, that Sandinista party discipline had declined to the point that the unions could act autonomously. The Chamorro government signed agreements ending the strike directly with the unions, not with the Sandinista leaders, however, indicating that the Sandinista leadership's control over the unions was limited.

The political situation in July 1990 further encouraged the government to cultivate good relations with Sandinista leaders and unions because, as the July disturbances suggested, the government had no alternative. Yet the Sandinistas' ability to incite followers to the streets waned quickly after the summer strikes. A call from the Sandinista leaders and the FNT for a nationwide strike in October 1990 prompted little response. An FNT rally against the government's economic policies turned out 3,000 rather than the expected 60,000 demonstrators. Probably as a result, the FNT agreed to join President Chamorro's discussions among unions, producers, and the government to reach a national understanding, the *concertación*, on economic and social policies. The *concertación* agreement, signed in October 1990, brought several months of peace before the property issue ignited. Another damper on Sandinista union activity may have been Humberto Ortega's cautionary remarks to the July 1991 Sandinista National Congress; he noted that irresponsible union demands and actions would condemn the country to crisis and imperil revolutionary goals.

The *concertación* agreement also appeared to temporarily defuse economic unrest. Strikes soon after the accord were of the uncontrolled variety, more likely to alienate than attract followers. However, a crisis developed in October 1991 when Daniel Ortega criticized the government as harking back to Somozaism with its policy of returning land to former owners and with the announcement that the mayor of Managua was contemplating the creation of a municipal police force. Ortega indicated that the people might have to exercise their right to civic rebellion, even with arms. President Chamorro accused the FSLN of calling for armed insurrection.

Protesting the new policy of privatization, Sandinista union members occupied a meat-packing plant and slaughterhouse in September 1991; five sugar refineries, a soap plant, and many large farms were taken over by early November. Workers

demanded that they be granted a 25 percent share in ownership when properties were returned to the private sector, some-
thing the Chamorro government had promised in August 1991
agreements. In Managua, police battled with students and
health workers, who marched to the Ministry of Labor armed
with clubs and homemade bombs. The violence escalated after
the FNT's rejection of a November 7 agreement between the
FSLN directorate and the government to end the strikes. There
reportedly were also violent incidents in Matagalpa and Estelí
and riots in Managua, where Sandinista followers destroyed
Radio Corporación, attacked Contra offices with rocket-
launched grenades, and looted and set fire to city hall. Earlier,
armed men had fired on the home of Vice President Godoy.
The rioting ended when President Chamorro said she would
call in the army and Daniel Ortega appealed to Sandinistas for
order.

The 1991 incidents displayed the distance between the Chamorro government and the UNO-affiliated unions. The CPT
complained when Vice President Godoy stated that the army
and police chiefs should be dismissed for not stopping the ram-
page that caused an estimated US$3 million in damage. On
November 13, the CPT went further, deploring the executive
branch's tolerance of and complicity in Sandinista terrorism
and crimes, a complaint that continued in 1992 and 1993.

The labor problem continued to present a serious challenge
to the Chamorro government through at least the midpoint of
her term. Former President Ortega emerged openly as the
champion of labor union mobilization against the Chamorro
economic policies. In the midst of a strike of transport workers
in September 1993, Ortega urged Sandinistas to support
marches protesting a vehicle ownership tax and a gasoline
price increase. He tied these new taxes to the need for a
change in the government's economic policies and the need to
resolve property issues.

Producers' Groups

The two major groups of producers, the UNO-affiliated
Cosep and the Sandinista-affiliated National Union of Farmers
and Cattlemen (Unión Nacional de Agricultores y Ganaderos—UNAG), began distancing themselves from the political
arena after the 1990 election and concentrating more narrowly
on serving their members' economic interests. On opposite
sides of the political scene during the Sandinista years, both

177

unions had played important political and economic roles. Different political positions after 1990, however, brought them closer in their attitudes toward the country's economic situation.

Formed in 1978, Cosep acts as a coordinating council for commercial and agricultural organizations. Cosep was viewed during the early Sandinista years as the major force in the anti-Sandinista opposition, trying in the early 1980s to engage in dialogues with the Sandinista government even as it adopted a highly confrontational stance. Cosep's position, however, was weakened in the mid-1980s by the flight of the middle class and by members' fears that their property would be confiscated, and in the late 1980s by pressure from the peace negotiations. Although one Cosep leader, Enrique Bolanos Geyer, had been a potential presidential candidate for the 1990 elections, Cosep supported Chamorro in the electoral campaign after she won internal elections within the UNO. Two Cosep members refused cabinet posts in the Chamorro government, however, protesting Chamorro's decision to maintain Humberto Ortega as chief of the army. The organization has continued to oppose decisions that allow the Sandinistas considerable influence in government, fearing that such a practice will produce an unfavorable investment climate.

UNAG is one of the Sandinista mass organizations; it was founded in April 1981 to organize small- and medium-sized farmers in support of the FSLN. Although always pro-Sandinista, UNAG tried to downplay ideology in the countryside in the 1980s and fought for nondogmatic, inclusive policies that would not alienate peasant property owners and would defend the interests of all efficient rural producers. After the Chamorro government took power, continued efforts to broaden its base. It sought to attract discontented, landless Contras to its ranks and to maintain its political influence by trying to develop joint positions on agricultural policy with Cosep and its large agricultural producers.

The two producers' groups continued to represent very different political, ideological, and economic positions. These differences were made clear during the Chamorro government's 1990 attempt to negotiate the economic and social national *concertación.* UNAG decided to participate in the negotiations even before the Sandinista unions agreed to do so. Cosep participated only after expressing objections that the result had been predetermined in previous discussions between the Sandinistas and the government. Cosep later refused to sign the final document, charging that the final agreement was unfair because the government had agreed to union demands that land and other confiscated and expropriated property should not be returned to former owners. The *concertación* opened a permanent breach between Cosep and the government.

The Church

The Roman Catholic Church hierarchy, which had been regarded by the Sandinista government as among its harshest critics, also became critical of the Chamorro government well before its second anniversary. From the beginning, the church's hierarchy had a role in the new Chamorro government: Cardinal Miguel Obando y Bravo, Archbishop of Managua, was named one of the guarantors of the peace accords signed during the 1990 transition period. The Roman Catholic Church also had a part in shaping society under the new government, according to some sources. Cardinal Obando was influential in revamping the national education system and curriculum to eliminate Sandinista influence. The educational revisions were carried out by Minister of Education Humberto Belli and his vice minister, Sofonías Cisneros Leiva, both of whom were close to Cardinal Obando, and by members of the City of God charismatic Roman Catholic sect.

For a short period at the beginning of the Chamorro government, the Roman Catholic Church abandoned the high-profile political and social posture it had assumed during the Sandinista years. However, the low profile was reversed when, on November 24, 1991, Cardinal Obando and Nicaragua's nine bishops, speaking as the Bishops' Conference of Nicaragua, signed a lengthy pastoral letter. This letter deplored the country's economic situation and faulted the government for a failure to establish justice. The letter also accused the government of corruption and accused, without naming them, the Sandinista labor unions of inciting violence. Finally, the letter criticized levels of military spending and the luxurious life-styles of many officials in the government in the face of poverty. In a statement that appeared to counter pressures from the United States for Nicaragua to open the economy totally to market forces, the bishops stated that poverty had reached "levels unprecedented for several decades" and noted their belief that "the free market alone cannot resolve underlying social problems."

179

The Universities

Nicaragua's two principal universities, the Central American University (Universidad de Centroamérica—UCA) and the National Autonomous University of Nicaragua (Universidad Nacional Autónoma de Nicaragua—UNAN), are viewed as strongholds of Sandinista thought and sympathy, but are not considered influential in the political system. In 1992 Xavier Gorostiaga, a well-known pro-Sandinista economist and a Jesuit priest, was the rector of the UCA, a Jesuit-run and church-financed institution. Alejandro Serrano Caldera, who served the Sandinista government as president of the Supreme Court and Nicaraguan ambassador to the United Nations, was the rector of the state-financed UNAN in 1993. Both are well-known intellectuals who are viewed as bringing academic credibility and strength to the universities.

The universities have actively sought to protect their own interests. During the transition period, the country's four state and two private universities were granted academic, financial, and administrative autonomy by the outgoing Sandinista legislature through the University Autonomy Law. The universities were also given the right to elect their own rectors, faculty council, and other governing bodies. Students, faculties, and administrators protested the Chamorro government's attempts in May 1990 to have the National Assembly suspend the electoral agreements in order to provide time for their review. The government backtracked, and the National Assembly eventually passed a law containing only minor reforms. University protests were not effective against the Chamorro government budget cuts for the universities, which passed the National Assembly in December 1991 with Sandinista support.

The Media

Noted during the Sandinista years for its virulently partisan and sensationalist character, the communications media began to show small signs of moderation and objectivity as the Chamorro regime progressed. However, partisanship was still a key word in the printed and broadcast press, and Sandinista dominance over the communications media largely continued, despite the transfer of power in the government. After the 1990 elections, however, important differences of opinion emerged in the relationship between the Sandinista-dominated media and official FSLN positions.

The greatest news source for most Nicaraguans is the radio. Some radio stations are considered so influential that opponents of their political position target them for attacks. The rightist Radio Corporación, for instance, was heavily damaged twice by Sandinistas in the early years of the Chamorro government, and the Sandinista Radio Ya was attacked by unknown assailants.

The three major dailies of the Sandinista period continued to dominate the print media market in 1993. *La Prensa*, founded in 1926, with an estimated circulation of 30,000 in early 1992, continued the family tradition built by the president's late husband, Pedro Joaquín Chamorro Cardenal. At the time of the transition, *La Prensa* was run by the president's daughter, Cristiana Chamorro de Lacayo, also the wife of Antonio Lacayo. Cristiana Chamorro's tight control over *La Prensa* and reported refusal to permit criticism of her mother's government led to a rebellion among the editorial board and staff within a year after the 1990 election. The editorial staff, which included other family members, took the opportunity presented by Cristiana Chamorro's official trip abroad with her mother in November 1990 to publish articles harshly critical of the government for its relations with Sandinista leaders. In January the staff forced Cristiana Chamorro to resign as editor and removed Violeta Chamorro from the board of directors. The changes were seen as an attempt by the editorial staff to establish *La Prensa* as an independent paper rather than the official voice of the government.

One of the two pro-Sandinista newspapers also moved in the 1990s to a position more critical of the Chamorro government and the FSLN. *Barricada*, founded in 1979, with an estimated circulation of 20,000 in 1992, declared in early 1992 that it would no longer serve as the house organ of the FSLN and would instead take independent positions. Always regarded by many observers as the most professional of the three major newspapers, *Barricada* became the first public forum in which Sandinista leaders expressed internal disagreements in February 1992. The shift in popular outlook may have been made possible by the division of powers among the Sandinista commanders after their electoral defeat. Bayardo Arce Castaño became head of the FSLN's newspapers, radio stations, and television programs and was planning to establish a Sandinista television station. Significantly, the first disagreement aired in *Barricada* was between Arce and Daniel Ortega.

The third main daily, *El Nuevo Diario,* which had an estimated circulation of 40,000 to 45,000 in 1992, was founded in 1980 by Xavier Chamorro Cardenal, one of Violeta Chamorro's brothers-in-law. It continued its uncritical support of the FSLN, despite expectations that with the end of the Contra war the newspaper would take more independent positions.

Several weekly newspapers also were published in the early 1990s. The Cosep group brought out *La Nicaragüense;* a group headed by former vice president Sergio Ramírez published *El Seminario* in the early 1990s; and a Sandinista group continued *Semana Cómica,* a satirical tabloid. A new weekly newspaper, *El Centroamericano,* also appeared in León in the early 1990s.

Foreign Relations

The Chamorro government had great difficulty translating its electoral victory into increased foreign aid, although much of its foreign policy during its first years appeared aimed at that end. The high levels of international interest that attended the Sandinista years (1979–90) and the 1990 electoral process quickly waned after the Chamorro inauguration. The end of the Cold War and the transfer of dependence from the Soviet bloc to the United States created a dilemma for the Chamorro government, which viewed foreign assistance as crucial to its economic recovery and development, and which had acquired a popular image during the campaign as the political force that would attract foreign funding, particularly from the United States. The Chamorro administration sought to address the declining international interest, particularly in the United States, with an active international lobbying effort. The United States, which many Nicaraguans had believed would help Nicaragua substantially if Chamorro were elected, became ambivalent about the Chamorro government when the UNO's policy of accommodation toward the Sandinistas persisted. As a result, the Chamorro government rapidly followed the path of other Latin American governments, seeking to diversify its foreign relations and decrease its reliance on the United States, despite United States predominance in the country's economic and political affairs.

By the end of the first year of the Chamorro government, Nicaragua was still highly dependent on foreign aid. Promises of foreign aid in 1990 totaled over US$700 million, more than twice the country's export earnings from its major products—coffee, cotton, and bananas. Nicaraguan experts estimated that it would take three years of aid at that level to generate economic recovery and growth and to service a US$9.9 billion debt. Soon after the government took office, it estimated the country's foreign aid needs at US$907 million for 1990 and US$582 million for 1991.

Relations with the United States

Although it had provided substantial support to UNO forces for the elections, the United States did not prove a staunch and uncritically supportive ally of the Chamorro government. Although initially the United States gave signals that it was willing to support the Chamorro government strongly, the relationship deteriorated when some officials within the United States government began to object to the Chamorro government's conciliatory policy toward the Sandinistas.

On March 13, 1990, in a first gesture to the Chamorro government-elect, United States president George H.W. Bush lifted the United States trade embargo imposed five years earlier. Bush also announced that he was presenting the United States Congress with a proposal for US$300 million in emergency supplemental appropriations for Nicaragua for the 1990 fiscal year (FY—see Glossary), which would extend through September 30, 1990. He also asked the United States Congress to add more than US$200 million for Nicaraguan aid to the budget request for FY 1991, which began on October 1, 1990. The emergency supplemental proposal included US$128 million for immediate economic needs and US$75 million for other economic, social, and political programs. The United States also contributed US$50 million to help clear Nicaragua's US$234 million arrearages with international financial institutions, in the hope that other countries also would contribute sizable funds. For repatriation efforts, the Bush administration's request included US$32 million for the demobilization and repatriation of the Contras and their families, and US$15 million for the repatriation of other Nicaraguan refugees.

In addition, Bush announced an immediate US$21 million aid package for the Chamorro government. The package included US$650,000 toward the Chamorro government's transition period expenses, US$13 million in surplus foodstuffs, and US$7.5 million for Contra repatriation. The Bush administration also announced that it had begun the process of restoring Nicaragua's sugar quota, its eligibility for preferential treatment under the Caribbean Basin Initiative (CBI) and the

Generalized System of Preferences, and its access to benefits of the Export-Import Bank and the Overseas Private Investment Corporation.

In its first action to assist President Chamorro, the United States Congress, although not acting as quickly as the Chamorro government wished on funds critical to its spring planting season, approved the emergency supplemental package on May 24, 1990. For FY 1991, the United States Congress did not specifically earmark funds for Nicaragua, but it indicated in the report accompanying the foreign aid legislation that it expected to provide Nicaragua with as much as possible of the administration's US$200 million request for the country. (The United States Congress also specified that no funds were to be provided for Contras who had not disarmed and were not abiding by the terms of the April 1990 cease-fire.) Continuing resolutions from October 1, 1991, through September 30, 1992, providing appropriations for FY 1992, allowed the Bush administration to continue funding Nicaragua at the FY 1991 US$200 million level, just under the administration's US$204.7 million request. The Bush administration obligated US$262.2 million in FY 1990, US$268.9 million in FY 1991, and an estimated US$185.5 million in FY 1992.

As a result of the actions, during FY 1991 and FY 1992 Nicaragua was the second-largest recipient of United States aid to Central America, behind El Salvador. In addition, in September 1991, the Bush administration signed an agreement with Nicaragua cancelling US$259.5 million in bilateral debt to the United States.

In exchange for its assistance, however, the United States expected the Chamorro government to adopt free-market reforms, privatize industries, restore property to former owners, and drop the international lawsuit that the Sandinista government had brought against the United States for the Contra war. All these provisions proved highly problematic for the new government. Complicating the matter, the United States conditioned disbursements of certain obligated funds on progress toward fulfillment of economic objectives. At times, pressures from the Bush administration and members of the United States Congress for political reform in Nicaragua appeared to be prerequisites for further aid from the United States.

United States discomfort with the continuing Sandinista leadership of the Nicaraguan military was highlighted in late 1990 and early 1991. During this period, Salvadoran guerrillas shot down two Salvadoran air force aircraft and a United States helicopter with Soviet surface-to-air missiles obtained from the Nicaraguan military. The accidents resulted in the deaths of three United States soldiers. Even though the Chamorro government arrested four officers in connection with the October 1990 sale of the missiles to the Salvadorans and the Nicaraguans said that the Salvadoran guerrillas would be forced to return unfired missiles, the incident accentuated United States fears that the Chamorro government was being used by the Sandinistas. Subsequent reports that Nicaraguan army soldiers had tried to smuggle arms and munitions to a Marxist group in Honduras, the assassination in Managua of former Contra leader Enrique Bermúdez, and the Salvadoran guerrillas' continued use of Nicaragua as a safe haven exacerbated United States concerns. For its part, the Nicaraguan government objected to the United States request to the Soviet Union that it cut the supply of spare parts needed by the Nicaraguan army to maintain its helicopters and trucks.

In April 1991, President Chamorro paid a state visit to the United States. She addressed a joint session of Congress in the hope of easing growing United States doubts about her administration and obtaining a long-term commitment for United States aid. Although President Bush and the United States Congress praised and applauded President Chamorro, she received no commitments other than a promise that the United States would lead efforts to obtain aid to clear Nicaragua's arrearages with international financial institutions, opening the way for new support.

At the time of President Chamorro's visit, a central issue in United States-Nicaraguan relations was unresolved. The United States wanted the Chamorro government to drop the suit that the Sandinista government had brought against the United States in the International Court of Justice (ICJ) on April 9, 1984. In the suit, the Sandinista government charged that the United States had violated international law in recruiting, training, arming, equipping, financing, supplying, and otherwise encouraging, supporting, aiding, and directing military and paramilitary actions in and against Nicaragua. The ICJ ruled against the United States on June 27, 1986.

In its decision, the ICJ ruled, twelve to three, that the United States had violated obligations not to intervene in another state's affairs, not to use force against another state, not to violate the sovereignty of another state, and not to interrupt peaceful maritime commerce. The ICJ also ruled that the United States had not abided by its 1956 Friendship, Commerce, and Navigation Treaty with Nicaragua. The ICJ ordered the United States to make reparations to Nicaragua but left a first attempt at setting the form and amount of reparations to agreement between the two parties. Because the United States rejected the ICJ's decision, no attempts were ever made at agreement, and in the 1990 transition period the National Assembly passed a law requiring future governments to proceed with the claim. Although the Chamorro government initially resisted spending its political capital to meet United States demands to drop the claim, President Chamorro told President Bush during her April 1991 state visit that she had introduced legislation to the National Assembly to repeal the law. In June 1991, forty-nine to one after the Sandinista deputies had walked out, the UNO coalition in the National Assembly voted to revoke the law. The Chamorro government subsequently notified the ICJ that it was dropping the claim.

Despite the Bush administration's public words of firm support for the Chamorro government's ongoing economic reforms, the Nicaraguan government's relations with the Sandinistas were a continuing irritant and a cause for the Bush administration's difficulties in shaping and implementing its Nicaragua policy. As Nicaragua sought foreign funds to help sustain the army, in late 1991 the United States discouraged Taiwan from giving between US$2 million and US$3 million for nonlethal assistance to the Sandinista military. Earlier, the United States apparently had ignored a request from the Chamorro government to help fund retirement and retraining benefits for 2,700 army officers. Without indications that the Sandinista military and police were firmly under President Chamorro's control, there seemed little prospect in 1993 that the United States would endorse her reconciliation policy.

Relations with Central American Countries

The elections in Nicaragua and the end of the Contra war, all achieved as part of the ongoing Central American peace process that began in 1983, raised hopes that Central Americans could turn to other issues of concern in the region. The Chamorro government maintained that it favored political and economic integration in Central America. In June 1990, President Chamorro joined the four other Central American presidents in a summit meeting in Antigua, Guatemala, part of an ongoing series of presidential summits that had taken place since the Esquipulas II agreement of August 1987. The five presidents announced on June 17, 1990, that they had agreed to a plan for regional cooperation in trade, financing, investment, and production. The plan included the revival of the Central American Common Market (CACM—see Appendix B) through a revision of tariff and nontariff barriers to trade.

Central America sought to increase trade as an important step to economic recovery and long-term growth, both through broad and steady access to the United States market and through increasing trade within the Central American region. As mandated by the 1987 Esquipulas II accords, Central Americans took steps to advance integration efforts among themselves. Various efforts to bring all the countries together have resulted in some liberalization of trade. Nicaragua participated in the first step in January 1991, when in a two-day meeting in Tuxtla, Mexico, the presidents of the five Central American countries signed an agreement outlining free-trade arrangements that would be phased in by December 31, 1996. This trade integration would start with each country bilaterally negotiating agreements by economic sector with Mexico. Subsequently, however, Nicaragua did not move with the same speed as other Central American countries toward regional economic integration; its delay was attributed to domestic economic conditions. Nicaragua also lagged on a regional political measure, namely, participation in the Central American Parliament. In a September 1991 meeting in San Salvador, the presidents of Guatemala, El Salvador, and Honduras decided to hold an inaugural session of the parliament the following month. Nicaragua, however, had not yet held elections for the twenty delegates each country would send to the body; this delay was attributed to the cost of holding special elections and to domestic political reasons. The three participating countries gave Nicaragua, Costa Rica (which had not yet ratified the treaty), and Panama (which had expressed interest in joining regional integration measures) thirty-six months to take the steps necessary to participate. After Nicaragua finally held elections for its delegates, the Central American Parliament, with delegates from Guatemala, El Salvador, Honduras, and Nicaragua in attendance, had its first meeting in Esquipulas, Guatemala, in 1993.

Relations with Other Countries

The Chamorro government maintained relations with the Soviet Union and Cuba, despite their identification with the Sandinista party and cause. Even before the 1990 election results were officially announced, the Soviet Union pledged to recognize whoever won, as long as the elections were fair, and quickly acknowledged Chamorro as the winner. Cuba's government kept more than a diplomatic presence in Nicaragua after Chamorro's inauguration, and Cuban medical personnel remained in some areas to continue assisting with Nicaraguan health programs.

Many countries provided economic assistance of various types, either through bilateral or Central American regional initiatives, although the amount of aid that the Chamorro government received was criticized as falling far short of its needs. In June 1990, at a two-day Conference of Donors meeting in Rome, the Chamorro government was successful in securing pledges toward the US$350 million it had requested in emergency aid. This amount was in addition to what friendly countries had already pledged. Nicaragua said that it needed US$220 million for social programs, infrastructure repair, and support for the producer sector, including small and medium producers, and US$130 million to finance the import of fuel and inputs for economic recovery. Pledges were made by nearly all of the thirty-four donors attending the conference, which included twelve European Community (now European Union) countries, the World Bank (see Glossary), and the International Monetary Fund (IMF—see Glossary). Most of the funds reportedly were contributed by Venezuela and Germany. Subsequently, in July 1990, Venezuela announced that it would resume oil exports to Nicaragua after the renegotiation of Nicaragua's US$150 million petroleum debt incurred during the Sandinista years. Mexico and Venezuela had supplied oil to Nicaragua under the concessionary San José oil supply agreement, but sales had been suspended in 1985 for nonpayment.

In September 1991, the Chamorro government rectified relations with multilateral institutions. It paid off US$270 million in arrearages to the World Bank and US$90 million to the Inter-American Development Bank (IDB), through donations and credits from the United States and other countries, including a bridge loan from Colombia, Mexico, Venezuela, and Spain. The same month, the IMF announced that it had approved an eighteen-month, US$55.7 million loan to support the Chamorro government's economic reform program.

A mid-March 1992 meeting of the "consultative group" of donor nations organized by the World Bank seemed promising as a source of substantial funds for 1992 and 1993. The government planned to use the funding for infrastructure, agricultural production, social programs, and balance-of-payments support.

Asian countries also expressed interest in new relations with Nicaragua. Japan and the Republic of Korea (South Korea) principally investigated investment possibilities, although Japan also looked into the prospect of building a new transisthmian canal across Nicaragua. Taiwan, which in 1990 had a political interest in reestablishing the diplomatic relations that the Sandinistas had broken in reaching out to China, offered not only substantial investments but also low-interest loans. However, Taiwanese plans to construct a sawmill and to manufacture plywood and veneers in the northeast to ship to United States and European markets ran afoul of Nicaraguan environmentalists.

Despite great strides taken in the previous several years, Nicaragua in late 1993 still had many hurdles to overcome in institutionalizing its democracy. The elections of 1990 were the first in over a half century when government control peacefully transferred from one party to another in fair elections. Plans for the next elections in 1996 were proceeding, and the country's largest party, the FSLN, showed promising signs of moving from its revolutionary and authoritarian past to a genuine democratic party. Whether these new trends would continue and would take hold at the grassroots level, replacing the centuries-old legacy of dictators and revolution, remained to be seen.

*   *   *

Post-Sandinista Nicaragua may fall into the same academic literature void as pre-Sandinista Nicaragua, with little reliable English-language public source material analyzing the political situation. Scholarly works in print on Nicaragua's internal politics in the postelectoral period were limited as of December 1993. All suffer from lack of study of the UNO parties, which were disregarded by academe during the Sandinista years much as the opposition was ignored during the Somoza years. Until that deficit is corrected, analysis of the politics of the Chamorro years is likely to remain superficial and/or susceptible to political bias. A worthwhile general overview of Nicaragua in the early postelectoral period is contained in the chapter on Nicaragua in Tom Barry's *Central America Inside Out: The Essential Guide to Its Societies, Politics, and Economies.* An informed discussion of the politics of the Chamorro government's first eight months is "Nicaragua in Transition," an article in *Current History,* by Jennifer McCoy, who served as the Carter Center's representative in Nicaragua during the preelectoral and postelectoral period.

Other studies that bear on the political situation are more specifically focused. Studies of the election itself are included in Philip J. Williams's "Elections and Democratization in Nicaragua: The 1990 Elections in Perspective," in the *Journal of Inter-American Studies and World Affairs.* Family relations in Nicaraguan politics from the 1800s through the early Chamorro years are treated in "Family Affairs: Class, Lineage and Politics in Contemporary Nicaragua," by Carlos Maria Vilas, in the *Journal of Latin American Studies.*

The Sandinistas continue to be a focus of study. *Latin American Perspectives,* a publication of the pro-Sandinista North American Congress on Latin America, devoted an entire postelectoral volume, *The Sandinista Legacy: The Construction of Democracy,* to the Sandinistas. *New York Times* reporter Mark Uhlig, who covered Nicaragua during the Sandinista years, has written an extensive postelectoral analysis of the FSLN in "Nicaragua's Permanent Crisis: Ruling from Above and Below," in *Survival.* A forthcoming book by Rose J. Spalding, *Capitalists and Revolution in Nicaragua,* will deal with the politics of the Sandinista years and the Chamorro government. (For further information and complete citations, see Bibliography.)

Chapter 5. National Security

Members of the Sandinista People's Army, Nicaragua's national army

FREE ELECTIONS IN NICARAGUA in 1990 ended eleven years of government by the Marxist Sandinista National Liberation Front (Frente Sandinista de Liberación Nacional—FSLN), but under the new government, the Sandinista People's Army (Ejército Popular Sandinista—EPS) is still controlled by the Sandinistas (see Glossary). The commanding general of the EPS, Humberto Ortega Saavedra, a former member of the Sandinista directorate, and his general staff, all Sandinistas, function independently of civilian authority, although President Violeta Barrios de Chamorro is nominally commander in chief and minister of defense.

Under the Sandinista administration (1979–90), the EPS grew from a force of a few thousand guerrillas to an army that at its peak had a strength of around 97,000 troops, augmented by militia and reserve forces. The estimated number of total active-duty personnel was 134,000. Since the restoration of peace, the armed forces have undergone comprehensive reform. Their strength was cut back to about 15,000 at the end of 1993, the militia has been disbanded, and obligatory military service has been terminated. During the 1980s, armor, heavy weapons, and aircraft supplied by the Soviet Union and its allies enabled the Sandinistas to field the most powerful army in Central America (see Glossary). Although some of these items have been sold, Soviet weaponry still predominates in the inventory of the depleted army. However, much of it is not in service because of lack of maintenance and personnel to operate it.

The conclusion of the civil war in 1990 was accompanied by the demobilization of some 22,000 Contra (short for *contrarevolucionario*—see Glossary) fighters of the Nicaraguan Resistance. Nevertheless, violence in the heavily armed society remains commonplace. The Chamorro government has not been able to deliver on many of its promises of land and credits to the former Contras to facilitate their reintegration into Nicaraguan society. Several thousand of them—known as Recontras—have formed armed bands in rural areas. Their targets are often local Sandinista officials and Sandinista farm cooperatives. Disgruntled veterans of the EPS, known as Recompas, have formed similar groups in protest against the government's failure to relieve their economic distress.

In 1993 government amnesties, offers of payments for arms, and assurances of fulfillment of campaign promises reduced the number of Recontras and Recompas threatening the countryside. Political murders and kidnappings remain serious threats in the polarized society, although the level of violence has eased significantly since the 1970s and 1980s. The National Police and the criminal justice system, however, are not effective in arresting and convicting persons responsible for the lawlessness. Harassment of former resistance members by local security forces is a source of friction, but few such crimes by the EPS or police result in any punishment. Under pressure from domestic and international critics, Chamorro has removed a number of high police officials to reduce Sandinista control over law enforcement, has replaced many Sandinista judges in the judicial system, and has sought to gain control over the state security apparatus, which had been one of the principal source of human rights abuse during the Sandinista era.

Military Heritage

During a prolonged period of political turmoil after the dissolution of the United Provinces of Central America in 1837, Nicaragua was rent by power rivalry between conservative and liberal political factions. The private armies of the main political factions, composed of officers of European descent commanding illiterate mestizos who had been pressed into service, were the only organized military forces in the country. The new country's main threat to its borders arose from Britain's continuing efforts to exercise domination over Nicaragua's Caribbean coast area, but the risk of armed confrontation with the United States persuaded the British to retreat from their attempts to formalize control of the area and to negotiate the Clayton-Bulwer Treaty, in which both countries agreed not to claim exclusive control over the region (see National Independence, ch. 1).

In 1854 and 1855, bloody fighting between liberal forces, aided by neighboring Honduras, and conservatives, aided by a conservative government in Guatemala, provided an opening for the United States adventurer William Walker, who landed in Nicaragua with a small band of followers (see Foreign Intervention (1850–68), ch. 1). Walker's power quickly grew, but after he installed himself as president, both contending political factions joined together with the armies of other Central American nations to drive Walker out. The conflict was prolonged and bitter, but in 1857, finally facing defeat, Walker and his remaining followers were evacuated under a truce organized by the United States Navy.

The first effort to build a professional military establishment did not occur until the administration of liberal president José Santos Zelaya (1893–1909). The plan was to raise an army of 2,000 regulars organized into sixteen infantry companies, augmented by cavalry, artillery, and engineering units. A flotilla of five armed vessels was also assembled. The envisaged strength was never reached, and the size of the army dwindled to fewer than 500 in the years following the arrival of United States marines, who were sent to Nicaragua in 1912 to suppress a revolt.

After the marines' last contingent, the legation guard, was withdrawn in 1925, a small United States training mission was introduced to organize a National Constabulary intended to replace the army and National Police. However, a coup and the outbreak of full-scale civil war led to a revival of the Nicaraguan army. The renewal of fighting precipitated another intervention by the United States that lasted from 1926 to 1933 (see United States Intervention, ch. 1).

National Guard, 1927–79

The long years of strife between the liberal and conservative political factions and the existence of private armies led the United States to sponsor the National Guard as what was intended to be an apolitical institution to assume all military and police functions in Nicaragua. The marines provided the training, but their efforts were complicated by a guerrilla movement led by Augusto César Sandino. Sandino opposed the United States-backed military force, which was composed mostly of his political enemies, and continued to resist the marines and the fledgling National Guard from a stronghold in the mountainous areas of northern Nicaragua.

Upon the advent of the United States Good Neighbor Policy in 1933, the marines withdrew from Nicaragua, but they left behind the best-organized, -trained, and -equipped military force that the country had ever known. Having reached a strength of about 3,000 by the mid-1930s, the guard was organized into company units, although the Presidential Guard component approached battalion size. Despite hopes for an apolitical force, however, the National Guard soon became the personal tool of the Somoza dynasty. Expanded to more than

10,000 during the civil war of 1978–79, the guard consisted of a reinforced battalion as its primary tactical unit, a Presidential Guard battalion, a mechanized company, an engineer battalion, artillery and antiaircraft batteries, and one security company in each of the country's sixteen departments.

The National Guard's main arms were rifles and machine guns, later augmented by antiaircraft guns and mortars. Although Nicaragua was not actively involved in World War II, it qualified for United States Lend-Lease military aid in exchange for United States base facilities at Corinto on the Pacific coast. Additional shipments of small arms and transportation and communication equipment followed, as well as some training and light transport aircraft. United States military aid to the National Guard continued under the Rio de Janeiro Treaty of Mutual Defense (1947), but stopped in 1976 after relations with the administration of Anastasio Somoza Debayle (1967–72, 1974–79) worsened. Some United States equipment of World War II vintage was also purchased from other countries: Staghound armored cars and M4 Sherman medium tanks from Israel and F–51 Mustang fighter aircraft from Sweden.

Except for minor frontier skirmishes with Honduras in 1957 over a border dispute, the National Guard was not involved in any conflict with its neighbors. In its only mission outside the country, one company participated in the peacekeeping force of the Organization of American States (OAS) in the Dominican Republic in 1965. The guard's domestic power, however, gradually broadened to embrace not only its original internal security and police functions but also control over customs, telecommunications, port facilities, radio broadcasting, the merchant marine, and civil aviation.

Upon the departure of the United States marines in 1933, General Anastasio Somoza García was selected by the president-elect of Nicaragua as first Nicaraguan commander of the National Guard. Although initially regarded as a malleable compromise candidate, Somoza soon indicated that he would exploit his position as head of the guard to consolidate power in what became the Somoza dynasty (see The Somoza Era, 1936–74, ch. 1). Through its control of all security, police, and intelligence functions, the guard became far more than simply a military institution. Command of the National Guard always remained in the hands of Somoza family members, and key officers were promoted mainly on the basis of personal loyalty

*Augusto César
Sandino*

to the ruling family. This loyalty was reinforced through kick-backs, perquisites, and special opportunities for personal gain that led to a pervasive system of corruption. At the time of Anastasio Somoza García's assassination in 1956, his oldest son, Luis Somoza Debayle, became president and his second son, Anastasio Somoza Debayle, took over as commander of the National Guard. When Luis Somoza Debayle's health deteriorated in 1967, control of the presidency passed to Anastasio Somoza Debayle.

The National Guard's close association with the Somoza family and its instinct for self-preservation through protection of the Somoza dynasty resulted in increasing alienation of large segments of the Nicaraguan population. This alienation was exacerbated by repressive measures, including the strafing of cities, and the ruthless urban warfare employed by the guard during the two years of fighting that preceded the ouster of Anastasio Somoza Debayle. As a result, many Nicaraguans saw the struggle of the FSLN against the government as an anti-National Guard crusade as well as an anti-Somoza crusade.

Sandinista Guerrilla Movement, 1961–79

The FSLN was officially founded in Honduras on the symbolic date of July 26, 1961, the eighth anniversary of the launching of the Cuban Revolution by Fidel Castro Ruz. The FSLN operated at first in the mountainous region that forms the border between Honduras and Nicaragua. Early successes were few, however, and the hardships and sheer effort of surviving led to discontent and desertions. Between 1970 and 1974, the FSLN struggled to broaden its bases of support by conducting guerrilla operations in the countryside while recruiting new supporters in the cities. Its rural guerrilla tactics were patterned after those of Castro's army, and FSLN forces were trained in Cuba. The tactics combined rural insurgency with popular insurrection, a mix which proved the key element in the FSLN's eventual victory.

For many observers, the FSLN first became a force to be reckoned with when it executed a spectacular raid and hostage-taking mission at a reception for the United States ambassador in Managua in December 1974 (see The End of the Anastasio Somoza Debayle Era, ch. 1). Subsequently, the Anastasio Somoza Debayle administration was obliged to accede to humiliating FSLN demands for ransom and political freedom for fourteen FSLN prisoners. The National Guard followed with a major counteroffensive that reduced armed resistance in the countryside. The FSLN remained on the defensive until 1977, but the guard's harsh reprisals caused popular feeling to swing even more toward the Sandinistas.

The seizure of the National Palace by a small group of Sandinistas in August 1978 sparked a mass uprising in the following month. The uprising was a turning point in the struggle to overthrow Anastasio Somoza Debayle. The FSLN no longer was fighting alone but rather was organizing and controlling a national insurrection of citizens eager to join the anti-Somoza movement. Hard-core Sandinista guerrillas numbered perhaps 2,000 to 3,000; untrained popular militias and foreign supporters added several thousand more to this total. Although the "first offensive," September 1978, declined toward the end of the year, fighting did not completely stop. The FSLN mounted its "final offensive" in May 1979, capturing a number of cities in June and launching a three-pronged assault against Managua in early July. Anastasio Somoza Debayle, strongly urged to do so by the United States, resigned on July 16 and fled the country; the National Guard collapsed two days later.

Sandinista People's Army, 1979–90

Sandinista ranks had ballooned during the final weeks of

the insurrection with the addition of thousands of untrained and undisciplined volunteers. These self-recruits, who had access to weapons, were the source of considerable crime and violence. By late 1979, the situation was clearly deteriorating; petty crime mounted and some Sandinistas were abusing their authority for personal gain. To end the chaotic situation and consolidate political power, FSLN combatants were regrouped into a conventional army framework. At its core were 1,300 experienced guerrilla fighters. Most of the remainder were members of the popular militias and others who had played some role in the defeat of Somoza. Cuban military personnel helped to set up basic and more advanced training programs and to advise the regional commands. The new army, known as the EPS, was placed under the command of Humberto Ortega, one of the nine FSLN commanders and brother of Daniel José Ortega Saavedra, the Sandinista junta coordinator.

The Sandinistas announced initially that their goal was to build a well-equipped professional military of some 25,000. Their primary missions were to deter attacks led by the United States, prevent a counterrevolutionary uprising, and mobilize internal support for the FSLN. The strength of the EPS increased steadily during the Contra war in the 1980s. At the time the peace accords for the war went into effect in 1990, the EPS's active-duty members numbered more than 80,000. Supplemented by reservists and militia, the Nicaraguan armed forces had an overall fighting strength of more than 125,000.

The buildup of the regular army depended at first on voluntary enlistments, but later in 1983 a universal conscription system, known as Patriotic Military Service, was adopted. Males between the ages of seventeen and twenty-six were obligated to perform two years of active service followed by two years of reserve status. Service by women remained voluntary. Mandatory conscription was bitterly resented. Thousands of youths fled the country rather than serve in the armed forces, and antidraft protests were widespread. The unpopularity of the draft was believed to have been a large factor in the Sandinista election defeat in 1990.

Inheriting only the battered remnants of the equipment of Somoza's National Guard, the Sandinistas eventually acquired enough Soviet heavy and light tanks and armored personnel carriers (APCs) to form five armored battalions. The Soviets and their allies delivered large amounts of other equipment, including 122mm and 155mm howitzers, 122mm multiple rocket launchers, trucks, and tank carriers. A mix of infantry weapons employed by the Sandinista guerrillas was gradually replaced by Soviet AK–47 assault rifles in the EPS and eventually among combat elements of the militia as well.

The Sandinistas upgraded the modest air force left by the National Guard after sending personnel to Cuba and East European countries for pilot and mechanic training. The most important acquisitions were Soviet helicopters for battlefield transport and assault missions. Although pilots were trained and runways constructed in preparation for jet fighters, neither the Soviet Union nor France was willing to extend credits for the purchase of modern MiG or Mirage aircraft. The United States warned that the introduction of sophisticated jet fighters might lead to retaliatory strikes because of the potential threat to the Panama Canal.

In an escalation of tensions, the United States mined Nicaraguan harbors and attacked boats in ports. In response, the Nicaraguan government, to defend against further attacks on harbors and shore installations, replaced the old patrol boats left by the National Guard with armed patrol craft and small minesweepers.

Sandinista People's Militia

Following the example of Cuba, the Nicaraguan government established the Sandinista People's Militia (Milicia Popular Sandinista—MPS) to augment the regular troops and to gain the services of enthusiastic supporters of the revolution who could not be accommodated in the EPS. The militia represented both a massive political mobilization and the primary means of defending the countryside against the forces of the Nicaraguan Resistance. Individual militias received weekend training in basic infantry weapons and were assigned as guards in sensitive installations or as neighborhood night watches. A typical militia battalion of 700 persons consisted of five infantry companies and various support units.

The principal weapons of the MPS were older-model rifles and machine guns and mortars. Militia members displaying aptitude during weekend training sessions were selected for several months of full-time training, followed by up to six months of service in the field. During 1982 and 1983, the militia had primary responsibility for border defense and sustained heavy casualties, while the regular army was concentrated at permanent bases. After the installation of the draft in 1983

Triumphant Sandinistas greeted by crowds in Managua,
July 19, 1979
Courtesy Susan Meiselas Magnum

enabled the EPS to widen its operations, the mobilized militia functioned mainly as a protector of rural communities. The FSLN claimed that 250,000 persons had received some form of military training, of whom 100,000 were mobilized in active units.

Before Anastasio Somoza Debayle's overthrow, women had constituted up to 40 percent of the ranks of the FSLN and 6 percent of the officers. Six women held the rank of guerrilla commander in the late 1970s. After the Sandinista victory, however, women were gradually shifted to noncombatant roles or to the Sandinista Police (Policía Sandinista—PS). Many women fighters resisted the redeployment, and their role became an issue. As a compromise, seven all-women reserve battalions were formed, but these were gradually converted into mixed battalions. Women's mobilization continued in other forms.

Women constituted 50 percent of the Sandinista Defense Committees (Comités de Defensa Sandinista—CDS) organized in the neighborhoods and up to 80 percent of Revolutionary Vigilance Patrols, volunteers who carried out nighttime watches in urban neighborhoods and at industrial sites.

Foreign Influences and Assistance

The influence of the United States on the National Guard was significant for many years. Between 1950 and 1976, when military relations were cut off, the total value of United States military aid was US$18.2 million. In addition, some 5,400 members of the guard received training in the United States. The National Guard managed to obtain some equipment and training assistance from Israel during the final years of the Somoza era to compensate for the loss of United States aid.

Cuba was the predominant influence on the FSLN during the period from its inception until July 1979. The Castro government provided advice, training, money, and moral support as well as some Soviet-made weapons. Captured National Guard weapons were at first used to arm the FSLN guerrillas, but as the struggle to overthrow Somoza escalated in the late 1970s, purchases on the international arms market reached the Sandinistas through Panamanian ports, transiting Costa Rica, which acquiesced in arms transshipment.

In addition to Panama and Costa Rica, Venezuela and other nations of the Andean Pact aided the anti-Somoza effort in the late 1970s in a variety of ways. A Simón Bolívar Brigade, formed in Colombia but also including sympathizers from a number of countries, participated in limited combat alongside the FSLN. Although both the Nicaraguan and Cuban governments downplayed the level of Cuban influence, the Cuban role was clearly paramount.

FSLN leaders requested military aid from the United States in mid-1979, but it was uncertain how serious their request was because they had already accepted Cuban military advisers. Although the request for military aid was rejected, the United States did offer to provide some training in the United States and to supply advisers, instructors, and some assistance in noncombat areas. All of these offers were refused by the Sandinista leaders. The United States administration criticized France for proceeding with a sale of US$15.8 million in equipment—consisting mainly of two patrol boats, two helicopters, trucks, and rocket launchers. As a result of the United States stance, no further military equipment was transferred from Western suppliers.

In March 1980, a high-level delegation that included Minister of Defense Humberto Ortega traveled to Moscow and signed a variety of agreements. Both Nicaraguan and Soviet officials hotly denied that these accords included secret military agreements. The FSLN leaders also visited Bulgaria and the German Democratic Republic (East Germany); both countries subsequently provided military advisers, and some Nicaraguan pilots were trained in Bulgaria.

Deliveries of Soviet weapons began soon after the visit to Moscow. They included the T–55 heavy tank mounted with a 100mm gun, which was an older model of a tank with capabilities that were limited under Nicaraguan conditions. Heavy artillery and multiple rocket launchers, far surpassing in range and firepower all other artillery in the region, also were delivered. APCs, jeep-like vehicles, trucks, tanker trucks, and mobile workshops followed and added mobility to the EPS. The Soviet Union also supplied helicopters to the Nicaraguan air force, giving the EPS the means to respond more rapidly to attacks and raids by the Nicaraguan Resistance. The United States Department of State estimated that the Soviet Union and its allies delivered some 120,000 tons of military and military-related equipment, valued at US$3.3 billion, between 1980 and 1990. In most cases, deliveries consisted of older equipment provided at discounted prices under generous terms or as donations.

Criticizing the Soviet-assisted buildup of the EPS, United States officials underscored the threat of Nicaragua's growing military potential to its neighbors. Other observers regarded the newly acquired weaponry as essentially defensive, noting that it added little to Nicaragua's capacity to wage war beyond its borders.

Prior to July 1979, Panamanian ties with the FSLN were strong, and Panama's support of the Sandinistas included volunteers in a Panamanian brigade that fought alongside the Sandinistas. A group of Panamanian National Guard officers arrived in Managua in late 1979 to offer advisory services, but found that Cubans had already arrived and were serving as the key advisers to the EPS and security organs. Venezuela briefly considered providing training for the nascent Sandinista air force but declined because of the strong Cuban presence. The United States claimed that as many as 3,500 Cuban military and security advisers were serving in Nicaragua by late 1985, although other sources said there were far fewer. Cuban officers were present during combat operations and served as pilots in some cases, but Nicaragua denied that they actively participated in the fighting. Of thousands of Soviet and Eastern European personnel in Nicaragua, only about thirty to forty Soviet citizens, fifty to sixty East Germans, and a few Bulgarians served with the Nicaraguan military. They mainly provided training in the use and maintenance of Soviet equipment.

The impact of the Sandinista success and the subsequent direction taken by the FSLN was considerable, especially in Central America and the Caribbean region. The FSLN victory, in effect, delivered a message to conservative, military-dominated administrations, putting them on notice that they could afford to ignore similar groups in their countries only at their own peril. In 1980 and 1981, the FSLN leadership did not hesitate to proclaim Sandinista moral support for guerrilla movements in Central America, especially in El Salvador, but was circumspect when issues of direct arms and military assistance were raised. In 1981 the United States cut off economic assistance to Nicaragua after publishing an extensive and controversial white paper claiming that Soviet and Cuban arms flowed through Nicaragua to the Salvadoran guerrillas of the Farabundo Martí National Liberation Front (Frente Farabundo Martí de Liberación Nacional—FMLN). There appeared to be no question, however, that FMLN guerrillas were trained by Nicaraguan and Cuban officers in Nicaragua. When the United States stated that Nicaragua's aid to the Salvadoran rebels was the reason for United States support for the Nicaraguan Resistance, the Nicaraguan government took steps to curtail the outward flow of weapons.

United States government charges that the FSLN supported rebel movements in other nations were not fully substantiated, in spite of repeated reports of Nicaraguan links with Guatemalan and South American insurgent groups. In 1993 the issue of the FSLN's ties with guerrillas and terrorists surfaced again when an arms cache exploded in Managua. The blast revealed tons of weapons, including Soviet surface-to-air missiles, assault rifles, and machine guns, plus ammunition and explosives. Ownership of the weapons was admitted by a faction of the FMLN, which had falsely informed the United Nations (UN) that its weapons had been destroyed in conformity with a UN-mediated peace process. In addition, many documents, including false passports, were discovered. The discovery suggested that a radical faction of Sandinistas with ties to left-wing Latin American and European terrorists continued to operate clandestinely. A second cache of explosives and light arms appeared soon afterward, linking the Sandinistas to Guatemalan guerrilla groups. An international investigation, however, found no evidence of active ties to international criminal or terrorist groups.

The Nicaraguan Resistance

Anti-Sandinista exile groups, backed by the United States Central Intelligence Agency (CIA), began in the spring of 1981 to plan paramilitary operations against the government of Nicaragua. A year later, new fighting was well under way. Together referred to as the Nicaraguan Resistance, the two main antigovernment organizations were the Nicaraguan Democratic Force (Fuerza Democrática Nicaragüense—FDN) and the Democratic Revolutionary Alliance (Alianza Revolucionaria Democrática—Arde). Based in Honduras, the FDN consisted largely of former members and officers of the National Guard in alliance with other groups, deserters from the FSLN militia, and disgruntled Miskito. According to a 1985 United States Congressional study, forty-six of the forty-eight command positions in the FDN were held by former members of the National Guard. In lower units, the majority of group and detachment leaders had no previous National Guard service. Ordinary soldiers were mainly disaffected peasants or peasant mercenaries with no guard affiliation. As the fighting continued, many field commanders were promoted from the ranks. Miskito, Sumo, and Rama (Misura), a right-wing Miskito group of 1,500 to 3,000 indigenous troops led by a former Somoza agent, operated in coordination with the FDN. Misurasata, a Costa Rican-based Miskito group under Brooklyn Rivera Bryan that was aligned with Arde, fought for Caribbean coast autonomy rather than against the Sandinista government.

Beginning with raids across the border, the FDN had by 1983 established a foothold along the Honduran border in the northern section of easternmost Zelaya Department. The FDN was estimated to have a strength of 10,000 to 15,000 persons by mid-1984. Advisory, financial, and material help from the CIA was crucial. According to the United States Department of State, military and nonmilitary assistance between 1982 and 1990 amounted to US$300 million. This figure did not include an additional US$100 million gathered by the United States National Security Council, and aid solicited from private organizations and foreign governments, much of it devoted to weaponry.

Operating out of Costa Rica, Arde included forces from several factions, including those of Edén Pastora Gómez (also known as Comandante Cero—Commander Zero). A hero of the 1978 FSLN takeover of the National Palace, Pastora had later become disenchanted with the FSLN. The Arde forces, which consisted of about 3,000 troops, had produced one well-publicized success by briefly occupying the town of San Juan del Norte. However, a split developed between Arde leaders in 1984 when Pastora pulled his forces out of Arde over the issue of unification with the FDN, and as a result the FDN's military campaign was severely weakened.

The funding of arms for the Contras, as members of the Nicaraguan Resistance had come to be known, was cut off by the United States Congress in 1984, contributing to a decline in Contra fortunes. The Contras were reduced to hit-and-run raids targeting civilian installations and sabotaging infrastructure. Subsequently revitalized as arms purchased with private funds reached them, the Contras were able to carry out numerous attacks on isolated military units and occupied the northeast border region with Honduras and some rural mountainous areas. Yet they failed to establish a liberated zone where they could set up a provisional government. The Contras' brutal practices of attacks on rural cooperatives, villages, and clinics, often involving the deaths of civilians and the torture and killing of Sandinista officials and soldiers, brought accusations that the Contras were conducting a deliberate campaign of terrorism.

By mid-1985, the military balance began to shift to the FSLN forces, which had been strengthened by draft call-ups and improved use of militia units. With the EPS numbering 40,000 troops and the active-duty militia 20,000, offensive operations of the government forces drove most of the Contras back into Honduras. Long-range artillery shelled suspected Contra camps just inside the Honduran border. Many Nicaraguan villagers in the war zones were evacuated to resettlement camps to give the government free-fire zones and to deny the Contras local support and intelligence. As part of its shift in tactics, the EPS formed thirteen Irregular Warfare Battalions (Batallones de Lucha Irregulares—BLIs) to carry on the fight against the

Contras. The BLIs were lightly armed, highly mobile, quick-reaction forces trained in counterguerrilla tactics. The use of Soviet-supplied helicopters to transport the BLIs added to the military pressure against the Contras.

Boosted by the resumption of weapons and ammunition supplies from the United States in 1986, the Contras mounted new offensives, briefly capturing a number of remote towns and cutting highway links. Some EPS helicopters were shot down with newly acquired shoulder-fired missiles. Although damaging to the Nicaraguan economy and costly in lives, the Contra campaign never posed a serious military threat to Managua or other large cities. The FDN claimed to have 10,000 of its 16,000 fighters operating inside Nicaragua; the FSLN said that there were only 6,000.

Although in 1988, while peace negotiations were under way, the United States Congress rejected the request of President Ronald Reagan's administration (1981–89) for additional military aid to the Contras, it approved nonlethal "humanitarian" aid that enabled the Contra forces to remain intact. After internationally monitored Nicaraguan elections were set for February 1990, five Central American presidents agreed that a new organization, the International Support and Verification Commission of the Organization of American States, would oversee the voluntary demobilization, repatriation, or relocation of the Contra forces over a ninety-day period. The demobilization process began on April 1, 1990.

Under the terms of the accords, former members of the resistance would have their confiscated property restored, be eligible for grants for rehabilitation and training, and receive parcels of land and credits enabling them to settle in autonomous rural development zones. Widows of slain Contras were to be provided with pensions. These commitments were, at best, only partially fulfilled. Many Contras who settled in the development zones soon abandoned them because the regions lacked the necessary infrastructure. Some ex-Contras also returned to their former homes as fears of Sandinista retribution subsided.

Armed Forces after 1990

Under an agreement between President-elect Chamorro of the National Opposition Union (Unión Nacional Opositora— UNO) and the defeated FSLN party, General Humberto Ortega, former minister of defense and commander in chief of

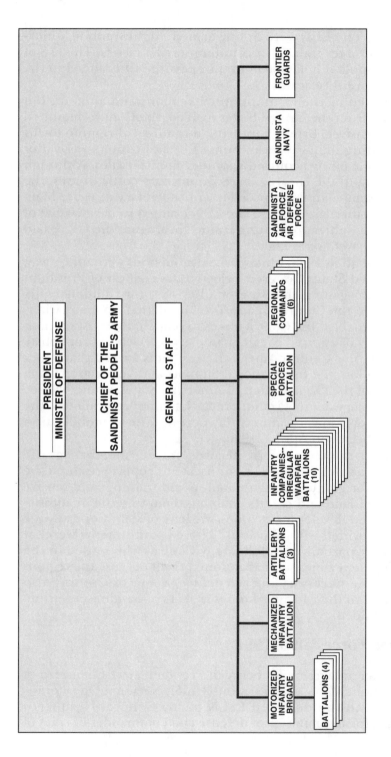

Figure 13. Organization of the Armed Forces, 1993

the EPS under the Sandinistas, remained at the head of the armed forces (see fig. 13). By a law that took effect in April 1990, the EPS became subordinate to President Chamorro as commander in chief. Chamorro also retained the Ministry of Defense portfolio. Chamorro's authority over the EPS was, however, very limited. There were no Ministry of Defense offices and no vice ministers to shape national defense policies or exercise civilian control over the armed forces. Under the Law of Military Organization of the Sandinista Popular Army enacted just before Chamorro's election victory, Humberto Ortega retained authority over promotions, military construction, and force deployments. He contracted for weapons procurement and drafted the military budget presented to the government. Only an overall budget had to be submitted to the legislature, thus avoiding a line-item review by the National Assembly.

Sandinista officers remained at the head of all general staff directorates and military regions. The chief of the army, Major General Joaquín Cuadra Lacayo, continued in his pre-Chamorro position. Facing domestic pressure to remove Humberto Ortega and the risk of curtailment of United States aid as long as Sandinistas remained in control of the armed forces, Chamorro announced that Ortega would be replaced in 1994. Ortega challenged her authority to relieve him and reiterated his intention to remain at the head of the EPS until the army reform program was completed in 1997. This date was later advanced to the first half of 1995.

The army reform measures were launched with deep cuts in personnel strengths, the abolition of conscription, and disbanding of the militia. The size of the army declined from a peak strength of 97,000 troops to an estimated 15,200 in 1993, accomplished by voluntary discharges and forced retirements. Under the Sandinistas, the army general staff consisted of numerous branches and directorates: artillery, combat readiness, communications, Frontier Guards, military construction, intelligence, counterintelligence, training, operations, organization and mobilization, personnel, and logistics. Most of these bodies appear to have been retained, although they have been trimmed and reorganized. The air force and navy are also subordinate to the army general staff.

Since 1990 the mission of the EPS has been to ensure the security of the national borders and to deal with internal disturbances. Its primary task has been to prevent disorder and

COMMISSIONED OFFICERS

NICARAGUAN RANK	TENIENTE SEGUNDO	TENIENTE	TENIENTE PRIMERO	CAPITÁN	MAYOR	TENIENTE CORONEL	CORONEL	GENERAL DE BRIGADA	MAYOR GENERAL*	NO RANK	GENERAL*
ARMY, AIR FORCE, AND NAVY											
U.S. ARMY AND AIR FORCE RANK TITLE	2D LIEUTENANT	1ST LIEUTENANT		CAPTAIN	MAJOR	LIEUTENANT COLONEL	COLONEL	BRIGADIER GENERAL	MAJOR GENERAL	LIEUTENANT GENERAL	GENERAL
U.S. NAVY RANK TITLE	ENSIGN	LIEUTENANT JUNIOR GRADE		LIEUTENANT	LIEUTENANT COMMANDER	COMMANDER	CAPTAIN	REAR ADMIRAL LOWER HALF	REAR ADMIRAL UPPER HALF	VICE ADMIRAL	ADMIRAL

* For Nicaraguan army only; no rank for Nicaraguan air force or navy.

ENLISTED PERSONNEL

NICARAGUAN RANK	NO RANK	SOLDADO DE PRIMERA	SARGENTO TERCERO		SARGENTO SEGUNDO		SARGENTO PRIMERO	NO RANK	NO RANK
ARMY, AIR FORCE, AND NAVY    									
U.S. ARMY RANK TITLE	BASIC PRIVATE	PRIVATE	PRIVATE 1ST CLASS	CORPORAL/SPECIALIST	SERGEANT	STAFF SERGEANT	SERGEANT 1ST CLASS	MASTER SERGEANT / FIRST SERGEANT	SERGEANT MAJOR / COMMAND SERGEANT MAJOR
U.S. AIR FORCE RANK TITLE	AIRMAN BASIC	AIRMAN	AIRMAN 1ST CLASS	SENIOR AIRMAN/ SERGEANT	STAFF SERGEANT	TECHNICAL SERGEANT	MASTER SERGEANT	SENIOR MASTER SERGEANT	CHIEF MASTER SERGEANT
U.S. NAVY RANK TITLE	SEAMAN RECRUIT	SEAMAN APPRENTICE	SEAMAN	PETTY OFFICER 3D CLASS	PETTY OFFICER 2D CLASS	PETTY OFFICER 1ST CLASS	CHIEF PETTY OFFICER	SENIOR CHIEF PETTY OFFICER	MASTER CHIEF PETTY OFFICER

Figure 14. Military Ranks and Insignia, 1993

violence wrought by armed bands of former Contra and Sandinista soldiers (see Internal Security, this ch.).

In November and December 1992, the EPS was deployed alongside the National Police to prevent violence during demonstrations by the National Workers' Front (Frente Nacional de Trabajadores—FNT) for improved pay and benefits. The EPS and the Frontier Guards also assist the police in narcotics control. A small EPS contingent works alongside demobilized Contras in a Special Disarmament Brigade to reduce the arsenal of weapons in civilian hands.

Army

As of 1993, the army's strength was estimated at 13,500 personnel. The EPS is organized into six regional commands and two military departments subordinate to the general staff (see fig. 14). The largest unit is a motorized infantry brigade of four battalions. In addition, there are a mechanized infantry battalion and three artillery battalions. The Irregular Warfare Battalions have been reduced to ten infantry companies. A Special Forces battalion has been formed from airborne and Special Forces personnel. Most of these units are neither fully staffed nor adequately equipped.

The army continues to depend on Soviet weapons delivered during the 1980s. Most of these are out-of-date and poorly maintained. The EPS's inventory of armor—heavy and light tanks, APCs, and reconnaissance vehicles—remains large by Central American standards. However, most of the Soviet T–55 tanks are reportedly in storage because of a lack of funds and personnel to maintain them. The PT–76 light tanks form the primary armor of the mechanized infantry battalion. Only about seventy-five APCs and reconnaissance vehicles are operational, and some of the armored weapons have been sold to other Latin American countries.

The army retains a considerable supply of 122mm and 152mm towed artillery pieces and multiple rocket launchers. Twelve of its APCs are mounted with Soviet AT–3 (Sagger) antitank guided missiles. The army retains numerous antitank guns and a stock of Soviet shoulder-fired antiaircraft missile launchers (see Table 12, Appendix A).

Air Force

When the Sandinistas assumed control in 1979, the Sandinista Air Force/Air Defense Force (Fuerza Aérea Sandinista/

Defensa Anti-Aérea—FAS/DAA) inherited only the remnants of the National Guard's small air force. Equipment included a few AT–33A armed jet trainers, Cessna 337s, and some transports, trainers, and helicopters. The time required to train pilots and construct airfields precluded a rapid FAS/DAA buildup. Beginning in 1982, the Sandinistas received from Libya the Italian-made SF–260A trainer/tactical support aircraft and the Czech L–39 Aero Albatros, a subsonic jet trainer that could be missile-armed for close-in air defense. In addition to light and medium transport aircraft, the air force acquired a fleet of helicopters from the Soviet Union that served as a vital asset in the war against the Contras. They included Mi–8 and Mi–17 transport helicopters and later the Mi–24, followed by its export variant, the Mi–25, a modern armored assault helicopter. After Humberto Ortega revealed that Nicaragua had approached France and the Soviet Union for Mirage or MiG fighter planes, the United States warned against introducing modern combat jets to the region. Although Nicaragua began construction of a new airbase with a longer runway and protective revetments, it did not succeed in acquiring new fighter aircraft.

A series of radar sites were constructed to give the Sandinistas radar coverage over most of Nicaragua, with the added capability of monitoring aircraft movements in neighboring countries. A Soviet-designed early-warning/ground-control intercept facility gave the air force the potential to control its combat aircraft from command elements on the ground.

After 1990 the FAS/DAA was no longer able to maintain its full aircraft inventory without Soviet support. The personnel complement fell from 3,000 in 1990 to 1,200 in 1993. Airbases at Bluefields, Montelimar, Puerto Cabezas, Puerto Sandino, and Managua remained operational. Combat aircraft were reduced to a single mixed squadron of Cessna 337s, L–39s, and SF–260As. However, the serviceability of all these aircraft was doubtful. In 1992 a number of helicopters and six radar units were sold to Peru. A small fleet of helicopters, transports, and utility/training aircraft was retained.

Navy

The "navy" of Somoza's National Guard consisted of a few old patrol boats. The Sandinistas acquired more modern vessels, although none was larger than fifty tons. The navy's mission was to discourage seaborne Contra attacks and to deter

Sandinista People's Army truck in Villa Nueva

CIA-run operations such as the destruction of diesel storage facilities at Corinto in 1983 and the mining of Nicaraguan harbors in 1984. The Sandinista Navy (Marina de Guerra Sandinista—MGS), which had reached a peak strength of 3,000 personnel in 1990, suffered a sweeping reduction to 500 by 1993.

The commander of the navy is an EPS officer with the rank of major. The principal bases of the MGS are at the ports of Corinto on the Pacific and Puerto Cabezas on the Caribbean. Other installations are at El Bluff near Bluefields and San Juan del Sur on the Pacific.

The Sandinistas had eight Soviet minesweeping boats, of which seven remained in 1993, but none is known to be in operating condition. Three Soviet Zhuk-class patrol boats are believed to be seaworthy, out of seven that remained at the end of 1990. Also believed to be operational are three North Korean fast patrol boats and two Vedette-type boats built in France and armed with Soviet 14.2mm machine guns.

Defense Spending

According to studies published by the United States Arms Control and Disarmament Agency (ACDA), Nicaraguan military spending totaled US$10 million in 1979, the year in which the Somoza administration was overthrown. This amount constituted 0.8 percent of the gross national product (GNP—see Glossary). Under the Sandinistas, military expenditures rose rapidly, going from US$53 million in 1980 to US$192 million in 1985. The latter figure was more than 17 percent of GNP and more than 26 percent of total government expenditures. ACDA was unable to estimate defense spending for the years 1986–89.

Valid comparisons of defense outlays between the Ortega and Chamorro administrations are difficult because of hyperinflation, the precipitous drop in value of the córdoba (C$— for value, see Glossary), and the chaotic exchange rate structure in the late 1980s. The United States Department of State estimated that military expenditures in 1989 were between US$76 million and US$90 million, a reduction of 44 percent from the previous year. In 1989 defense outlays constituted 36 percent of the entire budget. The announced defense budget figure for 1990 was US$166 million, corresponding to 25 percent of the total government budget that year. As military cutbacks continued, Chamorro's military budget proposal for 1991 of US$78.6 million was reduced by the National Assembly. According to ACDA, actual defense spending in 1991 was US$70 million, equivalent to 4 percent of the GNP and 14 percent of the national budget.

To some extent, the EPS has been able to compensate for these drastic curbs on spending by selling excess equipment. In 1992, for example, the EPS sold Soviet helicopters, APCs, cannons, and antiaircraft missiles to the Peruvian armed forces for US$25 million. All receipts from such sales went directly to the EPS.

United States concern over Sandinista control of the police and security forces precluded extending military aid to the Chamorro government and prohibited transactions under the United States Foreign Military Sales Program. In fiscal year (FY—see Glossary) 1994, however, the United States Department of Defense proposed allocating a small amount of money to the EPS for civil-military training. The EPS has sought further military cooperation with the United States, which the United States has made conditional on establishment of civilian control over the EPS and prosecution of alleged human rights violations by members of the EPS.

Internal Security

An end to war-related violence in 1990 brought a brief period of conciliation between the competing political factions in Nicaragua. That year, the last 1,000 persons detained in connection with the Contra conflict were released. That action followed the release in 1988 and 1989 of some 2,800 members of the National Guard and others held by the Sandinista government on security-related grounds.

Frequent episodes of political violence continue to plague the heavily polarized Nicaraguan society. Clashes resulting in bloodshed are often the outgrowth of demonstrations and protests in areas of the country where Chamorro's strength is greatest or in border areas where support for the Contras has been strong. Disputes over resettlement and land title have brought violent confrontations in many rural areas. By invading government-owned cooperatives, both ex-Contras and former EPS soldiers have attempted to regain land that had been expropriated from the Somozas. The assassination of former Contra leader Enrique Bermúdez Varela in February 1991, followed by an inept police investigation and the failure to identify any suspects, has undermined confidence in the ability of the government and the security forces to maintain order.

The Contra war left Nicaragua bitterly divided and heavily armed. An estimated 25,000 to 100,000 weapons remain in civilian hands. By mid-1991, some demobilized Contras had begun to rearm in small groups. These Recontras, as they were called, carried out numerous raids, originally intended to pressure the government into honoring its promises of jobs, farms, and credit for land purchases and to bring about an end to harassment by police and security forces. The Recontras' actions included kidnappings of Sandinistas for ransom and attacks on members of farm cooperatives. In 1993 the United States Department of State described the activities of the Recontras as principally criminal, with political overtones (see Interest Groups, ch. 4).

The best known of the Recontra groups is Northern Front 3-80 (Frente Norte 3-80), whose strength in 1993 was estimated at 1,400. The Recontra guerrillas survive because of support from sympathetic local peasants in mountainous areas north of Managua where police and army patrols rarely venture. They also receive some financial help from conservative Nicaraguan and anti-Castro Cuban groups in Miami.

A number of pro-Sandinista armed bands composed of dismissed members of the EPS call themselves Recompas, from *compas* (derived from *compañeros*), the term by which Sandinista soldiers referred to one another. The main Recompa group is the Revolutionary Front of Workers and Peasants (Frente Revolucionario de Obreros y Campesinos—FROC). In July 1993, the FROC gained control of the northern town of Estelí, reportedly looting some US$4 million from banks and shops before regular army troops drove them out, in the process incurring numerous civilian casualties. A month later, a large government delegation that had been invited to discuss an amnesty offer with the FROC was taken hostage by the right-wing Northern Front 3-80. In retaliation, pro-Sandinistas kidnapped thirty-four UNO government officials, including the country's vice president, who were meeting in Managua. Following intense negotiations, both sides released their hostages.

The grievances against the government by Recontras and Recompas are similar in many ways. Although the predecessor organizations of both groups fought each other in the 1980s, the Recontras and Recompas have, for the most part, avoided violent confrontations with each other in the 1990s. An amnesty proclaimed by the National Assembly in 1993 resulted in the surrender of large numbers of personnel from both rebel groups, leaving some 600 from each side still in the field.

Police and Law Enforcement

The collapse of the Somoza administration in 1979 left Nicaragua without any agency in charge of public order because the National Guard had performed police services, albeit in a repressive and corrupt fashion. For a brief period, FSLN veterans, working with the Sandinista Defense Committees and other mass organizations, provided rudimentary police functions, but this improvised system failed to prevent an upsurge of organized criminal activity, armed robbery, and attacks by youth gangs. The easy availability of weapons also contributed to the breakdown of law enforcement. A more professional police force was gradually put into place with the help of security training by the Panamanian National Guard and the Cuban government. Panama also donated vehicles and equipment and accepted several hundred Nicaraguans in Panama's police training academy.

Under the newly established Ministry of Interior, the Sandinista Police (Policía Sandinista—PS) was headed by a former

FSLN brigade commander. Individual operating sections were responsible for traffic, public safety, prisons, communications, surveillance, legal processing, and embassy protection. Women made up a substantial proportion of the force.

An eight-month training course for police cadets included a heavy dose of military training because in a national emergency the PS was expected to perform a support role in national defense. In addition to controlling street crime, the police were called on to combat the social legacy of the corrupt Somoza administration by enforcing morality and public welfare laws. Campaigns were launched against prostitution and alcoholism, but the new morality ordinances were enforced only sporadically. The crime rate was reduced somewhat when the police were granted authority to arrest "known delinquents" for "illegal association" when more specific charges could not be proven.

The police were later assisted by Revolutionary Vigilance Patrols organized by neighborhood Sandinista Defense Committees. These patrols conducted nighttime walks through neighborhoods and tended to discourage community crime. The PS also cooperated with the state security forces to suppress counterrevolutionary elements and to arrest political opponents of the administration.

Known as the National Police after 1990, the police force has continued to be controlled by Sandinistas despite the turnover of power to President Chamorro. The National Police's total complement was given as 11,000 by one source. The Sandinista police commander, René Vivas Lugo, remained its head. Police matters come under the Ministry of Government, which replaced the Ministry of Interior. The police, who act with substantial autonomy, have been repeatedly accused of human rights violations. A local human rights group has described the use of torture as an investigative tool as "systematic."

Many state security officials linked to serious human rights violations under the Sandinistas assumed positions as chiefs of police in provincial towns. To investigate and correct police wrongdoing, in 1991 a Civil Inspection Unit (also seen as Civil Inspectorate) was formed within the Ministry of Government. The following year, Chamorro appointed a civilian who had no Sandinista ties as vice minister of government responsible for supervising the police. Twelve police commanders, including Vivas, were removed and more moderate Sandinistas appointed from within the ranks. A new police law has instituted a regular system of promotion and retirement, emphasizing professionalism and subordination to civilian authority.

Although the counternarcotics efforts of the National Police are relatively weak, the drug problem in Nicaragua appeared to be quite modest as of 1993. Cocaine use appears to be the primary problem. The only local drug produced is marijuana, which is consumed domestically. Nicaragua is on an overland drug transit route from South America to the United States via the Pan American Highway, and drug movement by ship has been suspected through both Caribbean and Pacific ports. The effectiveness of drug law enforcement has been limited, although a law was passed in 1992 to authorize the establishment of an antinarcotics unit in the National Police.

Secret Police and Intelligence

Under the Sandinistas, the secret police and intelligence operations of the Ministry of Interior were the main instruments used to maintain FSLN control and suppress dissent. The secret police agency, the General Directorate of State Security (Dirección General de Seguridad del Estado—DGSE), carried out surveillance and operations against perceived opponents. The DGSE could detain suspected counterrevolutionaries and hold them indefinitely without charge. It operated its own detention and interrogation centers and clandestine prisons. The DGSE was reportedly assisted by at least 100 Cuban advisers.

After Chamorro's election in 1990, the DGSE, along with 1,200 of its 1,700 members, was transferred to the army and renamed the Directorate of Defense Information (Dirección de Información para la Defensa—DID). The DGSE's chief, Colonel Lenín Cerna Juárez, a militant Sandinista, became head of the DID. Human rights activists called on President Chamorro to remove Cerna from his position and to investigate human rights violations attributed to him while he headed the DGSE. In 1993 Chamorro established the Directorate of Intelligence Affairs in the Office of the Presidency to coordinate intelligence matters. This new directorate has not functioned effectively under its civilian head and the DID remains under EPS control. Cerna, however, was transferred from the DID to the post of inspector general of the EPS.

Little is known about DID functions in the military, but the organization is believed to conduct both military intelligence and internal intelligence gathering. Local human rights groups claim that the DID has followed the DGSE practice of operating wiretaps, intercepting mail, and conducting illegal searches of homes and businesses. Unlike the DGSE, however, DID does not have the power of arrest and therefore is not in a position to impose its authority on the civilian population, as was the case with its predecessor agency.

Human Rights

During the Sandinistas' eleven years in power, the Sandinista security forces were accused of widespread repression and numerous violations of human rights, often in conjunction with the army. These violations included the murder of perceived Contra supporters, kidnappings, disappearances, illegal detentions, and mistreatment and torture of prisoners. According to the human rights group Americas Watch, a high percentage of DGSE prisoners were coerced into signing confessions by deception, physical force, or deprivation. The security forces were also responsible in 1982 for the summary relocation of the Miskito under cruel conditions. Gross human rights abuses were also committed by the Contras. These abuses included systematic murder, torture, and kidnapping of civilian supporters of the FSLN. Undefended farm cooperatives and other facilities, such as clinics, associated with the Sandinistas were attacked. The raids led to many civilian casualties and executions.

According to local human rights groups, as many as 1,000 persons remained unaccounted for at the close of the Contra war in 1990. Numerous clandestine grave sites—most ascribed to the Sandinistas but some to the Contras—were discovered, providing evidence of the whereabouts of some persons who had disappeared. At one site, Correntada Larga on the south Caribbean coast, witnesses reported the torture and killing of sixty-seven peasants by the DGSE during a two-week period in 1981.

The end of armed conflict in 1990 brought improvement in the human rights situation; however, sporadic incidents of political or extrajudicial killings continue to occur. Rural violence is often associated with disputes in which demobilized Contras and peasants seek to negotiate a share of state-owned cooperatives. The disputes lead to clashes with police and often result in peasants occupying the cooperatives. The number of violent deaths of former Contras at the hands of the police, the army, or FSLN militants rose in 1993. In some incidents during which civilians were killed, government security forces were provoked by unruly and sometimes violent protesters. Even when it seems that the police have used disproportionate force or committed wanton murder, police actions are rarely investigated or punished.

Prison Conditions

The capacity of the Nicaraguan prison system was greatly expanded during the Sandinista period to keep pace with the incarceration of political prisoners. By the mid-1980s, the country had nine penitentiaries or public jails, holding cells in forty-eight local police stations, and some twenty-three DGSE detention centers. By the government's own estimate, there were 5,000 prisoners in 1984, of whom 2,000 were members of the National Guard or others accused of cooperation with the Contras. An independent human rights group in Nicaragua, the Permanent Human Rights Commission, claimed in 1986 that 10,000 were incarcerated, 70 percent of whom were political dissidents. The International Committee of the Red Cross, which periodically visited prisons, counted more than 1,000 members of the National Guard and 1,500 others accused of pro-Contra activity in early 1988. An estimated 500 to 600 additional persons were in DGSE facilities. After the release of thirty-nine inmates in February 1990, no further political prisoners were believed to be in Nicaraguan jails.

Under the Sandinistas, mistreatment and torture were reported to be common in the DGSE detention centers. The regular penitentiaries and public jails were known for primitive conditions and corruption emanating from the Prison Directorate under the Ministry of Interior. The largest penitentiary at Tipitapa outside Managua held most of the members of the National Guard and persons linked to the Contras. Tensions between inmates and guards were high, especially during peace talks, when releases appeared to be near. Tensions were aggravated by political prisoners who were unwilling to do work that they believed could help the Sandinista cause.

In late 1990, President Chamorro created a National Penitentiary Commission to oversee and improve the penal system. A report issued by a human rights group in 1992 described conditions in the national penitentiary system as "disastrous." The report accused the government of inexcusable indifference because it failed to allocate adequate funds. The prisoners were described as suffering from lack of food, clothing, medicine, and medical treatment. Cases of malnutrition were found, as well as contaminated water. Although physical abuse in the penitentiaries was rare, a high percentage of prisoners complained of torture and mistreatment in police detention cells. As a result of drastic cutbacks in the judicial system's budget, more than half of the prisoners in 1993 were persons awaiting trial.

Criminal Justice System

Immediately after the Sandinista victory in 1979, the FSLN government enacted by decree a Statute on the Rights and Guarantees of Nicaraguans. Among many provisions, the decree banned the death penalty and all forms of torture as well as cruel and degrading punishment. The maximum sentence for any crime was set at thirty years. Basic procedures were outlined for arrest and detention, including a defendant's right to legal counsel. Arbitrary violation of an individual's personal integrity, home, or correspondence was prohibited. These principles were gradually eroded by a series of measures, the first of which, the Law of National Emergency in 1982, legalized prolonged detention of opponents of the government and imposed constraints on political opposition and labor groups. An expanded State of Emergency, announced in 1985, virtually suspended all civil liberties, including the prohibition against arbitrary imprisonment, the presumption of innocence, the right to a fair and speedy trial, and habeas corpus.

An immediate problem faced by the new Sandinista administration in 1979 was how to handle the approximately 7,800 former members of the National Guard and former Somoza government officials who had been interned and then incarcerated. There was strong popular sentiment for executing those who were identified as torturers or "war criminals." Both Sandinista troops and the general public killed some captured Somoza supporters. The Sandinista junta later admitted that perhaps 100 Somoza officials had been put to death in the chaotic period following the July 1979 victory, but most were held for appearances before special tribunals that sat between November 1979 and February 1981. Trials by these politicized tribunals were heavily publicized to remind the public of the evils of the Somoza administration. Some 6,300 trials were conducted; there was a 78 percent conviction rate, and sentences ranged up to thirty years.

The proceedings of the tribunals were widely criticized by international human rights groups. Sandinistas who were not lawyers sat as judges and presented evidence. The charges were often vague and imprecise, and defendants had little time to prepare a defense. A proper appeals mechanism was lacking, and some of the accused were exposed to a campaign against them by the FSLN media. Nevertheless, the accused had legal representation, media access was permitted, and convictions were based on the previously existing legal code. Observers sympathetic to the Sandinistas argued that the justice administered by the special tribunals was relatively fair, especially when compared with actions taken by other newly victorious revolutionary governments in a similarly heated atmosphere.

A major problem of the early years of the Sandinista administration was the overcrowded criminal docket, which led to lengthy periods of detention for those awaiting trial and sentencing. In 1983 jury trials were limited to only the most severe felonies on the grounds that this limitation would help unclog the courts. A law of *amparo,* a feature of Spanish common law empowering courts to obtain redress of administrative excess or error, was suspended by the 1982 Law of National Emergency. The emergency law also suspended the limitation of seven days' detention without arraignment.

Two additional legal innovations were introduced by the FSLN junta. One was the People's Anti-Somoza Tribunals (Tribunales Populares Anti-Somocistas—TPAs). Similar to the special tribunals, members of the TPA panels were drawn from Sandinista mass organizations, and their jurisdiction was over persons charged as members of the Nicaraguan Resistance. The TPAs' jurisdiction later was expanded to include a broad category of acts construed to threaten the revolution. Defendants were held incommunicado for indefinite periods, and their legal counsels were unable to present a proper defense. In some cases, defendants were compelled to appear without benefit of attorney. Nearly all the accused were convicted, usually after long detention before trial. The TPAs were abolished in 1988, but many of the TPA judges were transferred to regular criminal courts.

The second legal innovation was an expansion of police power. In 1980 the Sandinista Police were given authority to adjudicate cases of cattle rustling, drug dealing, and insult to authority. Later, police power was further expanded to include the breaking up of unauthorized demonstrations and dealing with economic crimes such as hoarding, with sentences of up to two years. This new authority also extended the traditional powers of police judges to impose sentences of up to six months on such charges as vagrancy, drunkenness, or disturbing the peace. The police courts could impose sentences without granting defendants the right to counsel, the right to call witnesses, or the right to appeal to courts in the regular judicial system.

After the Chamorro government took office in 1990, it began efforts to depoliticize the judiciary. However, it was not until late 1993 that the Supreme Court, whose members serve six-year terms, had a non-Sandinista majority. Some progress was made in replacing Sandinista appointees to the 250 trial and appellate judgeships, yet Sandinista appointees remained in the majority in 1993. Nevertheless, because the Supreme Court appoints appeals and lower court judges, the prospect for more non-Sandinista judges seems favorable.

Military courts continue to be responsible for dealing with crimes committed by or against members of the armed forces or police. Proceedings of trials in military courts are secret, although information can be released at the discretion of the military. According to the United States Department of State's annual human rights reports, convictions by military courts are rare, and even when soldiers are convicted, they receive light sentences or the sentences are not enforced. According to a 1991 study by Americas Watch, almost no political crimes—whether committed by members of the military, ex-Contras, or civilians partial to the Sandinistas or to UNO—were prosecuted in the judicial system.

Procedures for the arrest of criminal suspects are set forth in the Police Functions Law. The law requires police to obtain a warrant before detaining a suspect, but the warrant is issued by a police official rather than a magistrate. The law also permits police to detain suspects for up to nine days for the purpose of collecting evidence before they are brought before a judge. Police are required to inform families when persons are detained but rarely do so, and detainees are not granted access to legal counsel once charged, as required by the constitution. The Reform Law of Penal Procedures, passed in 1991, provides for a maximum of three days' detention, but police continue to follow the Police Functions Law, which has not been amended.

The 1991 reform law also provides for bail; previously only compelling reasons such as ill health qualified accused criminals to remain at liberty while awaiting trial.

Defendants have the right to legal counsel at their trials. Although indigents are entitled to *pro bono* counsel, public defenders do not exist. In spite of the constitutional right to a speedy trial, arrested persons often spend months in jail before appearing in court. Under the 1991 law reforming penal procedures, jury trials have been restored. However, the jury system has not proven effective, partly because prospective jurors seek to evade jury duty, delaying trials. Those convicted have the right of appeal.

In 1993 Nicaragua had made strides in respecting human rights and its legal system. The mission of the Nicaraguan military, however, was still in a state of flux. Only established as a modern national entity in the 1930s, the Nicaraguan army was first a tool of the Somozas (as the National Guard) and then the military arm of the FSLN during the Sandinistas' eleven years in government. Despite massive downsizing and attempts to increase professionalism in the 1990s, in 1993 the Nicaraguan army was still controlled by its former FSLN leaders and unsure of its role. Whether the country's armed forces could become a truly national army was a question still unanswered.

*   *   *

The history of the Nicaraguan armed forces from the country's beginnings until the first years of the Sandinista era is traced in *Armed Forces of Latin America* by Adrian J. English. *Revolution and Foreign Policy in Nicaragua* by Mary B. Vanderlaan reviews the Sandinista military buildup and defense policy during the Sandinistas' first six years. Supplementary information on the Sandinista People's Army can be found in an article by Stephen M. Gorman and Thomas W. Walker in *Nicaragua: The First Five Years*. The brief article, "Nicaragua in Crisis," by Julio Montes in *Jane's Intelligence Review* summarizes the effects of the tremendous cutback in the armed forces since 1990.

Much of the data on the Nicaraguan weapons inventory cited in this chapter is based on *The Military Balance, 1993–94* and information from *Jane's Fighting Ships, 1993–94.*

Nicaraguan internal security, law enforcement, and court and prison conditions are surveyed in reports from Americas Watch and in the United States Department of State's annual

Country Reports on Human Rights Practices. (For further information and complete citations, see Bibliography.)

Appendix A

Table

Table 1. *Metric Conversion Coefficients and Factors*

When you know	Multiply by	To find
Millimeters	0.04	inches
Centimeters..........................	0.39	inches
Meters	3.3	feet
Kilometers	0.62	miles
Hectares (10,000 m^2)	2.47	acres
Square kilometers	0.39	square miles
Cubic meters	35.3	cubic feet
Liters	0.26	gallons
Kilograms	2.2	pounds
Metric tons	0.98	long tons
....	1.1	short tons
....	2,204.0	pounds
....		
Degrees Celsius	1.8	degrees
(Centigrade)	and add 32	Fahrenheit

Table 2. Total Population and Population Density by Department, 1990

Department	Population	Inhabitants per Square Kilometer
Boaco	117,900	28
Carazo	150,000	137
Chinandega	330,500	69
Chontales	129,600	21
Estelí	169,100	78
Granada	162,600	164
Jinotega	175,600	18
León	344,500	66
Madriz	88,700	55
Managua	1,026,100	305
Masaya	230,800	335
Matagalpa	322,300	47
Nueva Segovia	122,100	34
Río San Juan	52,200	7
Rivas	149,800	68
Zelaya[1]	298,900	5
NICARAGUA	3,870,700	32

[1] As of 1993, divided into Región Autonómista Atlántico Norte and Región Autonómista Altántico Sur.

Source: Based on information from Germany, Statistisches Bundesamt, *Länderbericht: Nicaragua, 1991*, Wiesbaden, 1991, 24.

Table 3. Socioeconomic Classes and Their Percentage of the Labor Force, 1980[1]

Class	Number	Percentage of Labor Force
Upper class (large landowners or owners of large industrial, commercial, and service enterprises employing more than 100 persons)	22.000	2.0
Middle class (medium landowners and owners of medium urban enterprises, independent professionals, and salaried administrators and technicians)	176,500	19.4
Upper peasants (middle-income smallholders and their unpaid family workers)	25,900	13.9
Lower peasants (poor smallholders)	149,300	16.4
Rural workers (landless agricultural workers: permanent, seasonal, and unemployed)	100,500	11.1
Working class (salaried workers in construction, mining, industry, commerce, services, and government)	153,500	16.9
Self-employed workers (nonsalaried artisans, peddlers, and unskilled workers)	79,700	8.8
Domestics and urban unemployed	120,400	13.3
TOTAL	908,000	100.0

[1] Landholding categories are defined by size and land use. Medium landowners hold 50–500 manzanas (one manzana is equal to 0.7 hectares) in domestic consumption crops; 14–65 manzanas in coffee; 50–200 manzanas in cotton; or 200–1,000 manzanas in cattle. Upper peasants possess 10–50 manzanas in domestic consumption crops; 5–15 manzanas in coffee; 5–50 manzanas in cotton; or 20–200 manzanas in cattle. Large landowners and lower peasants, respectively, have holdings above and below these limits.

Source: Based on information from Richard L. Harris, "The Economic Transformation and Industrial Development of Nicaragua," in Richard L. Harris and Carlos M. Vilas (eds.), *Nicaragua: A Revolution under Siege*, London, 1985, 47–48.

Table 4. Enrollment by Level of Education, Selected Years, 1970–87

Level of Education	1970	1980	1985	1987
Primary school	285,300	472,200	561,600	583,700
Middle school and high school	42,200	120,500	100,000	132,700
Vocational school	4,441	16,661	41,749	33,241
Teachers' college	1,757	2,560	9,570	11,228
University	9,385	35,268	29,000	26,878

Source: Based on information from Germany, Statistisches Bundesamt, *Länderbericht: Nicaragua, 1991*, Wiesbaden, 1991, 35.

Table 5. Selected Economic Indicators, 1980–92
(in billions of United States dollars unless otherwise indicated)

Indicator	1980	1981	1982	1983	1984	1985	1986	1987	1988	1989	1990	1991	1992[1]
Real GDP[2]	2.08	2.19	2.17	2.27	2.23	2.15	2.13	2.11	1.88	1.82	1.75	1.72	1.71
Real GDP growth[3]	4.6	5.4	-0.8	4.6	-1.6	-4.1	-1.0	-0.7	-10.9	-3.0	-4.0	-0.7	-0.5
Real GDP per capita[4]	750	765	734	743	708	656	628	603	520	487	453	435	423
Real GDP per capita growth[3]	1.2	1.9	-4.0	1.2	-4.7	-7.3	-4.3	-4.0	-13.6	-6.2	-7.1	-4.0	-12.1
Inflation[3]	35	24	25	31	35	220	682	912	14,316	4,770	12,338	400	10
Trade balance[5]	-397	-472	-364	-397	-399	-562	-495	-522	-562	-312	-230	-415	-507
Overall balance of payments[5]	-511	-195	-236	-461	-405	-417	-943	-715	-567	-651	-728	-682	n.a.[6]
External debt	1.59	2.30	2.78	3.38	3.95	4.58	5.32	6.27	6.77	8.07	10.6	10.5	10.1

[1] Estimated.
[2] GDP—gross domestic product; in constant 1980 United States dollars.
[3] In percentages.
[4] In United States dollars.
[5] In millions of United States dollars.
[6] n.a.—not available.

Source: Based on information from United States, Agency for International Development, *Latin America and the Caribbean: Selected Economic Data*, Washington, 1992, 122; and *Latin America Monitor*, London, 10, No. 6, July 1993, 1174.

Table 6. Major Trading Partners, 1984, 1989, and 1991
(in percentages)

Country	1984	1989	1991
Exports			
Germany[1]	14.2	21.1	14.0
Japan	11.5	6.7	11.0
Soviet Union	2.2	2.9	n.a.[2]
Canada	0.4	21.1	11.0
United States	n.a.	0.0	16.4
Imports			
Mexico	41.1	12.2	n.a.
Costa Rica	12.2	9.0	7.8
Soviet Union	10.3	19.4	10.1
Cuba	8.1	15.3	8.0
United States	n.a.	0.0	21.3
Venezuela	n.a.	n.a.	7.1

[1] Prior to 1990, for West Germany only. In 1991 for Germany.
[2] n.a.—not available.

Source: Based on information from Economist Intelligence Unit, *Country Profile: Nicaragua, Costa Rica, Panama, 1991–92*, London, 1991, 26; and Economist Intelligence Unit, *Country Report: Nicaragua, Costa Rica, Panama*, London, No. 4, 1992, 8.

Table 7. Production of Selected Commodities, 1985–89
(in thousands of tons)

Commodity	1985	1986	1987	1988	1989
Bananas	127	101	119	144	132
Beef	42	45	40	33	29
Coffee	50	43	37	43	42
Corn	234	234	277	280	299
Cotton	69	49	49	33	22
Rice	156	144	149	111	104
Shrimp and lobster ...	3	3	2	3	3
Sugarcane	2,831	2,810	2,575	1,932	2,300

Source: Based on information from Economist Intelligence Unit, *Country Profile: Nicaragua, Costa Rica, Panama, 1991–92*, London, 1991, 18.

Table 8. Principal Exports, 1984–88
(in millions of United States dollars)

Commodity	1984	1985	1986	1987	1988
Bananas	12	16	16	15	15
Coffee	122	118	110	133	85
Cotton	134	94	44	46	53
Beef	18	11	5	15	19
Shrimp and lobster . . .	13	13	9	14	4
Sugarcane	21	7	17	14	5

Source: Based on information from Economist Intelligence Unit, *Country Profile: Nicaragua,
Costa Rica, Panama, 1991–92*, London, 1991, 25.

Table 9. National Assembly Seats, Elections of 1985 and 1990

Party	1985	1990
FSLN[1]	61	39
MAP-ML[2]	2	—[3]
MUR[4]	0	1
PCdeN[5]	2	—[3]
PCD[6]	14	—[3]
PLI[7]	9	—[3]
PPSC[8]	6	—[3]
PSC[9]	0	1
PSN[10]	2	—[3]
UNO[11]	n.a.[12]	51
TOTAL	96	92

[1] Frente Sandinista de Liberación Nacional (Sandinista National Liberation Front).
[2] Movimiento de Acción Popular–Marxista-Leninista (Popular Action Movement–Marxist-Leninist).
[3] Part of the UNO coalition in 1990.
[4] Movimiento de Unidad Revolucionaria (Revolutionary Unity Movement).
[5] Partido Comunista de Nicaragua (Communist Party of Nicaragua).
[6] Partido Conservador Demócrata (Democratic Conservative Party).
[7] Partido Liberal Independiente (Independent Liberal Party).
[8] Partido Popular Social Cristiano (Popular Social Christian Party).
[9] Partido Social Cristiano (Social Christian Party).
[10] Partido Socialista Nicaragüense (Nicaraguan Socialist Party).
[11] Unión Nacional Opositora (National Opposition Union). Coalition formed to compete in the 1990
    election.
[12] n.a.—not applicable.

Source: Based on information from *The Europa Year Book, 1988*, 2, London, 1988; and *South
America, Central America, and the Caribbean, 1993*, London, 1993, 475.

Table 10. UNO Political Parties, 1992[1]

Party	Orientation	Leader
APC[2].............	right	Míriam Argüello Morales
MDN[3]..........	center	Roberto Urroz Castillo
PAN[4]............	-do-	Eduardo Rivas Gasteazoro
PANC[5]	right	Hernaldo Zúñiga Montenegro
PCdeN[6].........	left	Eli Altimirano
PCN[7].............	right	Silviano Matamoros Lacayo
PDCN[8]	center	Agustín Jarquín Anaya
PICA[9]	-do-	Alejandro Pérez Arévalo
PL[10]	-do-	Andrés Zúñiga Mercado
PLC[11]	right	José Somarriba
PLI[12]............	center	Virgilio Godoy Reyes
PPSC[13]	-do-	Luis Guzmán
PSD[14]	-do-	Guillermo Potoy
PSN[15]	left	Gustavo Tablada Zelaya

[1] UNO–Unión Nacional Opositora (National Opposition Union). The APC, PANC, and PCN announced in 1992 that they would merge as the National Conservative Party (Partido Conservador Nationalista–PCN) for the 1996 elections.
[2] Alianza Popular Conservadora (Popular Conservative Alliance).
[3] Movimiento Democrático Nicaragüense (Nicaraguan Democratic Movement).
[4] Partido de Acción Nacional (National Action Party).
[5] Partido de Acción Nacional Conservadora (Conservative National Action Party).
[6] Partido Comunista de Nicaragua (Communist Party of Nicaragua).
[7] Partido Conservador Nacional (National Conservative Party).
[8] Partido Demócrata de Confianza Nacional (Democratic Party of National Confidence).
[9] Partido Integracionalista Centroamericano (Central American Integrationist Party).
[10] Partido Liberal (Liberal Party).
[11] Partido Liberal Constitucionalista (Liberal Constitutionalist Party).
[12] Partido Liberal Independiente (Independent Liberal Party).
[13] Partido Popular Social Cristiano (Social Christian Popular Party).
[14] Partido Social Demócrata (Social Democratic Party).
[15] Partido Socialista Nicaragüense (Nicaraguan Socialist Party).

Table 11. Non-UNO Political Parties, 1992[1]

Party	Orientation	Leader
FSLN[2]	left	Daniel José Ortega Saavedra
MUR[3]	-do-	Moisés Hassan Morales
PCD[4]	right	José Brenes
PCSN[5]	center	Erick Ramírez Benevente
PLIUN[6]	-do-	Rodolfo Robelo
PMLN[7]	left	Isidro Téllez Toruño
PPSCA[8]	center	Mauricio Díaz Dávila
PRT[9]	left	Bonifacio Miranda
PS[10]	right	Fernando Agüero
PUCA[11]	-do-	Blanca Rojas
PUNC[12]	-do-	William Estrada

[1] UNO—Unión Nacional Opositora (National Opposition Union). The PCD announced that it would merge with three UNO parties as the Nicaraguan Conservative Party (Partido Conservador Nicaragüense) for the 1996 elections.
[2] Frente Sandinista de Liberación Nacional (Sandinista National Liberation Front).
[3] Movimiento de Unidad Revolucionaria (Revolutionary Unity Movement).
[4] Partido Conservador Demócrata (Democratic Conservative Party).
[5] Partido Social Cristiano Nicaragüense (Nicaraguan Social Christian Party).
[6] Partido de Liberal Independiente de Unidad Nacional (Independent Liberal Party of National Unity).
[7] Partido Marxista-Leninista de Nicaragua (Nicaraguan Marxist-Leninist Party).
[8] Partido Popular Social Cristiano Auténtico (Authenthic Popular Social Christian Party).
[9] Partido Revolucionario de los Trabajadores (Workers' Revolutionary Party).
[10] Partido Socialconservadismo (Social Conservative Party).
[11] Partido Unionista Centroamericano (Central American Unionist Party).
[12] Partido de Unidad Nacional Conservadora (National Conservative Unity Party).

Table 12. Major Items of Military Equipment, 1993

Type and Description	Country of Origin	In Inventory
Sandinista People's Army		
Tanks		
T–55 (heavy)	Soviet Union	130[1]
PT–76 (light)..........................	-do-	22
Armored reconnaissance		
BRDM–2	-do-	80[1]
Armored personnel carriers		
BTR–60	-do-	19
BTR–152 (wheeled)	-do-	100[1]
Towed artillery		
D–30 (122mm)	-do-	36
D–20 (152mm)	-do-	60
Mortars		
82mm	–do–	500
M–43 (120mm).......................	-do-	20
M–160 (160mm)......................	-do-	n.a.[2]
Multiple rocket launchers		
Type 63 (107mm).....................	China	30
BM–21 (122mm)	Soviet Union	30
Antitank weapons		
AT–3 Sagger missile	-do-	12
ZIS–2 57mm gun	-do-	325
ZIS–3 76mm gun	-do-	84
M–1944 100mm gun...................	-do-	24
Surface-to-air missiles		
S–7/–14/–16 shoulder-fired.............	-do-	500
Sandinista Air Force/Air Defense Force		
Combat and counterinsurgency		
Cessna 337..........................	United States	6[3]
SF–260A............................	Italy	4
Transport		
An–2 (light)	Soviet Union	8
An–26 (medium)	-do-	5

Table 12. Major Items of Military Equipment, 1993

Type and Description	Country of Origin	In Inventory
Helicopters		
Mi–24/25 (attack)	-do-	2
Mi–8/–17	-do-	19
Air defense guns		
14.5mm, 23mm, 37mm, 57mm, 100mm ...	Various	800
Sandinista Navy		
Patrol craft		
Sin Hung	North Korea	3
Zhuk	Soviet Union	3
Vedette	France	2
Minehunters and minesweepers		
K–8	Poland	4[3]
Yevgenya	Soviet Union	7[3]

[1] Some stored.
[2] n.a.—not available.
[3] May be nonoperational.

Source: Based on information from *The Military Balance, 1993–1994*, London, 1993, 190; and *Jane's Fighting Ships, 1993–94*, Alexandria, 1993, 442.

Appendix B

Central American Common Market

THE CENTRAL AMERICAN COMMON MARKET (CACM), established by Guatemala, Honduras, El Salvador, and Nicaragua (and later joined by Costa Rica) with the signing of the General Treaty of Central American Economic Integration (Tratado General de Integración Económica Centroamericana) in Managua on December 15, 1960, was one of four regional economic integration organizations created during the Latin American export boom of the 1960s. The CACM and the three other Latin American trading blocs, the Latin American Free Trade Area, the Caribbean Free Trade Association (Carifta), and the Andean Group, were generally alike in their initial endorsement of regional integration behind temporary protectionist barriers as a way to continue import-substitution industrialization (ISI—see Glossary).

The basic strategy for development in Latin America was pioneered in the 1950s by Raúl Prebisch and the Economic Commission for Latin America and the Caribbean (ECLAC). The "ECLAC approach" applied a structuralist model of development that emphasized increasing private and public investment in manufacturing and infrastructure in order to overcome dependence on exports of primary commodities. Prebisch argued that continued overreliance on primary commodity exports as a source of foreign exchange would eventually lead to economic stagnation and economic contraction, as population growth and falling commodity prices would exert downward pressure on per capita gross domestic product (GDP—see Glossary). Concurrently, Prebisch and ECLAC recognized the inherent limitations of ISI based solely on manufacturing for single-country domestic markets. Particularly for the smaller countries of the Western Hemisphere, strictly domestic production of manufactured goods would quickly saturate local demand and would prematurely reduce returns on capital investment.

In order to overcome the limitations of single-country ISI, ECLAC proposed to expand the "local" market by means of common markets among like groups of countries. A common external tariff (CET) would allow nascent industries to develop by protecting local manufacturers from extraregional competition.

The ECLAC approach was advanced and widely accepted throughout the Western Hemisphere as an alternative to both the liberal export-led growth model and the previous single-country ISI approach. In practice, however, elements of all three models coexisted uneasily in most Latin American economies until the mid-1980s.

Despite their common adherence to the ECLAC model of intraregional free trade within a protectionist framework, the various Latin American trading blocs differed from each other in the size and economic structure of their member states, their intermediate goals, their institutions, their cohesiveness, and their relationships to the global economy. In the case of the CACM, economic disequilibria among member states, incomplete and unbalanced implementation of the ECLAC-inspired integration scheme, and the inherent limitations of a development model based on protection from global competition eventually undermined the CACM as originally conceived by ECLAC. The CACM's effectiveness waned following Honduras's withdrawal in the wake of the 1969 Soccer War with El Salvador. The CACM stagnated throughout the 1970s and virtually collapsed during the prolonged Central American (see Glossary) political and debt crises of the 1980s, revitalizing only after its overhaul and the partial inclusion of Panama in the early 1990s.

Institutions

The post-World War II movement toward Central American economic integration began with a wave of bilateral free trade treaties signed among Guatemala, Honduras, El Salvador, Nicaragua, and Costa Rica between 1950 and 1956. By the end of this period of bilateral negotiations, each country had become party to at least one of the treaties, which involved free trade in a limited range of products. The trend toward economic integration was further bolstered by the formation of the Organization of Central American States (Organización de Estados Centroamericanos—Odeca) in 1951. Although primarily a political entity, Odeca represented a significant step toward the creation of other regional multilateral organizations.

Economic cooperation at the multilateral level began to take shape under the auspices of ECLAC, which in August 1952 began sponsoring regular meetings of the Committee of Economic Cooperation, comprising the ministers of economic affairs of the five Central American republics. It was through the committee that ECLAC advanced the Prebisch model of coordinated industrialization within regional trading blocs. ECLAC's active consultancy efforts facilitated the signing in 1958–59 of three important integration agreements: the Multilateral Treaty on Free Trade and Central American Economic Integration (Tratado Multilateral de Libre Comercio e Integración Económica Centroamericana), the Integration Industries Convention (Régimen de Industrias de Integración—RII), and the Central American Tariff Equalization Convention (Convenio Centroamericano sobre Equiparación de Gravámenes a la Importación).

The Multilateral Treaty on Free Trade and Central American Economic Integration provided for intraregional free trade in 239 groups of Central American products and a ten-year phase-in of intraregional free trade in all Central American goods. The Central American Tariff Equalization Convention was a complementary agreement to the multilateral treaty, establishing a CET on 270 products, including all those listed under the treaty, and proposing a harmonization of tariffs on an additional 200 products within five years. The tariff equalization convention would thereby provide the common barrier to extraregional imports under which Central American producers would conduct a liberalized trade.

The RII was the most controversial component of the ECLAC program and would be the most difficult to implement. As originally conceived, the RII was to direct the flow of capital investment into the region by granting incentives and privileges to firms given "integration industries" status. In order to prevent costly duplication of capital investment, firms whose products had small consumer markets in the region would be given a virtual monopoly within the CACM. The Central American countries were supposed to distribute integration industry plants among themselves in an equitable and efficient manner.

The integration regime envisioned by the ECLAC-sponsored agreements never entered fully into force, but was instead superseded by the General Treaty of Central American Economic Integration, which became the basis for the CACM. The general treaty represented a compromise between the ECLAC-inspired approach and the policy preferences of the United States. The latter proposed several significant changes to the ECLAC integration scheme, the main difference being the establishment from the outset of intraregional free trade as the norm, rather than as the exception as provided for in the multilateral treaty. Under the United States plan, all products would be subject to intraregional free trade unless exempted. The United States was also opposed to the granting of monopoly status to integration industries within the region. In exchange for adoption of its plan, the United States would provide funding for the various institutions of the CACM and increase its economic aid to Central America.

In February 1960, Guatemala, El Salvador, and Honduras accepted the United States-sponsored integration scheme and signed the Tripartite Treaty (Tratado Tripartito) in Esquipulas, Guatemala, establishing intraregional free trade as the norm and excluding an RII mechanism. The Tripartite Treaty evoked strong objections from ECLAC, which saw its guiding role in Central American integration undermined by United States involvement in the process. In response to protests from ECLAC and the government of Nicaragua, the United States and the parties to the Tripartite Treaty agreed to negotiate a compromise integration treaty to supersede all prior free-trade agreements. The General Treaty of Central American Economic Integration was signed in Managua, Nicaragua, by four of the five republics (Costa Rica delayed signing by two years) on December 13, 1960, with ECLAC conceding on the free trade issue and the United States conceding on the inclusion of the RII. The general treaty went into effect for Guatemala, El Salvador, and Nicaragua in June 1961 and for Honduras and Costa Rica in April and July 1962, respectively.

In addition to the RII, the general treaty established a permanent secretariat, Secretaría Permanente del Tratado General de Integración Económica Centroamericana (SIECA), and a development bank, Banco Centroamericano de Integración Económica (BCIE). A Central American Clearing House (Cámara Centroamericana de Compensación de Monedas) was established in 1963 to promote the use of local currencies in the settlement of short-term trade deficits between pairs of CACM member states. A Central American Monetary Council (Consejo Monetario Centroamericano) was set up the following year to promote monetary union.

The CACM Experiment

During the 1960s and 1970s, the CACM had a significant

positive impact on trade flows in Central America. Intra-regional exports as a percentage of total exports grew dramatically—from 7 percent of total exports in 1960 to 26 percent in 1970—before declining to 23.4 percent in 1975 and to 14.7 percent in 1985. The total value of trade within the region grew from US$33 million in 1960 to US$1.1 billion in 1980, dropping to US$421 million in 1986. By 1967, 95 percent of all goods traded within the region had attained duty-free status, and 90 percent of traded goods were covered by the CET. The goods exempted from intraregional free trade were mainly traditional agricultural exports destined for global markets.

Most of the new intraregional trade was in consumer goods, a large share of which consisted of processed foods. By 1970 food processing was the single most prominent industrial activity within the CACM, accounting for approximately 50 percent of gross industrial output. The preference for consumer goods production was built into the CACM tariff structure, which imposed a high CET on extraregional consumer goods but did not impede the import of intermediate or capital goods.

In addition to the protection afforded to consumer goods production by the CET on consumer imports, CACM member states also promoted investment in industry by introducing generous tax incentives and exemptions for new and existing industrial firms. To help promote balanced development, the Central American Convention of Fiscal Incentives for Industrial Development (Convenio Centroamericano de Incentivos Fiscales al Desarollo Industrial) was signed among the then four CACM member states in 1962 to equalize the granting of tax incentives to industrial firms. The convention allowed Honduras and Nicaragua to offer temporarily broader tax breaks to industrial firms than the other two more industrialized republics. Honduras became the main beneficiary of this differentiated treatment, gaining in 1969 an extension of its preferential taxation status.

Another important incentive to industrial development within the CACM was the implementation of regional infrastructure development projects. Several development organizations were established during the 1960s to improve intraregional transport and communications: the Regional Telecommunications Commission (Comisión Técnica de las Telecomunicaciones de Centroamérica—Comtelca), the Central American Corporation of Air Navigation Services (Corporación Centroamericana de Servicios de Navegación Aérea—

Cocesna), the Central American Maritime Commission (Comisión Centroamericana de Transporte Marítimo—Cocatram), and the Central American Railways Commission (Comisión Centroamericana de Ferrocarriles—Cocafer). These organizations were financed mainly by the Regional Office for Central America and Panama (ROCAP) of the United States Agency for International Development (AID) as part of the Alliance for Progress initiative. AID/ROCAP also financed a Regional Highway Program to improve highway routes considered vital to intraregional trade.

Stagnation of the CACM

Despite the considerable expansion of intraregional trade and investment in Central America during the 1960s, by the end of the decade, the region had not yet achieved the balanced industrial growth nor the diversification of extraregional exports that was needed to maintain the momentum of the CACM.

This failure resulted in part from the Central American governments' inability to implement fiscal modernization or to overcome persistent structural trade deficits by the less developed economies of the region. Moreover, the gradual abandonment by regional economic planners of key components of the ECLAC model, particularly the goal of monetary union and the Integration Industries Convention, reduced the potential for joint action on a broad range of common challenges. Lack of progress on structural reforms of the Central American economies meant that the CACM would exist primarily as a customs union, rather than become an economic community. By the early 1980s, Central America's profound economic problems and political upheavals had undermined most CACM activities and institutions.

During the 1960s, Central American policy makers charged with implementing the ECLAC model were faced with a series of deeply ingrained social and political obstacles to economic modernization. Foremost among these were the structural biases in favor of traditional export agriculture that diverted capital from industrial investment and discouraged export diversification. Among the most pervasive structural biases were the antiquated tax systems that relied primarily on import tariffs as a source of revenue while undertaxing property and personal income. As free trade entered into force within the CACM, governments found themselves forfeiting a large share of their traditional revenues. In all of the republics except Costa Rica, political opposition to fiscal reform from the powerful landowning sector prevented governments from recovering the lost funds through property and income taxes. Pressure for fiscal reform was offset by a surplus of commercial bank credit during the 1970s, which allowed Central American governments to run consecutive fiscal deficits. When the flow of lending to Latin America ended abruptly in 1982, the burden of servicing Central American public and private debts caused a severe regional economic depression. The "lost decade" of the 1980s was characterized by macroeconomic instability, massive capital flight, and severe cutbacks in public services.

Monetary and credit policies were also strongly biased in favor of the traditional export sector, which enjoyed a sharp increase in commercial bank lending throughout the 1960s. In 1970 a large share of domestic credit was still being channeled to traditional export agriculture, which received three times as much credit as did industry. Moreover, interest rates for traditional agriculture were in some cases kept artificially much lower than the rates paid by industry and by nontraditional agriculture.

Despite these inconsistencies in public policy toward industrialization, manufacturing's contribution to GDP grew modestly in all of the region except Honduras during the 1960s. Industrial growth associated with the CACM was generally more capital intensive than manufacturing for domestic markets, where small, labor-intensive firms employing ten to twenty workers were the norm. Rather than producing the desired diversification of extraregional exports, however, Central America's industrial development stagnated at the stage of consumer goods production and became heavily dependent on capital-goods imports paid for with foreign exchange from traditional agricultural exports. The foreign exchange constraint that had existed before formation of the CACM remained essentially unchanged, as competitive export industries oriented toward global markets failed to develop under the CACM's protective CET.

Another major drawback of the CACM was its inability to compensate for disequilibria in capital endowments, in net export volume, and in productivity among more- and less-developed member states. As a result, intraregional trade imbalances became pronounced, and the CACM became polarized between the net creditors, Guatemala and El Salvador, and the net debtors, Honduras and Nicaragua. Costa Rica evolved from a net debtor to a net creditor.

The institutions created by the general treaty to alleviate structural imbalances among member states failed to operate as planned. One of the first CACM institutions to be deactivated was the Integration Industries Convention, which had been negotiated to help allocate capital investment rationally and fairly among member states. The convention had been a source of controversy from the beginning, having been opposed by the United States and excluded from the earlier Tripartite Treaty. When rivalries arose over the proposed location of plants, CACM institutions were unable to mediate the conflicts or to impose solutions. As a result, only two firms ever attained integration industries status, and the convention was effectively scrapped in the mid-1960s when a tire plant was established in Costa Rica to compete with an integration industries plant in Guatemala.

Another CACM institution that abandoned its original purpose was the Central American Clearing House. The clearing house had originally been designed to promote the use of local currencies in the settlement of intraregional trade deficits. The clearing house and the Central American Monetary Council were supposed to represent initial steps toward monetary union. By 1963, however, the CACM member states had allowed the monetary cooperation effort to lapse and were settling their trade deficits in United States dollars twice yearly. Little impetus remained to maintain exchange rate stability or currency convertibility within the CACM.

Rupture of the CACM

As the 1960s progressed, unbalanced growth and development among CACM member states began to take a serious toll on cooperative efforts in trade, monetary policy, and investment promotion. By the end of the decade, the CACM had reverted to an amorphous grouping of economies at different stages of development pursuing uncoordinated and sometimes antagonistic macroeconomic policies. The most acute conflict arose between Honduras and El Salvador over the issues of unbalanced trade, investment, and migration.

By the mid-1960s, chronic Honduran trade deficits with El Salvador and highly visible Salvadoran investment in Honduras had led to widespread Honduran indignation and a virtual Honduran boycott of Salvadoran products. Meanwhile,

300,000 Salvadoran migrants displaced by the expansion of export agriculture in their country had settled across the border in Honduras. Capitalizing on the widespread sentiment against Salvadoran "encirclement," the government of Honduran President Oswaldo López Arellano (1963–71) attempted to expel Salvadoran squatters under the pretext of land reform. Increasing tensions throughout the summer of 1969 erupted into hostilities on July 14, when Salvadoran air and land units made an incursion into Honduran territory. The ensuing four-day war claimed 2,000 lives and led to the forced repatriation of about 150,000 Salvadorans.

Diplomatic and commercial relations between El Salvador and Honduras were suspended for a decade thereafter, as was air transport between the two countries. Honduras withdrew from the CACM in December 1970, after it failed to persuade the other member states to enact further reforms in its favor. Honduras subsequently conducted trade with CACM countries on a bilateral basis until 1986. Honduras's withdrawal from the CACM, although not significant in terms of lost trade volume, represented a symbolic collapse of the organization as a vehicle for promoting coordinated regional growth. The prospects for integration had already dimmed considerably prior to the Soccer War, as evidenced by the piecemeal abandonment of major components of the original ECLAC integration plan.

Reactivation of Integration

Despite Honduras's withdrawal from the CACM and its suspension of commercial relations with El Salvador, Central American intraregional trade rose steadily throughout the 1970s, exceeding US$1 billion by 1980, before halving in the mid-1980s as a result of accumulated intraregional debts, the overall debt crisis, and the disruption caused by civil wars in El Salvador and Nicaragua. Most efforts to coordinate industrial and macroeconomic policies had been abandoned, however, well before the general treaty expired in 1982.

A reactivation of Central American economic integration was made possible with the signing of the Central American Peace Agreement (Esquipulas II) in August 1987. Esquipulas II laid the political groundwork for concerted action to renew the integration system following restoration of peace and democracy in the region. Formal action to restart the integration process was taken at the eighth summit of Central American presidents, held in Antigua, Guatemala, in June 1990. The participants at the Antigua summit approved the Economic Action Plan for Central America (Plan de Acción Económico de Centroamérica—Paeca), which foresaw a new conceptual and legal basis for a Central American economic community.

The new integration initiative emphasizes insertion of the region's economy into the global economy based on export-led growth. The industrial base established under the CACM will be retrofitted and modernized to compete in the international marketplace, and nontraditional exports will be promoted more vigorously. Concurrently, the maximum CET for the region is to be reduced from 40 percent to 20 percent and is expected to average between 10 percent and 15 percent for most products. With assistance from the European Community (EC), now the European Union (EU), a new Central American Payments System is being established to settle intraregional debts. The main components of this new payments system are a revised Central American Clearing House and a Special Foreign Currencies Fund. The new payments system, backed by a 120 million European Currency Unit (ECU—see Glossary) support fund, is designed to manage intraregional creditor-debtor relations multilaterally, rather than bilaterally as under the previous regime, so that trade deficits will be incurred against the system rather than against individual countries. In addition, the Special Currencies Fund, which is backed by an initial EU support fund of 30 million ECUs, will help the less developed countries in the region finance the building and improvement of export-related infrastructure.

Further progress toward integration was made at the tenth Central American presidential summit, held in San Salvador, El Salvador, in July 1991, when the original participants agreed to include Panama in certain aspects of the new economic community. The eleventh summit, held in Tegucigalpa, Honduras, modified several CACM institutions and incorporated them into the System of Central American Integration (Sistema de Integración Centroamericana—SICA), an umbrella organization encompassing both political and economic integration efforts. Honduras fully rejoined the integration process in February 1992, upon the signing of the Transitional Multilateral Free Trade Agreement with the other Central American republics.

Central American integration was given a further boost with the signing of the North American Free Trade Agreement (NAFTA) among Canada, Mexico, and the United States. In

August 1992, a Framework Free Trade Agreement was signed among the five Central American republics and Mexico, establishing the procedures for the formation of a free-trade area projected to enter into force in December 1996. Inclusion of Central America in a free-trade area with Colombia and Venezuela was also foreseen in the Caracas Commitment adopted at a regional summit in February 1993. Guatemala's recognition of Belize in September 1991 made it possible to begin free-trade agreement talks with the Caribbean Community and Common Market (Caricom), the successor to Carifta. Central America's economic convergence with NAFTA, the G-3 (Mexico, Colombia, and Venezuela), and Caricom is expected to further the objectives of the United States-sponsored Enterprise for the Americas Initiative (see Glossary), which foresees the eventual formation of a Western Hemisphere free-trade zone.

*   *   *

Several detailed studies of the institutional development of the CACM through the 1980s are available; however, no comprehensive treatment of Central American economic integration efforts since Esquipulas II has yet been published. The earlier works include *Economic Integration in Central America*, an extensive 1978 study edited by William R. Cline and Enrique Delgado; and Victor Bulmer-Thomas's *The Political Economy of Central America Since 1920*, which places the CACM within the context of historical patterns of development in the region. More recent information on economic and political integration efforts in Central America can best be obtained from biannual issues of *Revista de la Integración y el Desarollo de Centroamérica*, published by the BCIE, and various numbers of *Panorama Centroamericano*, published by the Instituto Centroamericano de Estudios Políticos. Statistical data on CACM member states are available from various SIECA publications, including *Cuadernos de la SIECA, Estadísticas Analíticas del Comercio Intracentroamericano*, and *Series Estadísticas Seleccionadas de Centroamérica*. Current reporting of Central American economic developments is available from *Latin American Weekly Report, Latin America Monitor,* and the Economist Intelligence Unit's *Country Reports* and *Country Profiles* on Central American countries. (For further information and complete citations, see Bibliography.)

Bibliography

Chapter 1

Anderson, Thomas P. *Politics in Central America: Guatemala, El Salvador, Honduras, and Nicaragua.* New York: Praeger, 1988.

Bailey, T.A. "Interest in a Nicaraguan Canal, 1903–1931," *Hispanic American Historical Review,* 16, No. 1, February 1936, 2–28.

Bermann, Karl. *Under the Big Stick: Nicaragua and the United States since 1848.* Boston: South End Press, 1986.

Blachman, Morris J., William LeoGrande, and Kenneth E. Sharpe (eds.). *Confronting Revolution: Security Through Diplomacy in Central America.* New York: Pantheon, 1986.

Black, George. *Triumph of the People: The Sandinista Revolution in Nicaragua.* London: Zed Press, 1981.

Booth, John A. "Celebrating the Demise of *Somocismo*: Fifty Recent Sources on the Nicaraguan Revolution," *Latin American Research Review,* 17, No. 1, 1982, 173–89.

_____. *The End and the Beginning: The Nicaraguan Revolution.* Boulder, Colorado: Westview Press, 1985.

Brody, Reed. *Contra Terror in Nicaragua. Report of a Fact-finding Mission: September 1984-January 1985.* Boston: South End Press, 1985.

Burns, E. Bradford. *Patriarch and Folk: The Emergence of Nicaragua, 1798–1858.* Cambridge: Harvard University Press, 1991.

Carr, Albert H.Z. *The World and William Walker.* Westport, Connecticut: Greenwood Press, 1975.

Castro, Vanessa, and Gary Prevost (eds.). *The 1990 Elections in Nicaragua and Their Aftermath.* Lanham, Maryland: Rowman and Littlefield, 1992.

Child, Jack. *The Central American Peace Process, 1983–1991: Sheathing Swords, Building Confidence.* Boulder, Colorado: Lynne Rienner, 1992.

Cole Chamorro, Alejandro. *Desde Sandino hasta los Somoza.* Granada, Nicaragua: Editorial el Mundo, 1971.

Collinson, Helen (ed.). *Women and Revolution in Nicaragua.* London: Zed Press, 1990.

Conrad, Robert Edgar (ed.). *Sandino: The Testimony of a Nicaraguan Patriot, 1921–1934.* Princeton, New Jersey: Princeton University Press, 1990.

Crawley, Eduardo. *Nicaragua in Perspective.* New York: St. Martin's Press, 1984.

Dematteis, Lou (ed.). *Nicaragua: A Decade of Revolution.* New York: Norton, 1991.

Denny, Harold Norman. *Dollars for Bullets: The Story of American Rule in Nicaragua.* Westport, Connecticut: Greenwood Press, 1980.

Diederich, Bernard. *Somoza and the Legacy of U.S. Involvement in Central America.* New York: Dutton, 1981.

Dodson, Michael, and Laura Nuzzi O'Shaughnessy. *Nicaragua's Other Revolution: Religious Faith and Political Struggle.* Chapel Hill: University of North Carolina Press, 1990.

Dore, Elizabeth. "Nicaragua: The Experience of the Mixed Economy." Pages 319–50 in Jonathan Hartlyn and Samuel A. Morley (eds.), *Latin American Political Economy: Financial Crisis and Political Change.* Boulder, Colorado: Westview Press, 1986.

Dunkerley, James. *Power in the Isthmus: A Political History of Modern Central America.* London: Verso, 1990.

Edwards, Mike. "Nicaragua, Nation in Conflict." *National Geographic,* 168, No. 6, June 1985, 786.

Eich, Dieter, and Carlos Rincón. *The Contras: Interviews with Anti-Sandinistas.* San Francisco: Synthesis, 1985.

Floyd, Troy S. *The Anglo-Spanish Struggle for Mosquitia.* Albuquerque: University of New Mexico Press, 1967.

Folkman, David I., Jr. *The Nicaragua Route.* Salt Lake City: University of Utah Press, 1972.

Gilbert, Dennis L. *Sandinistas: The Party and the Revolution.* New York: Basil Blackwell, 1988.

Goodman, Louis W., William M. LeoGrande, and Johanna Mendelson Forman (eds.). *Political Parties and Democracy in Central America.* Boulder, Colorado: Westview Press, 1992.

Gutman, Roy. *Banana Diplomacy: The Making of American Policy in Nicaragua, 1981–87.* New York: Simon and Shuster, 1988.

Halftermeyer, Gratus. *Historia de Managua: data desde el siglo XVIII hasta hoy.* (5th ed.) Managua: Talleres de la Impresa Nacional, 1972.

Hartlyn, Jonathan, and Samuel A. Morley (eds.). *Latin American Political Economy: Financial Crisis and Political Change.* Boulder, Colorado: Westview Press, 1986.

Heyck, Denis Lynn Daly (ed.). *Life Stories of the Nicaraguan Revolution.* New York: Routledge, 1990.

Hodges, Donald Clark. *Intellectual Foundations of the Nicaraguan Revolution.* Austin, Texas: University of Texas Press, 1986.

Kamman, William. *A Search for Stability: United States Diplomacy Toward Nicaragua, 1925–1933.* Notre Dame, Indiana: University of Notre Dame Press, 1968.

Karnes, Thomas L. *The Failure of Union: Central America, 1824–1975.* Tempe, Arizona: Center for Latin American Studies, Arizona State University, 1976.

Keen, Benjamin. *A History of Latin America.* (4th ed.) Boston: Houghton Mifflin, 1992.

_____. *Latin American Civilization: History and Society, 1492 to the Present.* (5th ed.) Boulder, Colorado: Westview Press, 1991.

Latin American Studies Association (LASA). *The Nicaraguan Elections of November, 1984: Report of the Delegation of the Latin American Studies Association.* Austin, Texas: University of Texas Press, 1984.

López, Julio, and Serres Chamorro. *La caída del Somocismo y la lucha Sandinista en Nicaragua.* San José, Costa Rica: Editorial Universitaria Centroamericana, 1979.

Macaulay, Neill. *The Sandino Affair.* Durham, North Carolina: Duke University Press, 1985.

MacLeod, Murdo J. *Spanish Central America: A Socioeconomic History, 1520–1720.* Berkeley: University of California Press, 1973.

Mijeski, Kenneth J. (ed.). *The Nicaraguan Constitution of 1987: English Translation and Commentary.* Athens: Ohio University, Center for International Studies, 1991.

Millett, Richard L. "Anastasio Somoza García: A Brief History of Nicaragua's 'Enduring' Dictator," *Revista Interamericana* [San Juan, Puerto Rico], 7, No. 3, Fall 1977, 486–508.

_____. *Guardians of the Dynasty.* Maryknoll, New York: Orbis Books, 1977.

_____. "Nicaragua: A Glimmer of Hope?" *Current History,* 89, No. 543, January 1990, 21–24, 35–37.

Miranda, Roger, and William Ratliff. *The Civil War in Nicaragua: Inside the Sandinistas.* New Brunswick, New Jersey: Transaction, 1992.

Pastor, Robert A. *Condemned to Repetition: The United States and Nicaragua.* Princeton, New Jersey: Princeton University Press, 1987.

Ortega Saavedra, Humberto. *Cincuenta años de lucha Sandinista.* Havana: Editorial de Ciencias Sociales, 1980.

Robinson, William I., and Kent Norsworthy. "Elections and U.S. Intervention in Nicaragua," *Latin American Perspectives,* 12, No. 2, Spring 1985, 83–110.

Rosset, Peter, and John Vandermeer (eds.). *Nicaragua: Unfinished Revolution. The New Nicaragua Reader.* New York: Grove Press, 1986.

Skidmore, Thomas E., and Peter H. Smith. *Modern Latin America.* (3d ed.) New York: Oxford University Press, 1992.

Spalding, Rose J. (ed.). *The Political Economy of Revolutionary Nicaragua.* Boston: Allen and Unwin, 1987.

Stimson, Henry Lewis. *American Policy in Nicaragua: The Lasting Legacy.* New York: Markus Wiener, 1991.

Stone, Doris Z. "Synthesis of Lower Central American Ethnohistory." Pages 209–33 in Robert Wauchope (ed.), *Handbook of Middle American Indians,* 4. Austin: University of Texas Press, 1966.

Uhlig, Mark A. "Nicaragua's Permanent Crisis: Ruling from Above and Below," *Survival,* 33, September/October 1991, 401–23.

United Nations. Economic Commission for Latin America and the Caribbean. *Damage Caused by Hurricane Joan in Nicaragua: Its Effect on Economic Development and Living Conditions, and Requirements for Rehabilitation and Reconstruction.* New York: December 2, 1988.

Walker, Thomas W. (ed.). *Nicaragua: The First Five Years.* New York: Praeger, 1985.

_____. (ed.). *Revolution and Counterrevolution in Nicaragua.* Boulder, Colorado: Westview Press, 1991.

Williams, Mary Wilhelmine. *Anglo-American Isthmian Diplomacy 1815–1915.* (American Historical Association series.) Gloucester, Massachusetts: P. Smith, 1965.

Woodward, Ralph Lee, Jr. *Central America: A Nation Divided.* (2d ed.) New York: Oxford University Press, 1985.

Wyden, Peter. *Bay of Pigs: The Untold Story.* New York: Simon and Schuster, 1979.

(The following periodicals were also used in the preparation of this chapter: *Barricada* [Managua], 1990–92; *Central America Report* [Guatemala], 1989–92; *El Nuevo Diario* [Managua], 1990–92; *Latin America Political Report* [London], 1989–92; and *La Prensa* [Managua], 1990–92.)

Chapter 2

Arnove, Robert R. *Education and Revolution in Nicaragua.* New York: Praeger, 1986.

Banberger, Ellen L. *Construcción de la democracia en Nicaragua.* Managua: Escuela de Sociología, Universidad Centroamericana, 1989.

Barndt, Deborah. "Popular Education." Pages 317–46 in Thomas W. Walker (ed.), *Nicaragua: The First Five Years.* New York: Praeger, 1985.

Barry, Tom. *Central America Inside Out: The Essential Guide to Its Societies, Politics, and Economics.* New York: Grove Weidenfeld, 1991.

Baumeister, Eduardo. "Agrarian Reform." Pages 229–45 in Thomas W. Walker (ed.), *Revolution and Counterrevolution in Nicaragua.* Boulder, Colorado: Westview Press, 1991.

Biondi-Morra, Brizio N. *Revolución y política alimentaria: un análisis crítico de Nicaragua.* Mexico, D.F.: Siglo Ventiuno Editores, 1990.

Bossert, Thomas John. "Health Policy: The Dilemma of Success." Pages 346–64 in Thomas W. Walker (ed.), *Nicaragua: The First Five Years.* New York: Praeger, 1985.

Bourgois, Philippe I., and Charles Holy. "The Atlantic Coast of Nicaragua." Pages 135–40 in Neil Snarr (ed.), *Sandinista Nicaragua: An Annotated Bibliography with Analytical Introductions.* Ann Arbor: Pierian Press, 1989.

Bradstock, Andrew. *Saints and Sandinistas: The Catholic Church in Nicaragua and Its Response to the Revolution.* London: Epworth Press, 1987.

Brown, Phyllidia. "Decline of Public Health Takes Its Toll in Nicaragua," *New Scientist,* 130, No. 1,763, April 6, 1991, 10.

Bulmer-Thomas, Victor. *The Political Economy of Central America since 1920.* New York: Cambridge University Press, 1987.

The Cambridge Encyclopedia of Latin America and the Caribbean. (Eds., Simon Collier, Harold Blakemore, and Thomas E. Skidmore.) New York: Cambridge University Press, 1985.

Centro de Investigaciones y Documentación de la Costa Atlántica. *Trabil Nani: Miskito For "Many Troubles": Historical Background and Current Situation of the Atlantic Coast of Nicaragua.* Managua: 1985.

Centro de Investigación y Estudios de la Reforma Agraria (CIERA). *La Mosquitia en la Revolución.* Managua: 1981.

Chuchryk, Patricia M. "Women in the Revolution." Pages 143–65 in Thomas Walker (ed.), *Revolution and Counterrevolution in Nicaragua.* Boulder, Colorado: Westview Press, 1991.

Close, David. *Nicaragua: Politics, Economics, and Society.* New York: Pinter, 1988.

Collins, Joseph, and Paul Rice. *Nicaragua: What Difference Could a Revolution Make?* San Francisco: Institute for Food and Development Policy, 1985.

Collinson, Helen, and Lucinda Broadbent (eds.). *Women and Revolution in Nicaragua.* Atlantic Highlands, New Jersey: Zed Books, 1990.

Covington, Paula (ed.). *Latin America: A Critical Guide to Research Sources.* New York: Greenwood Press, 1992.

Criguillion, Ana. "La rebeldía de las mujeres Nicaragüenses: semillero de una nueva democracia." Pages 159–95 in Ellen L. Banberger, *Construcción de la democracia en Nicaragua.* Managua: Escuela de Sociología, Universidad Centroamericana, 1989.

Diskin, Martin. "The Manipulation of Indigenous Struggles." Pages 80–96 in Thomas W. Walker (ed.), *Reagan Versus the Sandinistas: The Undeclared War on Nicaragua.* Boulder, Colorado: Westview Press, 1987.

Dodson, Michael, and Laura Nuzzi O'Shaughnessy. *Nicaragua's Other Revolution: Religious Faith and Political Struggle.* Chapel Hill: University of North Carolina Press, 1990.

Donahue, John M. *The Nicaraguan Revolution in Health: From Somoza to the Sandinistas.* South Hadley, Massachusetts: Bergin and Garvey, 1986.

Dozier, Craig L. *Nicaragua's Mosquito Shore: The Years of British and American Presence.* Tuscaloosa, Alabama: University of Alabama Press, 1985.

Enrique, Laura J. *Harvesting Change: Labor and Agrarian Reform in Nicaragua, 1979–90.* Chapel Hill: University of North Carolina Press, 1991.

The Europa World Year Book, 1991. London: Europa, 1991.

Fagen, Richard, Carmen Diana Deere, and José Luis Corragio (eds.). *Transition and Development: Problems of Third World Socialism.* New York: Monthly Review Press, 1986.

Federal Republic of Germany. Statistisches Bundesamt. *Länderbericht: Nicaragua, 1988.* Wiesbaden: 1988.

_____. Statistisches Bundesamt. *Länderbericht: Nicaragua, 1991.* Wiesbaden: 1991.

Garfield, Richard. "War-Related Changes in Health and Health Services in Nicaragua," *Social Science and Medicine,* 28, No. 7, 1989, 669–76.

Garfield, Richard, and Glen Williams. *Health and Revolution: The Nicaraguan Experience.* New York: Oxford University Press, 1992.

Gilbert, Dennis L. *Sandinistas: The Party and the Revolution.* New York: Basil Blackwell, 1988.

Gilbert, Dennis L., and Braulio Muñoz. "Sociology." Pages 711–20 in Paula Covington (ed.), *Latin America: A Critical Guide to Research Sources.* New York: Greenwood Press, 1992.

Girald, Giulo. *Faith and Revolution in Nicaragua: Convergence and Contradictions.* Maryknoll, New York: Orbis Books, 1989.

Harris, Richard L. "The Economic Transformation and Industrial Development of Nicaragua." Pages 47–48 in Richard L. Harris and Carlos M. Vilas (eds.), *Nicaragua: A Revolution under Siege.* London: Zed Books, 1985.

Harris, Richard L., and Carlos M. Vilas (eds.). *Nicaragua: A Revolution under Siege.* London: Zed Books, 1985.

Haslam, David. *Faith in Struggle: The Protestant Churches in Nicaragua and Their Response to the Revolution.* London: Epworth Press. 1987.

Inter-American Development Bank. *Economic and Social Progress in Latin America: Annual Report.* Washington: 1991.

Jenkins Molieri, Jorge. *El desafío indígena en Nicaragua: el caso de los mískitos.* Managua: Editorial Vanguardia, 1986.

Karnes, Thomas L. *Tropical Enterprise: The Standard Fruit and Steamship Company in Latin America.* Baton Rouge: Lousiana State University Press, 1978.

Lancaster, Roger N. *Thanks to God and the Revolution: Popular Religion in the New Nicaragua.* New York: Columbia University Press, 1988.

McLean, George F., Raul Molina, and Timothy Ready (eds.). *Culture, Human Rights, and Peace in Central America.* Lanham, Maryland: University Press of America, 1989.

Massey, Doreen B. *Nicaragua.* Philadelphia: Open University Press, 1988.

Mexico and Central American Handbook, 1991. (Ed., Ben Box.) Bath, United Kingdom: Trade and Travel, 1990.

Molyneux, Maxine. "Women." Pages 145–62 in Thomas W. Walker (ed.), *Nicaragua: The First Five Years.* New York: Praeger, 1985.

"Nicaragua: The Informal Sector in Transition." (Research paper.) Washington: Pan American Development Foundation, May 31, 1985.

Nicaragua. Instituto Nacional de Estadísticas y Censos. *Nicaragua: 10 años en cifras.* Managua: 1988.

Norsworthy, Kent. *Nicaragua: A Country Guide.* Albuquerque, New Mexico: Inter-Hemispheric Education Resource Center, 1990.

O'Shaughnessy, Laura Nuzzi, and Luis H. Serra. *The Church and the Revolution in Nicaragua.* Athens: Ohio University, Center for International Studies, Latin American Studies Program, 1986.

Peachy, Paul. "Modernization and the Sociology of the Family System in Central America." Pages 65–82 in George F. McLean, Raul Molina, Timothy Ready (eds.), *Culture, Human Rights, and Peace in Central America.* Lanham, Maryland: University Press of America, 1989.

Pérez Alemán, Paola. *10 Años de investigaciones sobre la mujer en Nicaragua, 1976–1986: informes.* Managua: Ministerio de la Presidencia, Oficina de la Mujer, 1986.

Pérez Alemán, Paola, and Ivonne Siu. *La mujer en la economía Nicaragüense: cambios y desafíos.* Managua: Ministerio de la Presidencia, Oficina de la Mujer, 1986.

Political Handbook of the World: 1991. (Ed., Arthur S. Banks.) Binghamton, New York: McGraw Hill, 1991.

Programa nacional de desarrollo social y superación de la pobreza. Managua: Ministerio de la Presidencia, March 1991.

Rodríguez, Ileana. *Obstáculos a la promoción y aplicación de la "Convención sobre la eliminación de todas las formas de discriminación contra la mujer: caso de Nicaragua".* Managua: Ministerio de la Presidencia, Oficina de la Mujer, 1987.

Sandiford, Peter. "Why Do Child Mortality Rates Fall? An Analysis of the Nicaragua Experience," *American Journal of Public Health,* 81, No. 1, January 1991, 30–38.

Snarr, Neil (ed.). *Sandinista Nicaragua: An Annotated Bibliography with Analytical Introductions.* Ann Arbor: Pierian Press, 1989.

Spalding, Rose J., (ed.). *The Political Economy of Revolutionary Nicaragua.* Boston: Allen and Unwin, 1987.

Stoll, David. *Is Latin America Turning Protestant? The Politics of Evangelical Growth.* Berkeley: University of California Press, 1990.

The Statesman's Yearbook, 1990–1991. (Ed., John Paxton.) New York: St. Martin's Press, 1990.

Stephens, Beth. "Women in Nicaragua," *Monthly Review,* 40, No. 4, September 1988, 1–18.

Strachan, Harry W. *Family and Other Business Groups in Economic Development: The Case of Nicaragua.* New York: Praeger, 1976.

United Nations. Centro Latinoamericano de Demografía. *Boletín Demográfico.* Santiago, Chile: January 1990.

_____. Economic Commission for Latin America and the Caribbean. *Statistical Yearbook for Latin America and the Caribbean, 1989.* Santiago, Chile: 1989.

_____. Statistical Office. *Statistical Yearbook, 1991.* New York: 1991.

United States. Agency for International Development. *Country Development Strategy, Nicaragua, 1991–1996.* Washington: 1990.

_____. Central Intelligence Agency. *The World Factbook, 1991.* Washington: GPO, 1991.

Vilas, Carlos María. *The Sandinista Revolution: National Liberation and Social Transformations in Central America.* New York: Monthly Review Press, 1986.

_____. *State, Class, and Ethnicity in Nicaragua: Capitalist Modernization and Revolutionary Change on the Atlantic Coast.* Boulder, Colorado: Lynne Rienner, 1989.

Walker, Thomas W. *Nicaragua: The Land of Sandino.* (3d ed.) Boulder, Colorado: Westview Press, 1991.

Walker, Thomas W. (ed.). *Nicaragua: The First Five Years.* New York: Praeger, 1985.

_____. *Reagan Versus the Sandinistas: The Undeclared War on Nicaragua.* Boulder, Colorado: Westview Press, 1987.

_____. *Revolution and Counterrevolution in Nicaragua.* Boulder, Colorado: Westview Press, 1991.

Webster's New Geographical Dictionary. Springfield, Massachusetts: Merriam-Webster, 1988.

West, Robert, and John P. Augelli. *Middle America: Its Lands and Peoples.* Englewood Cliffs, New Jersey: Prentice-Hall, 1989.

Williams, Harvey. "The Social Programs." Pages 87–93 in Thomas W. Walker (ed.), *Revolution and Counterrevolution in Nicaragua.* Boulder, Colorado: Westview Press, 1991.

The World Bank. *World Development Report, 1990.* New York: Oxford University Press, 1990.

_____. *World Development Report: The Challenge of Development.* New York: Oxford University Press, 1991.

(Various issues of the following publications were also used in the preparation of this chapter: *Business Latin America,* 1992; *Business Outlook,* 1991; *Central America Report* [London], 1991; *Christian Science Monitor,* 1990; *Envío* [Managua], 1990–93; *Latin America Monitor* [London]; *Latin American Newsletter* [London], 1993; *Natural History; New York Times; This Week in Central America.*)

Chapter 3

The Americas Review/World of Information, 1991–92. Saffron Walden, Essex, United Kingdom: World of Information, 1992.

Annis, Sheldon (ed.). *Poverty, Natural Resources, and Public Policy in Central America.* New Brunswick, New Jersey: Transaction, 1992.

Baez, William. *Nicaragua: The Informal Sector in Transition.* Washington: Pan American Development Foundation, 1985.

Biondi-Morra, Brizio N. *Hungry Dreams: The Failure of Food Policy in Revolutionary Nicaragua, 1979–90.* Ithaca, New York: Cornell University Press, 1993.

"Bottom Line: Tough Choices for Violeta." *This Week in Central America* [Guatemala City], 17, No. 43, November 5, 1990, 258.

Colburn, Forrest D. *Post-Revolutionary Nicaragua: State, Class, and the Dilemmas of Agrarian Policy.* Berkeley: University of California Press, 1986.

Conroy, Michael. *Nicaragua: Profiles of the Revolutionary Public Sector.* Boulder, Colorado: Westview Press, 1987.

Crosby, Benjamin. "Central America." Pages 103–38 in Anthony Lake (ed.), *After the Wars: Reconstruction in Afghanistan, Indochina, Central America, Southern Africa, and the Horn of Africa.* (United States-Third World Policy Perspectives Series, No. 16.) New Brunswick, New Jersey: Transaction, 1990.

Economist Intelligence Unit. *Country Profile: Nicaragua, Costa Rica, Panama, 1991–92.* London: 1992.

The Europa World Year Book, 1990. London: Europa, 1990.

Gibson, Bill, "The Inflation-Devaluation-Inflation Hypothesis in Nicaragua." *Journal of Development Studies,* 27, No. 2, January 1991, 241–42.

Inter-American Development Bank. *Economic and Social Progress in Latin America: Annual Report.* Washington: 1991.

International Monetary Fund, Office of Press Relations. "IMF Press Release No. 91/49." Washington: September 19, 1991.

Jenkins, Tony. *The United States Embargo Against Nicaragua–One Year Later.* Washington: Overseas Development Council, May 1986.

Lake, Anthony (ed.). *After the Wars: Reconstruction in Afghanistan, Indochina, Central America, Southern Africa, and the Horn of Africa.* (United States-Third World Policy Perspectives Series, No. 16.) New Brunswick, New Jersey: Transaction, 1990.

Leiken, Robert S., and Barry Rubin (eds.). *The Central American Crisis Reader.* New York: Summit Books, 1987.

Leonard, H. Jeffrey. *Environment and the Poor: Development Strategies for a Common Agenda.* (United States-Third World Policy Perspectives Series, No. 11.) New Brunswick, New Jersey: Transaction, 1989.

McCargar, James. "El Salvador and Nicaragua: The AFL-CIO Views on the Controversy." (Policy paper.) Washington: AFL-CIO, Department of International Affairs, 1985.

Nicaragua. Instituto Nacional de Estadísticas y Censos. *Nicaragua: 10 años en cifras.* Managua: 1989.

"Nicaragua Open for Business," *LA/C Business Bulletin,* 1, No. 3, March 1991, 1–4.

"Nicaragua Starts on the Long Road Back to the Future," *World Bank News,* October 3, 1991, 2–3.

Nietschmann, Bernard. "The Ecology of War and Peace," *Natural History,* 99, November 1990, 34–42, 44–48.

Norsworthy, Kent, and Tom Barry. *Nicaragua: A Country Guide.* Albuquerque, New Mexico: Inter-Hemispheric Education Resource Center, 1990.

Parry, Robert, and Peter Kornbluh. "Iran-Contra's Untold Story," *Foreign Policy,* 72, Fall 1988, 3–30.

Pelupessy, Wim (ed.). *Perspectives on the Agro-Export Economy in Central America.* Pittsburgh: University of Pittsburgh Press, 1991.

Ramírez, Sergio. "Election Night in Nicaragua," *Granta,* 36, Summer, 1991, 109–30.

Somoza Debayle, Anastasio, as told to Jack Cox. *Nicaragua Betrayed.* Boston: Western Islands, 1980.

United States. Agency for International Development. *Latin America and the Caribbean: Selected Economic Data.* Washington: 1992.

_____. Embassy in Managua. *1990 Foreign Economic Trends.* Washington: GPO, 1990.

Walker, Thomas W. (ed.) *Reagan Versus the Sandinistas: The Undeclared War on Nicaragua.* Boulder, Colorado: Westview Press, 1987.

Williams, Harvey. "The Social Impact in Nicaragua." Pages 247–64 in Thomas W. Walker (ed.), *Reagan Versus the Sandinistas: The Undeclared War on Nicaragua.* Boulder, Colorado: Westview Press, 1987.

World Refugee Survey, 1991. New York: United States Committee for Refugees, 1991.

(Various issues of the following publications were also used in the preparation of this chapter: *Business Latin America,* 1992; *Business Outlook,* 1991; *Central America Report* [London], 1991;

Christian Science Monitor, 1990; Economist Intelligence Unit, *Country Report: Nicaragua, Costa Rica, Panama* [London], 1991–92; Economist Intelligence Unit, *Country Report: Nicaragua, Honduras* [London], 1993–94; *Envío* [Managua], 1990–93; *Latin America Monitor* [London]; *Latin American Newsletter* [London], 1993; *Natural History; New York Times; This Week in Central America.*)

Chapter 4

Banks, Arthur S., (ed.), *Political Handbook of the World, 1993.* New York: McGraw-Hill, 1993.

Barry, Tom. *Central America Inside Out: The Essential Guide to Its Societies, Politics, and Economies.* New York: Grove Weidenfeld, 1991.

Bedard, Paul. "U.S. Searches for a Way to Bolster Chamorro's Tottering Government," *Washington Times,* September 7, 1990, A5.

Castro, Vanessa, and Gary Prevost (eds.). *The 1990 Elections in Nicaragua and Their Aftermath.* Lanham, Maryland: Rowman and Littlefield, 1992.

Christian, Shirley. "Disenchanted with Chamorro, Some Contras Are Taking Up Arms Again," *New York Times,* April 22, 1991, A3.

_____. "Ex-Contras Clash with Sandinistas," *New York Times,* August 2, 1991, A3.

_____. "Nicaragua Holds Suspect in Killing of Contra Chief," *New York Times,* March 6, 1991, A3.

_____. "Panicky Need for Farm Land Leads Nicaraguan Peasants into Fatal Clash," *New York Times,* March 6, 1991, A3.

_____. "Victors' Lament: To the Losers Belong the Spoils," *New York Times,* June 8, 1991, A2.

Cisneros, Julio, and José Luis Abalos, (eds.). *Legislación municipal de Nicaragua.* Valencia, Spain: Generalitat Valenciana, 1991.

Cody, Edward. "Up to 200 Disenchanted Contras Take Up Arms Again," *Washington Post,* April 9, 1991, A15.

Coone, Tim. "Nicaraguan Rights Battle Turns Violent," *Financial Times,* June 19, 1991, 3.

Díaz Lacayo, Aldo. *Diplomacia con dignidad.* Caracas, Venezuela: Ediciones Centauro, 1989.

Dickens, Samuel T. "Assassins in Managua," *New York Times,* April 16, 1991, A23.

Dillon, Sam. "Sloppy Work Slows Contra Death Probe," *Miami Herald,* May 13, 1991, A1, A11.

Dillon, Sam, and Karen Branch. "Managua: We'll Probe Contra's Death," *Miami Herald,* February 18, 1991. A6.

Doherty, William C. "Nicaragua's Second Piñata," *Wall Street Journal,* November 22, 1991, A3.

The Europa World Year Book, 1988, 2. London: Europa, 1988.

The Europa World Year Book, 1993, 2. London: Europa, 1993.

Gilbert, Dennis L. *Sandinistas: The Party and the Revolution.* New York: Basil Blackwell, 1988.

Hockstader, Lee. "Former Contra Rebels Take Up Arms Again in Nicaragua," *Washington Post,* June 29, 1991, A14, A16.

Howard, Jan. "Chamorro Faces New Contra Demands," *Miami Herald,* August 12, 1991, A6.

_____. "Nicaraguan Economic Plan Leaves Many Unemployed," *Miami Herald,* September 12, 1991, A12.

_____. "Taiwan Gives Nicaragua Loan to Help Repay Debt," *Miami Herald,* August 27, 1991, A5.

Hull, Jennifer Bingham. "Sandinistas Opt for Stability," *Christian Science Monitor,* July 24, 1991, 3.

Krauss, Clifford. "Chamorro Pleads with Congress for Aid," *New York Times,* April 17, 1991, A6.

Kurian, George Thomas (ed.). *Encyclopedia of the Third World,* 2. New York: Facts on File, 1993.

Lacayo, Antonio. "A New Nicaragua Deserves a New Reputation," *Wall Street Journal,* April 12, 1991, 1.

Meyer, Cord. "Confrontation in Nicaragua," *Washington Times,* November 15, 1991, A3.

Oppenheimer, Andres. "Sandinistas' New Careers May Refocus Their Politics," *Miami Herald,* April 2, 1991, C2.

Oquist, Paul. *Dinámica socio-política de las elecciones Nicaragüenses de 1990.* (2d ed.) Caracas: Fundación Friedrich Ebert, 1991.

Prevost, Gary. "The FSLN in Opposition." Pages 109–22 in Vanessa Castro and Gary Prevost (eds.), *The 1990 Elections in Nicaragua and Their Aftermath.* Lanham, Maryland: Rowman and Littlefield, 1992.

Robinson, Linda. "Nicaragua's $1 Billion Battle," *U.S. News and World Report,* July 29, 1991, 35–36.

Scott, David Clark. "Nicaraguan Government Seeks to Pacify Rearming Contras," *Christian Science Monitor*, August 14, 1991, 1–2.

Serafino, Nina M. "Nicaragua Chronology since the February 25, 1990, Elections: The Transition and President Chamorro's First 100 Days." (Library of Congress, Congressional Research Service, Report 90–423 F.) Washington: September 5, 1990.

_____. "Nicaragua's 'Civic' Opposition: Players, Problems and Prospects." (Library of Congress, Congressional Research Service, Report 87–735 F.) Washington: August 5, 1987.

South America, Central America, and the Caribbean, 1993. London: Europa, 1993.

Spalding, Rose J. *Capitalists and Revolution in Nicaragua: Opposition and Accommodation, 1979–93*. Chapel Hill: University of North Carolina Press, 1994.

Sullivan, Mark P. "Central America and U.S. Foreign Assistance: Congressional Action." (Library of Congress, Congressional Research Service, Major Issues System, IB84075.) Washington: December 7, 1992.

Tamayo, Juan O. "Nicaraguan Wants U.S. to Fund Sandinista Army Retirements," *Miami Herald*, June 26, 1991, A10.

Uhlig, Mark A. "Chamorro Party OKs Tough Property Law," *Miami Herald*, August 21, 1991, A8.

_____. "Chamorro's Kin Moving Against Her," *New York Times*, January 12, 1991, A3.

_____. "Nicaragua's Permanent Crisis: Ruling from Above and Below," *Survival*, 33, September-October 1991, 401–23.

_____. "Sandinistas' Booty Sets Off a Bitter Battle in Nicaragua," *New York Times*, June 25, 1991, A1, A2.

United States. Department of State. *Communiqué of the International Court of Justice: Military and Paramilitary Activities in and Against Nicaragua (Nicaragua v. United States of America) Judgment of the Court*. (Department of State Publication No. 86/8.) Washington: GPO, June 27, 1986.

_____. Department of State. Dispatch. *Nicaraguan President's Visit*. Washington: GPO, April 29, 1991.

Walker, Thomas W. *Nicaragua: The Land of Sandino*. (3d ed.) Boulder, Colorado: Westview Press, 1991.

(Various issues of the following publications were also used in the preparation of this chapter: *Barricada* [Managua]; *Christian Science Monitor*; *Current History*; *El Nuevo Diario* [Managua]; *Envío* [Managua]; *Financial Times*; Foreign Broadcast Information Service, *Daily Report: Latin America*; *Journal of Inter-American Studies and World Affairs*; *Journal of Latin American Studies*; *La Prensa* [Managua]; *Latin American Regional Reports. Mexico and Central America* [London]; *Miami Herald*; *New York Times*; *Wall Street Journal*; *Washington Post*; and *Washington Times* .)

Chapter 5

Americas Watch. *Fitful Peace: Human Rights and Reconciliation under the Chamorro Government.* New York: 1991.

_____. *Human Rights in Nicaragua: August 1987–August 1988.* New York: 1988.

Booth, John A. *The End and the Beginning: The Nicaraguan Revolution.* Boulder, Colorado: Westview Press, 1985.

Brás, Marisabel. "The Transformation of the Nicaraguan Army," *How They Fight: Armies of the World.* Washington: Department of Defense, Army Intelligence and Threat Analysis Center, July 1993, 47–56.

Dyer, Gwynne, and Adrian English. "Nicaragua." Pages 423–26 in John Keegan (ed.), *World Armies.* Detroit: Gale Research, 1983.

English, Adrian J. *Armed Forces of Latin America.* London: Jane's, 1984.

The Europa World Year Book, 1993, 2. London: Europa, 1993.

Gorman, Stephen M., and Thomas W. Walker. "The Armed Forces." Pages 91–118 in Thomas W. Walker (ed.) *Nicaragua: The First Five Years.* New York: Praeger, 1985.

Gutman, Roy. *Banana Diplomacy: The Making of American Policy in Nicaragua, 1981–87.* New York: Simon and Shuster, 1988.

Jane's Fighting Ships, 1993–94. (Ed., Richard Sharp.) Alexandria, Virginia: Jane's, 1993.

Keegan, John (ed.). *World Armies.* Detroit: Gale Research, 1993.

Kornbluh, Peter. "The Covert War." Pages 21–38 in Thomas W. Walker (ed.), *Reagan Versus the Sandinistas: The Underclared War on Nicaragua.* Boulder, Colorado: Westview Press, 1987.

McCoy, Jennifer L. "Nicaragua in Transition," *Current History,* 90, No. 554, March 1991, 117–20.

The Military Balance, 1993–94. London: Institute for Strategic Studies, 1993.

Montes, Julio. "Nicaragua in Crisis," *Jane's Intelligence Review* [London], 6, No. 1, January 1994, 45–47.

Norsworthy, Ken, and Tom Barry. *Nicaragua: A Country Guide.* Albuquerque, New Mexico: Inter-Hemispheric Education Resource Center, 1990.

Political Handbook of the World, 1993. New York: McGraw Hill, 1993.

Rosset, Peter, and John Vandermeer (eds.). *Nicaragua: Unfinished Revolution: The New Nicaragua Reader.* New York: Grove Press, 1986.

United States. Arms Control and Disarmament Agency. *World Military Expenditures and Arms Transfers, 1990.* Washington: GPO, 1991.

_____. Congress. 102th, 2d Session. Senate. Committee on Foreign Relations. *Nicaragua Today: A Republican Staff Report to the Committee on Foreign Relations, United States Senate.* Washington: GPO, 1992.

_____. Department of State. *Background Notes: Nicaragua.* Washington: GPO, 1993.

_____. Department of State. *Country Reports on Human Rights Practices for 1990.* (Report submitted to United States Congress, 102d, 1st Session, Senate, Committee on Foreign Relations and House of Representatives, Committee on Foreign Affairs.) Washington: GPO, 1991.

_____. Department of State. *Country Reports on Human Rights Practices for 1991.* (Report submitted to United States Congress, 102d, 2d Session, Senate, Committee on Foreign Relations and House of Representatives, Committee on Foreign Affairs.) Washington: GPO, 1992.

_____. Department of State. *Country Reports on Human Rights Practices for 1992* (Reported submitted to United States Congress, 103rd, 1st Session, Senate, Committee on Foreign Relations and House of Representatives, Committee on Foreign Affairs.) Washington: GPO, 1993.

_____. *Human Rights in Nicaragua under the Sandinistas: From Revolution to Repression.* Washington: GPO, 1986.

_____. *Inside the Sandinista Regime: A Special Investigator's Perspective.* Washington: GPO, 1986.

_____. *Nicaragua's Interior Ministry: Instrument of Political Consolidation.* Washington: GPO, 1987.

Vanderlaan, Mary B. *Revolution and Foreign Policy in Nicaragua.* Boulder, Colorado: Westview Press, 1986.

Walker, Thomas W. *Nicaragua: The Land of Sandino.* (3d ed.) Boulder, Colorado: Westview Press, 1991.

Walker, Thomas W. (ed.). *Nicaragua: The First Five Years.* New York: Praeger, 1985.

_____. *Reagan Versus the Sandinistas: The Undeclared War on Nicaragua.* Boulder, Colorado: Westview Press, 1987.

(Various issues of the following periodicals were also used in the preparation of this chapter: *The Economist* [London]; Economist Intelligence Unit, *Country Report: Nicaragua, Honduras* [London]; *Facts on File; Jane's Intelligence Review* [London]; *Latin American Monitor: Central America* [London]; *Latin American Regional Reports: Caribbean and Central American Report* [London]; *New York Times;* and *Washington Post.*)

Appendix B

Bulmer-Thomas, Victor. *The Political Economy of Central America since 1920,* Cambridge: Cambridge University Press, 1987.

_____. *Studies in the Economics of Central America.* New York: St. Martin's Press, 1988.

Cline, William R., and Enrique Delgado (eds.). *Economic Integration in Central America.* Washington: Brookings Institution, 1978.

Edwards, Sebastian. "Latin American Economic Integration: A New Perspective on an Old Dream," *The World Economy,* 16, No. 3, May 1993, 317–37.

Salazar, José Manuel. "Present and Future Integration in Central America," *Cepal Review,* No. 42, December 1990, 157–80.

Secretaría Permanente del Tratado General de Integración Económica Centroamericana. *Cuadernos de la SIECA, No. 17: 25 años de integración (en cifras).* Guatemala City: 1986.

_____. *Series Estadísticas Seleccionadas de Centroamérica.* Guatemala City, No. 24, May 1991.

(Various issues of the following publications were also used in the preparation of this appendix: *Estadísticas analíticas del comercio Intracentroamericano* [Guatemala City]; Economist Intelligence Unit, *Country Report: Guatemala, El Salvador* [London];

Economist Intelligence Unit, *Country Report: Nicaragua, Honduras,* [London]; Economist Intelligence Unit, *Country Report: Panama, Costa Rica* [London]; *Latin American Monitor: Central America* [London]; *Latin American Weekly Report* [London]; *Panorama Centroamericano* [Guatemala City]; and *Revista de la integración y el desarollo de Centroamérica* [Tegucigalpa].)

Glossary

Central America—Here, used in a geographic sense. Central America is considered to be the entire isthmus between Mexico and Colombia, including present-day Belize, Guatemala, Honduras, El Salvador, Nicaragua, Costa Rica, and Panama. A more traditional political view of the term, most often used in the region itself, is that Central America encompasses only the five successor states to the United Provinces of Central America (1821–38): Guatemala, Honduras, El Salvador, Nicaragua, and Costa Rica.

compadrazgo—Literally, "copaternity." A system of ritual "coparenthood" that links parents, children, and godparents in a close social or economic relationship.

Constituent Assembly—A deliberative body made up of elected delegates who are charged with the responsibility of drafting a new constitution and, in some instances, electing a new president. Traditionally, after it completes its work, a Constituent Assembly reverts to a Congress (former title of Nicaraguan legislatures), which then serves as the country's legislative body until the next scheduled elections.

Contadora—A diplomatic initiative launched by a January 1983 meeting on Contadora Island off the Pacific coast of Panama, by which the "Core Four" mediator countries of Mexico, Venezuela, Colombia, and Panama sought to prevent through negotiations a regional conflagration among the Central American states of Guatemala, El Salvador, Honduras, Nicaragua, and Costa Rica. In September 1984, the negotiating process produced a draft treaty, the Contadora Acta, which was judged acceptable by the government of Nicaragua but rejected by the other four Central American states concerned. The process was suspended unofficially in June 1986 when the Central American governments refused to sign a revised Acta. The Contadora process was effectively superseded by direct negotiations among the Central American states.

Contra—Short form of *contrarevolucionario* (counterrevolutionary). Member of the Nicaraguan Resistance, an armed resistance movement in the 1980s supported by the United States and fighting against the national Sandinista government.

córdoba (C$)—Nicaraguan monetary unit from 1912 to 1988. Relatively stable for most of that period, the córdoba's value plummeted in 1985. By mid-1988 the official rate was US$1 = C$20,000 (US$1 = C$60,000 on the black market), and the córdoba was replaced by the new córdoba (C$n; *q.v.*) at a rate of 1,000 córdobas to 1 new córdoba.

Creole—In Nicaragua a term used for an English-speaking person of African or mixed African and indigenous ancestry.

Enterprise for the Americas Initiative (EAI)—A plan announced by President George H.W. Bush on June 27, 1990, calling for the United States to negotiate agreements with selected Latin American countries to reduce their official debt to the United States and make funds available through this restructuring for environmental programs; to stimulate private investment; and to take steps to promote extensive trade liberalization with the goal of establishing free trade throughout the Western Hemisphere.

European Currency Unit (ECU)—Instituted in 1979, the ECU is the unit of account of the European Union (EU). The value of the ECU is determined by the value of a basket that includes the currencies of all EU member states. In establishing the value of the basket, each member's currency receives a share that reflects the relative strength and importance of the member's economy. One ECU was equivalent to about US$1.15 in 1993.

fiscal year (FY)—Nicaragua's fiscal year is the calendar year. Where reference is made to United States aid appropriations or disbursements, the United States government's FY, which runs from October 1 to September 30, is used with the date of reference drawn from the year in which the period ends. For example, FY 1992 began on October 1, 1991, and ended on September 30, 1992.

gold córdoba (C$o, sometimes C$)—Nicaraguan monetary unit divided into 100 centavos. Introduced in mid-1990, the gold córdoba replaced the new córdoba at a rate of 1 gold córdoba to 5 million new córdobas (*q.v.*). In mid-1993, US$1 = C$o6.15.

gross domestic product (GDP)—A measure of the total value of goods and services produced by the domestic economy during a given period, usually one year. Obtained by adding the value contributed by each sector of the economy in the form of profits, compensation to employees, and depreciation (consumption of capital). Only domestic production is included, not income arising from investments and possessions owned abroad, hence the use of the word *domestic* to distinguish GDP from gross national product (*q.v.*).

gross national product (GNP)—The total market value of all final goods and services produced by an economy during a year. Obtained by adding the gross domestic product (*q.v.*) and the income received from abroad by residents and subtracting payments remitted abroad to nonresidents.

import-substitution industrialization (ISI)—An economic development strategy that emphasizes the growth of domestic industries, often by import protection using tariff and nontariff measures. Proponents favor the export of industrial goods over primary products.

International Monetary Fund (IMF)—Established along with the World Bank (*q.v.*) in 1945, the IMF is a specialized agency affiliated with the United Nations (UN) that takes responsibility for stabilizing international exchange rates and payments. The main business of the IMF is the provision of loans to its members when they experience balance-of-payments difficulties. These loans often carry conditions that require substantial internal economic adjustments by the recipients.

liberation theology—An activist movement led by Roman Catholic clergy who trace their inspiration to Vatican Council II (1965), where some church procedures were liberalized, and the Second Latin American Bishops' Conference in Medellín, Colombia (1968), which endorsed greater direct efforts to improve the lot of the poor. Advocates of liberation theology—sometimes referred to as "liberationists"—work mainly through Christian Base Communities (Comunidades Eclesiásticas de Base—CEBs). Members of CEBs meet in small groups to reflect on scripture and discuss its meaning in their lives. They are introduced to a radical interpretation of the Bible, one that employs Marxist terminology to analyze and condemn the wide disparities between the wealthy elite and the impoverished masses in most underdeveloped countries. This reflection often leads members to organize to improve their living standards through cooperatives and civic improvement projects.

new córdoba (C$n)—Nicaraguan monetary unit from 1988 to 1990. Replaced the former currency, the córdoba (*q.v.*), in an attempt to control inflation; the value of the new córdoba dropped to US$1 = C$n3.2 million in less than three years. Replaced by the gold córdoba (*q.v.*) in 1990 at a rate of 5 million new córdobas to 1 gold córdoba.

San José Accord—An agreement between Mexico and Venezuela, signed in 1980 in San José, Costa Rica, whereby the two oil producers committed themselves to supply crude oil on concessionary terms to ten Central American and Caribbean nations.

Sandinista—Originally a member of the Marxist group attempting to overthrow the Somozas or their hand-picked president in the 1960s and 1970s. The group took its name from Augusto César Sandino, who led a guerrilla struggle against United States occupation of Nicaragua in the 1930s. The political arm of the group, the Sandinista National Liberation Front (Frente Sandinista de Liberación Nacional—FSLN), was the national government of Nicaragua from July 1979 to April 1990. After the late 1970s, the term *Sandinista* is used for a member or supporter or the FSLN or as the adjectival form of the FSLN.

World Bank—The informal name used to designate a group of four affiliated international institutions: the International Bank for Reconstruction and Development (IBRD), the International Development Association (IDA), the International Finance Corporation (IFC), and the Multilateral Investment Guarantee Agency (MIGA). The IBRD, established in 1945, has the primary purpose of providing loans at market-related rates of interest to developing countries at more advanced stages of development. The IDA, a legally separate loan fund but administered by the staff of the IBRD, was set up in 1960 to furnish credits to the poorest developing countries on much easier terms than those of conventional IBRD loans. The IFC, founded in 1956, supplements the activities of the IBRD through loans and assistance designed specifically to encourage the growth of productive private enterprises in less developed countries. The MIGA, founded in 1988, insures private foreign investment in developing countries against various non-commercial risks. The president and certain officers of the IBRD hold the same positions in the IFC. The four institutions are owned by the governments of the countries that subscribe their capital. To participate in the World Bank group, member states must first belong to the International Monetary Fund (*q.v.*).

Index

abortion, 83
Accessory Transit Company, 13
acquired immune deficiency syndrome (AIDS), 77
agrarian reform. *See* land reform
Agrarian Reform Law (1981), 39, 68-69, 110-11
agricultural: cooperatives, 69, 111; development, 115, 134; policy, 126-27
agricultural production, 126-27; in civil war, xxxii, 36, 43; and natural disasters, 48, 126; neglect of, xxvi
agricultural products (*see also under individual crops*), 5, 125-26, 127-30; diversification of, 101, 126; export of, 10, 17, 18, 101, 116, 126; nontraditional, 126
agriculture, 125-31; decline in, 126; employment in, 119; export crops, 107; indigenous, 100; nationalization in, 108; as percentage of gross domestic product, 126, 127; slash-and-burn, 5; subsistence, 92
Aguado, Enoc, 27
Agüero, Fernando, 29
AID. *See* United States Agency for International Development
AIDS. *See* acquired immune deficiency syndrome
air force, 209, 211-12; bases, 212; matériel, 200, 212; number of personnel, 212; radar, 212; restructured, 200; training, 200
Alemán, Arnoldo, 162
Alianza Popular Conservadora. *See* Conservative Popular Alliance
Alianza Revolucionaria Democrática. *See* Democratic Revolutionary Alliance
American Baptist Church, 86
Americas Watch, 219, 223
Amnesty International, 40
amnesty law, 174, 194, 216
AMNLAE. *See* Luisa Amanda Espinoza Nicaraguan Women's Association
Andean Group, 239
ANDEN. *See* National Association of Nic-

araguan Teachers
Antigua (Guatemala), 8
APC. *See* Conservative Popular Alliance
Arce Castaño, Bayardo, 181
archaeological excavations, 4
Arde. *See* Democratic Revolutionary Alliance
Argüello, Leonardo: as president, 27
Argüello Morales, Míriam, 161, 162
Arias Dávila, Pedro (Pedrarias), 8
Arias Plan (Esquipulas II) (1987), 47-48, 149, 160, 187, 247
Arias Sánchez, Oscar, 47-48
armed forces (*see also* National Guard; Sandinista People's Army), 207-13; commander of, xxxvii, 143, 146, 193, 207-9; demobilization of, xxxvii, 48, 74, 115-16, 153, 193, 209; foreign influences on, 202-5; in government transition, 146; history of, 194-95; human rights violations by, 219; military assistance to, 202-5; missions of, 209-11; number of personnel in, xxxvii, 193, 209; organization of, 209; political role of, xxxvii; reform of, 209; restructuring of, 209; Sandinista control of, xxxv, 146, 153, 193; Somoza family control of, 25; under Zelaya, 195
army, 211; commander of, xxxvii, 143, 146; creation of, xxvii; matériel of, 211; number of troops in, 211; organization of, 211
Army for the Defense of Nicaraguan Sovereignty (Ejército Defensor de la Soberanía de Nicaragua—EDSN), 22, 24; destruction of, 24; number of personnel in, 22
Asociación de Mujeres Nicaragüenses Luisa Amanda Espinoza. *See* Luisa Amanda Espinoza Nicaraguan Women's Association
Asociación de Trabajadores del Campo. *See* Association of Agricultural Workers

of, 107; from Mexico, 118, 188; promises of, 182; from Spain, 118, 188;
from the United States, 26, 117-18,
183-84, 186, 204; from Venezuela, 118,
188; from World Bank, 118, 119, 188,
189
foreign borrowing, 102
foreign debt, 39; rescheduled, 39; servicing, 245
foreign exchange, 126, 127, 245
foreign investment, 103, 104; under
Díaz, 20; loss of, 107; under Zelaya, 18
foreign relations, 182-89
forestry, 100, 131
forests: in central highlands, 56; rain, 59,
131, 134; regeneration of, 134
FPN. *See* National Patriotic Front
Framework Free Trade Agreement
(1992), 249
France: matériel from, 202, 212; pirates
from, xxvi, 9, 90
Frente Nacional de Trabajadores. *See*
National Workers' Front
Frente Amplio de Oposición. *See* Broad
Opposition Front
Frente de Trabajadores Socialcristianos.
See Social Christian Workers' Front
Frente Farabundo Martí de Liberacíon
Nacional. *See* Farabundo Martí
National Liberation Front
Frente Nacional de Trabajadores. *See*
National Workers' Front
Frente Norte 3-80. *See* Northern Front 3-
80
Frente Obrero. *See* Workers' Front
Frente Patriótico Nacional. *See* National
Patriotic Front
Frente Revolucionario de Obreros y
Campesinos. *See* Revolutionary Front
of Workers and Peasants
Frente Sandinista de Liberación Nacio-
nal. *See* Sandinista National Liberation
Front
FROC. *See* Revolutionary Front of Work-
ers and Peasants
FSLN. *See* Sandinista National Liberation
Front
FTS. *See* Social Christian Workers' Front
Fuerza Aérea Sandinista/Defensa Anti-
Aérea. *See* air force
Fuerza Democrática Nicaragüense. *See*
Nicaraguan Democratic Force

Fundamental Statute of the Republic of
Nicaragua (1979), xxxii, 40, 45
G-3. *See* Group of Three
Garifuna people, 90
GC. *See* Center Group
GDP. *See* gross domestic product
General Confederation of Workers-Inde-
pendent (Confederación General de
Trabajadores-Independiente—CGT-
I), 122, 173
General Directorate of State Security
(Dirección General de Seguridad del
Estado—DGSE), 218; human rights
violations by, 219
Generalized System of Preferences, 184
General Treaty of Central American Eco-
nomic Integration (Tratado General
de Integración Económica Cen-
troamericana) (1960), 239, 241-42
geographic regions, 55-59
German Democratic Republic (East Ger-
many): relations with, 203
Germany: relations with, 18, 19
GNP. *See* gross national product
Godoy Reyes, Virgilio, 46, 175, 177; in
elections of 1990, 49, 160, 161
Golfo de Fonseca, 56
González Dávila, Gil, 6-8; exploration by,
6-8; rivalry of, with Hernández, 8
Gorostiaga, Xavier, 180
government, local: under constitution of
1987, 151-52; powers of, 152; regions
of, 151-52
Gracias (Honduras), 8
Granada: agriculture in, xxvi; competition of, with León, 10-11; conservatives in, 10-11, 103; destroyed, xxvi, 9,
15; elite class in, 10, 103; founded, 8;
population in, 62
Great Depression, xxix
gross domestic product (GDP), 74, 102,
104; agriculture, 126, 127; construction, 124; defense spending, 214;
industry, 124; manufacturing, 245; per
capita, xxxiv, 70; private sector, 68,
108, 109; state enterprises, 110; tax
revenues, 115
gross national product (GNP): defense
spending as percentage of, 214
Group of Three (G-3), 249
Group of Twelve. *See* Los Doce
Grupo de Centro. *See* Center Group

Published Country Studies

(Area Handbook Series)

550–65	Afghanistan	550–28	Ethiopia
550–98	Albania	550–167	Finland
550–44	Algeria	550–173	Germany, East
550–59	Angola	550–155	Germany, Fed. Rep. of
550–73	Argentina	550–153	Ghana
550–169	Australia	550–87	Greece
550–176	Austria	550–78	Guatemala
550–175	Bangladesh	550–174	Guinea
550–170	Belgium	550–82	Guyana and Belize
550–66	Bolivia	550–151	Honduras
550–20	Brazil	550–165	Hungary
550–168	Bulgaria	550–21	India
550–61	Burma	550–154	Indian Ocean
550–50	Cambodia	550–39	Indonesia
550–166	Cameroon	550–68	Iran
550–159	Chad	550–31	Iraq
550–77	Chile	550–25	Israel
550–60	China	550–182	Italy
550–26	Colombia	550–30	Japan
550–33	Commonwealth Caribbean, Islands of the	550–34	Jordan
550–91	Congo	550–56	Kenya
550–90	Costa Rica	550–81	Korea, North
550–69	Côte d'Ivoire (Ivory Coast)	550–41	Korea, South
550–152	Cuba	550–58	Laos
550–22	Cyprus	550–24	Lebanon
550–158	Czechoslovakia	550–38	Liberia
550–36	Dominican Republic and Haiti	550–85	Libya
550–52	Ecuador	550–172	Malawi
550–43	Egypt	550–45	Malaysia
550–150	El Salvador	550–161	Mauritania

550–79	Mexico	550–179	Spain
550–76	Mongolia	550–96	Sri Lanka
550–49	Morocco	550–27	Sudan
550–64	Mozambique	550–47	Syria
550–35	Nepal and Bhutan	550–62	Tanzania
550–88	Nicaragua	550–53	Thailand
550–157	Nigeria	550–89	Tunisia
550–94	Oceania	550–80	Turkey
550–48	Pakistan	550–74	Uganda
550–46	Panama	550–97	Uruguay
550–156	Paraguay	550–71	Venezuela
550–185	Persian Gulf States	550–32	Vietnam
550–42	Peru	550–183	Yemens, The
550–72	Philippines	550–99	Yugoslavia
550–162	Poland	550–67	Zaire
550–181	Portugal	550–75	Zambia
550–160	Romania	550–171	Zimbabwe
550–37	Rwanda and Burundi		
550–51	Saudi Arabia		
550–70	Senegal		
550–180	Sierra Leone		
550–184	Singapore		
550–86	Somalia		
550–93	South Africa		
550–95	Soviet Union